Rethinking Embodiment in Feminist Media Studies

Rethinking Embodiment in Feminist Media Studies

Sudhir Kumar Singh

MD Publications Pvt Ltd
New Delhi
www.mdppl.com

Published by :

MD Publications Pvt Ltd
"MD House", 11, Darya Ganj,
New Delhi - 110 002
Phone : +91-11-45355555
E-mail : contact@mdppl.com
Website: www.mdppl.com

ISBN: 978-81-7533-256-0

Published and Printed by Mr. Pranav Gupta on behalf of **MD Publications Pvt Ltd** at Mohit Enterprises, Delhi.

Preface

Feminism - movement for the political, social, and educational equality of women with men; the movement has occurred mainly in Europe and the United States. It has its roots in the humanism of the 18th century and in the Industrial Revolution. Feminist issues range from access to employment, education, child care, contraception, and abortion, to equality in the workplace, changing family roles, redress for sexual harassment in the workplace, and the need for equal political representation.

Feminists have long recognized the significance of the media as a site for the expression of - or challenges to - existing constructions of gender. In this broad-ranging analysis, Liesbet van Zoonen explores the ways in which feminist theory and research contribute to the fuller understanding of the multiple roles of the media in the construction of gender in contemporary societies.

Influential historiographies of anti-colonial nationalism suggest that women's cultural identities-laid out in codes by which they belong to their kin group and share in its collective future are determined by the male elite's contentious relationship with imperialist modernity. Construed to be spiritually superior to the materialistic Westerner, this traditional self posits an alternate racial-cultural hierarchy against the dominant one. The Orientalist sexual politics of nationalism give men some flexibility in experimenting with modern concepts and tools; but they confine the new woman's identity in a spatiotemporal dichotomy. She has to keep tradition in the home and community and superficially adapt to the nation's social and economic teleologies in the private and public spheres.

The implication of such studies is that the new woman's investment in her people's goals of gaining freedom from racial-masculinist domination and building independent nations inhibits her ability to self-actualize and intervene in patriarchal national history. This raises the central question: To what extent can woman claim agencies in her personal thought and practice and over her historical role without discarding commitments to her cultural community and its ongoing liberation struggle, during and after colonization? The challenge to attaining this political stance within, not outside, the communal realm is that the woman must stake her affiliation according to the terms defined by a community-reconfigured-as-nation: she must define herself and her role in terms of a past she shares with her people, and a future she collectively imagines.

I am very grateful to Mr. Pranav Gupta, Director of MD Publications Pvt Ltd, New Delhi, for his kind cooperation and support for this book.

Sudhir Kumar Singh

CONTENTS

1

Rethinking Embodiment in Feminist Media Studies

An Introduction

The question of how to engage the thought of classic male theorists and philosophers faces feminist theorists across cultures, disciplines, and social locations. Historically, the exclusion of women from the public sphere has meant that men alone had access to the resources that allowed them to become socially respected and acknowledged intellectuals. As a result, men have claimed the authority to speak for all, to define universal human concerns. As the authors included in this collection well know, there is no escaping the influence of these thinkers, given their domination of intellectual and political life.

All the writers in this collection face the challenge of untangling the strands of the thought of these authoritative figures - to distinguish their originality and insight into broad political and social questions from their blindness to their own male privilege and failure to see the human experience whole when they do not acknowledge or see the lives of women. Thus there is a continuing tension in feminist appropriations and use of the ideas of male theorists who are themselves unconcerned with questions of gender.

Education feminists, like other feminist theorists, have been profoundly influenced by classic male theorists. Despite the claims of some feminists that women must create a new language and a new imaginary, it seems self-defeating to ignore the work of male thinkers who have addressed questions of knowledge, culture, and power. Education feminists have shared both a language and political goals with these democratic and liberatory writers. John Dewey and Paulo Freire, in particular, were an inspiration for an earlier generation of education feminists, who appropriated their rhetoric and commitment to democracy and equity to feminist goals in education.

Feminists have also built upon the insight and analysis of such figures as Antonio Gramsci, W. E. B. DuBois, and Stuart Hall to analyze the cultural processes through which power is exercised in terms of class, race, and colonialism. Education feminists have been drawn to and in turn have redeployed the conceptions of culture, hegemony, and race put forth by these theorists to develop a feminist analysis of women, knowledge, and education. Within the last decade, poststructuralist theory has profoundly shaped feminist educational theory, and the impact of theorists such as Michel Foucault and Jacques Lacan has been immense.

But the relationship between education feminists who share a commitment to education as a site for possible progressive political action and critical and democratic male theorists continues to be complex. Education feminists, like others, must consider not only their relationship to a male intellectual and political tradition that has more often than not ignored and excluded them, but also to the relationships among women themselves across divides of race, class, and sexuality.

In an ideal world, individuals would exchange their ideas, speak and listen in conversations between equals. The French feminist philosopher and psychoanalyst Luce Irigaray, for example, envisions her writing as a conversation-between herself as author and the reader, but also between herself as critic and those she is critiquing, saying that "the only reply that can be given to the question of the meaning of the text is: read, perceive, feel.... Who are you? Would be a more pertinent question provided that it does not collapse into a demand for an identity card or an autobiographical anecdote.

The answer would be: and who are you? can we meet? Talk: Love: Create something together? Thanks to which milieu? What between-us (entrenous)?" (cited in Whitford 1991, 14; emphasis in the original). But we are not yet at a point at which such exchanges or conversations "entre nous" occur between feminists and those unconcerned with women's issues. Most male theorists, including most of those addressed in these essays, have failed to engage feminist thought at all.

It is still the case that intellectual and material exchanges tend to be between men, and women in many cultures continue to be the symbolic objects of exchanges solidifying male ties. Thus the feminist use of the work of male theorists who have historically ignored our own work contains profound contradictions. Numerous feminist theorists have considered the question of how to establish a woman's voice and ground for feminist politics and theorizing distinct from the patriarchal tradition of Western thought. Feminism and its relationship to the dominant patriarchal intellectual tradition has been a major issue facing women at least since the Enlightenment.

A famous example is Mary Wollstonecraft's early reading of Jean-Jacques Rousseau in A Vindication of the Rights of Women. Sharing Rousseau's enlightenment concerns with individual freedom and a desire for radical democracy, Wollstonecraft nonetheless rejects Rousseau for his sexism and assumption that only men could be citizens. For Rousseau, women should be educated only to be the nurturers and sexual playthings of men. As Wollstonecraft writes, "Rousseau declares that a woman should never for a moment feel herself independent, That she should be governed by fear to exercise her natural cunning, and made a coquettish slave in order to render her a more alluring object of desire, a sweeter companion to man, whenever he chooses to relax himself.

He carries the arguments, which he pretends to draw from the indications of nature, still further, and insinuates that truth and fortitude, the corner-stones of all human virtue, should be cultivated with certain restrictions, because, with respect to the female character, obedience is the grand lesson which ought to be impressed with unrelenting vigor. What nonsense!" From her rejection of Rousseau's sexual politics, Wollstonecraft proceeds to argue the need for an equal and challenging education for women, an education that will awaken the moral as well as rational parts of their being.

The need to challenge patriarchal assumptions is also at the heart of Virginia Woolf's brilliant analysis of gender, war, and education, Three Guineas. In Three Guineas Woolf uses requests for support of three different causes- an organisation to end war, a woman's college, and a group seeking help for women in the professions-as a way to organize a meditation on women's position in a society in which both institutions and knowledge itself are male defined or male controlled. Woolf asks how, as a woman, she should position herself in relation to a civilisation that has ignored and silenced her. Should she want to join what she calls "the procession of the sons of educated men"?

As she comments in a famous passage, "Let us never cease from thinking - what is this 'civilisation' in which we find ourselves? What are these ceremonies and why should we take part in them? What are these professions and why should we make money out of them? Where in short is it leading us, the procession of the sons of educated men?" If the civilisation dominated by "the sons of educated men" is one based on war, violence, and exploitation, says Woolf, then we should approach entry into it very cautiously.

At the end of Three Guineas Woolf suggests what she calls an "outsider's society" of women, one in which women could share a commitment to seeking "freedom, equality, and peace" but could at the same time disassociate themselves from the aggression and violence of male-dominated society and knowledge. "Broadly speaking," she explains, "the main distinction between us who are outside society and you who are inside society must be that whereas you will make use of the means provided by your position-measures such as your wealth and the political influence placed within your reach-we, remaining outside, will experiment not with public means but with private means in private. Those experiments will not be merely critical but creative".

Woolf's metaphor of the three guineas can stand in for the continuing uneasiness of women theorists committed to democratic goals of peace and justice about their relationship to the intellectual heritage of men. Our ultimate goals may be very similar, but what do we take on if we imagine ourselves as the inheritors of these "gender-blind" theories and then apply them to our own concerns as feminist women? A powerful philosophical answer to Woolf's concerns can be found in the work of Irigaray, who attempts to write through what she calls a female imaginary.

Irigaray calls on feminists to examine dominant beliefs carefully for their assumptions of who speaks and who labors, saying, "The culture, the language, the imaginary and the mythology in which we live at the moment ... I say to myself ... let's have a look ... this edifice that looks so clean and so subtle ... let's see what ground it is built on. Is it all that acceptable? The substratum is the woman who reproduces the social order, who made this order's infrastructure".

Irigaray argues that the fundamental imagery and metaphors with which we think (both in terms of philosophy and common sense discourse) are framed by a perspective that only seems authentic if you are male. Rather than accept the idea of the discursive construction of gender and then assume women and men can create themselves differently, she argues that it is first necessary to subject Western philosophy to a feminist analysis to reveal the patriarchal nature of Western thought and to begin to construct an alternative feminine imaginary, one from which women can speak and think. If this project is not undertaken, then women will be faced with the choice of accepting their traditional identity as "other," as the object and foil of male thought and action, or of becoming women-as-men-that is, taking on the qualities of the subject position, the actor, which are only imagined and symbolized in terms of men.

What Irigaray is suggesting is not the abolition of rationality, but the proposal of a new embodied female subject, who literally can think and not just feel. She argues that a female symbolic does not imply that an overarching and universally "true" woman will be discovered by philosophy to replace the universal Western man whose shadow looms over us, but rather that all women's identities must be understood as existing within/through a symbolic and imaginary discourse that itself is shaped by material structures of power and privilege.

Irigaray's concern with the "edifice that looks so clean and so subtle," like Woolf's warning to women about following "the procession of the sons of educated men," is taken up and expanded in the work of the lesbian poet and theorist Audre Lorde, whose concerns are captured in her famous phrase "the master's tools will never dismantle the master's house." As Lorde writes, "[The] master's tools will never dismantle the master's house. They may allow us temporarily to beat him at his own game, but they will never enable us to bring about genuine change. And this fact is only threatening to those women who still define the master's house as their only source of support".

Although this passage is often cited as a caution to women about the danger of using a male intellectual tradition that has objectified or ignored women as the theoretical foundation of a critique of that same tradition, if we return to Lorde's original essay we see that she is cautioning not just about patriarchy, but about racism as well, speaking directly to white and heterosexual women about their blindesses to their own privilege and their ignorance of the profundity of differences among women. Lorde continues, "Women today are still being called upon to stretch across the gap of male ignorance and to educate men as to our existence and our needs.

This is an old and primary tool of all oppressors to keep the oppressed occupied with the master's concerns". But Lorde goes on to point out that asking women of colour to educate white women about their lives and concerns follows exactly the same logic and must be combated in just the same way. Expanding the concerns of Woolf and Irigaray, Lorde challenges feminist theorists to locate ourselves self-consciously in relation to women as well as men.

What then are the possibilities for a feminist engagement with male theorists who have ignored women's concerns or who have continued to enact male privilege? The essays in this collection are not monolithic in approach; they take a number of different stances in relation to the male theorists who have influenced them. Broadly - though these divisions are not rigid or fast - there seem to be three approaches represented here. First, there is a kind of negative engagement that uses critique as a point of departure for a feminist analysis; second, there is the appropriation and application of the ideas of male theorists to feminist concerns with little or no critique; and third, there is the application of the conceptual framework of the male theorist, in a critical way, to a feminist analysis.

The division of feminist critique into these three stances-critical analysis and rejection, uncritical appropriation, and critical appropriation - is of course artificial. Most feminist educational theorists, including the writers in this collection, have moved among these stances, sometimes rejecting, sometimes appropriating, and sometimes undertaking extensive critique and reinterpretation of the work of classic male theorists. The choice of how to read and use these male theorists depends in part on the social location of the feminist critic and in part on the historical and political context, the strategic need to make theoretical alliances for common political goals.

When male theorists imagine students and political actors as men and assume that the work of the private world, the world of reproduction and emotional nurturance, will be done "offstage" by anonymous women, their theories may be rejected as so deeply flawed that they cannot be useful for a feminist analysis of the education of women. The analysis of these patriarchal assumptions and silences in the work of classic male theorists is one example of a feminist engagement.

On the other hand, other feminist theorists have argued that powerful ideas can be extracted from their patriarchal place of origin to be applied to women's condition.

Gramsci's idea of hegemony, Foucault's conception of power, Freire's passionate defense of the possibility of human liberation-all these ideas have at different times been taken and reimagined by feminist teachers and thinkers without engaging in a feminist critique of the patriarchal nature of the original theories. Women of colour, positioned in complex relationships of oppression, may well feel more solidarity with male theorists of colour than they do with white women across a racial divide. Despite the inadequate understanding of gender in the work of these male antiracist thinkers and political figures, feminist women of colour share a strong sense of collectivity with them.

Feminist poststructuralist theorists have also employed and elaborated on the ideas of male theorists, in many cases using the ideas of one male theorist to critique the ideas of another without providing a feminist critique of their ideas. Perhaps the most complex attitude taken by feminist theorists in relation to male theorists is one of critical engagement-the stance most frequently taken by the writers in this collection. Feminists committed to alliances across race and ethnic lines frequently put forward complex readings of male antiracist theorists who have often articulated goals of liberation and human rights in a powerful and poetic rhetoric but who have ignored women's concerns. In this case, these are strategic readings, in which the feminist theorist is aware of limitations but nonetheless uses these theories for defined political goals. Bell hooks's reading of Freire can be seen in this light.

Hooks makes clear her debt to Freire and his meaning for her own personal development, yet she is aware of what she calls his "blind spot" to male privilege, the way he, like other political leaders, has constructed "a phallocentric paradigm of liberation- wherein freedom and the experience of patriarchal manhood are always linked as though they are one and the same". What hooks is trying to hold is the contradiction between

Freire's blindness to sexism and the value of his ideas when they are abstracted from these blinders. The frequent feminist citation of Foucault is another example of a feminist engagement with a powerful male theorist who himself showed little if any concern with analyzing patriarchal privilege.

Nonetheless, Foucault's ideas have provided a powerful impetus for feminist critiques of discourse and power. The essays in this collection address these complex questions within educational studies, providing a reading of influential male theorists who have shaped the broadly defined critical democratic tradition in education. The authors represented here take different positions in their readings, some speaking from the context of their own previous scholarly engagement, some providing a more general critique.

In each chapter, however, the feminist reading provided offers a new and challenging perspective on the work of classic educational and cultural theory by examining this work through the lens of gender. Frances Maher addresses the foundational thought of John Dewey and his influence in later progressive pedagogies in her essay, "John Dewey, Progressive Education, and Feminist Pedagogies: Issues in Gender and Authority." Maher argues that it is important for educators who see themselves as "progressive" to return to reading John Dewey through the lens of gender.

As Maher notes, issues of power, authority, and gender are central to any attempt at developing a pedagogy that respects and addresses all students. Conceptions of women's natures and teaching as work have been profoundly shaped by these conceptions - both the assumed natures of women teachers and the natures of students, both boys and girls. Maher argues that Dewey's conceptions of teaching and learning are profoundly limited by the absence of a consideration of the role of the teacher.

That failure, Maher argues, rests on Dewey's unstated acceptance of gender differences. The same acceptance of gender difference and failure to address male privilege can be seen in the democratic, liberatory critics of the 1960s. Maher turns to the work of three feminist educational theorists, Jane Roland Martin, Valerie Walkerdine, and Jane Miller, to explore alternative visions of progressive teaching. In their work, Maher finds attention to questions of power and authority that she sees as central to pedagogy.

In her essay "DuBois and the Invisible Talented Tenth," Cally L. Waite rereads W. E. B. DuBois's classic essay "The Talented Tenth" against the lives and accomplishments of three powerful black women, Anna Julia Cooper, Mary Church Terrell, and Ida B. Wells-Barnett. By examining their work as educators and community leaders, Waite shows that these women embody precisely the attributes DuBois was calling for in his conception of the talented tenth. Each of these women was committed to education as key to racial uplift.

These women were not only intellectuals but also activists whose lives embody exactly the values and beliefs DuBois was calling for. Moreover, DuBois was well acquainted with all three and worked closely with Wells-Barnett, in particular. Yet in his published work, DuBois was strikingly silent about the accomplishments of these three women, failing to identify them even when he quoted their writings. As Waite argues, recognizing and engaging the accomplishments of these women contemporaries of DuBois not only challenge us to read his work anew, it changes our understanding of this whole period of history.

The contributions of the Italian theorist Antonio Gramsci on feminist educational thinking have been eclipsed in the past decade by poststructuralist thought and in particular by the work of Michel Foucault. In her essay "Remembering and Regenerating Gramsci," Jane Kenway makes a strong argument for a reconsideration of Gramsci by education feminists. After briefly summarizing his life, she uses the interpretations of Chantal Mouffe and Ernesto Laclau to examine Gramsci's key ideas, in particular his ideas of ideology and hegemony. She then turns to appropriations of Gramsci by feminist writers in the 1980s to show the ways in which Gramsci provided powerful conceptual tools for examining the construction of gender relations in schooling.

As Kenway makes clear, one of Gramsci's great strengths is his grounding in a materialist analysis. Madeleine Arnot, R. C. Connell and his colleagues, and Patti Lather in her early work used Gramsci to suggest ways to tie constructions of gender to power and control of material resources. Kenway suggests that this Gramscian approach should be reconsidered by contemporary education feminists seeking to understand the ways male power continues to be reproduced and reconfigured in the contemporary world.

The assumptions of male privilege embedded in the thought of Paulo Freire through the complex tradition of feminist pedagogy. Along with Foucault, Freire is one of the male theorists most frequently cited and admired by feminist educational theorists. Freire's passionate prose and commitment to social justice have inspired activist teachers and scholars throughout the world. As women have come to analyze our own oppression, Freire's call for pedagogy of the oppressed seems to speak directly to our own concerns.

While I am sympathetic to the humanity and power of Freire's life and thought, in this chapter I am concerned about the silences and patriarchal assumptions in Freire's writings. I look at his acceptance of a gendered division of public and private as well as his infrequent discussion of women's concerns and responses to feminist critiques of his thought. The broad generalisations and universalism of Freire's work seemingly make it possible to apply him to almost any situation of oppression, but I argue here that Freire's conception of the liberatory teacher is based on assumptions of patriarchal privilege and women's subordination in the domestic sphere.

In her essay "The Dreamwork of Autobiography: Felman, Freud, and Lacan" Alice Pitt considers the uneasy relationship of feminist theorists and the great patriarchs of the psychoanalytic tradition. She explores the complex thought of Sigmund Freud and Jacques Lacan through the feminist reading of Shoshana Felman: For Pitt, the theoretical contributions of classic psychoanalytic theory as represented by Lacan and Freud challenge feminist educational theorists to account for the unconscious in their readings of pedagogy. Pitt approaches these questions obliquely through a reading of dreams and women's autobiographies.

For Pitt, the power of the psychoanalytic conception of the unconscious makes it tool feminist educators cannot ignore. Using Felman's appropriation of these ideas, she challenges feminist educational theorists to reimagine these ideas in their own thinking about women's lives and learnings. While Pitt engages Lacan and Freud with caution, she also calls for feminist theorists to examine the workings of desire and the unconscious in their own thinking about knowledge and teaching.

Like Freud and Lacan, the British sociologist Basil Bernstein largely ignored gender in his theoretical writings. Yet, as Madeleine Arnot argues in her chapter, "Bernstein's Sociology of Pedagogy: Female Dialogues and Feminist Elaborations," his ideas have been highly influential in the work of a number of women sociologists, both those who define their work as explicitly feminist and those who do not. In preparation for this chapter, Arnot asked a number of senior women academics who had been influenced by Bernstein to discuss the importance of his work.

She uses their responses to explore the multifaceted uses of Bernstein's work in addressing questions of gender and education. Out of the rich material she collected in preparing this chapter, she selected two primary themes to explore: the power and attraction of Bernstein's work for women educationalists and the specific gender research that has been developed by women using Bernstein's theories. Arnot argues that although Bernstein failed to address gender issues in the development of his theory, it is precisely the universal and abstract nature of his theorizing that makes it applicable to any pedagogical context-thus providing the possibility for a feminist use.

As one respondent wrote, "Bernstein's models are essentially beyond gender," but as Arnot explains, a feminist application of Bernstein's categories requires a reworking and specific grounding of his overarching theory to the specificity of gender relations. Bernstein himself has acknowledged his failure to engage feminist theory or his own specific location within a gendered social structure. Although Arnot and many of her respondents are aware of the complexities of the application of a Bernsteinian theoretical model to gender issues in education, they are confident that Bernstein's work has great potential for feminist elaboration and application.

In her essay "Coming to Theory: Finding Foucault and Deleuze" Elizabeth Adams St. Pierre reflects on her own intellectual journey and engagement with poststructural and feminist theory. St. Pierre is concerned with theorizing subjectivity and explores the complex relationship of the feminist reading subject and poststructuralist texts. She names Michel Foucault and Gilles Deleuze as representative of the theorists who have challenged her own thinking. Grounding her approach in what she calls the "feminist work of paying attention to my lived experiences," St. Pierre traces her own intellectual engagement with theory as a student and writer; but her use of experience here is complicated by her understanding that experience itself is produced through theoretical understanding-that "theory produces people."

From this beginning, she traces out her own journey from student to ethnographer deeply concerned with the subject position woman. St. Pierre discusses her own ongoing research with older white Southern women and her developing understanding of them as human subjects located in space as well as time. St.Pierre sees herself as using the theoretical works of both men and women and rejects the canonical boundaries of rigid definitions of theoretical schools. Instead, she heterogeneously employs theories that allow her to understand her own subjectivity and that of the older women she is studying and to explore ways of thinking differently about the practices and discourses that construct her and others.

Stuart Hall, sociologist, critic, and one of the founders of the British cultural studies movement, has been one of the most influential figures in late-twentieth-century cultural criticism. Annette Henry approaches his work from her perspective as a black feminist educational researcher. As she points out, the depth and range of Hall's writings, along with his great influence, make any engagement with his work a daunting project. In her essay, "Stuart Hall, Cultural Studies: Theory Letting You off the Hook?"

Henry sets out Hall's powerful ideas about language, culture, and power in the context of her own concern with the lives of black girls in schools. She emphasizes Hall's engagement with questions of subjectivity and identity and his continued concern with material structures of power. Although Hall himself rarely engaged questions of gender, Henry makes clear that the central issues of his work provide a powerful tool for exploring the culture of schools and what Henry terms "the invisibility and the self-effacement of girls"-particularly girls of colour.

By applying the theoretical lens of cultural studies, Henry highlights the complexity and hybridity of social identities while at the same time emphasizing the need to move beyond a theoretical analysis to social action. In her essay "Ten Years Later, Yet Again: Critical Pedagogy and Its Complicities" Patti Lather uses an analysis of a 1998 essay by Peter McLaren in a special collection of Educational Theory on "The State of Critical Theory Today" to explore the assumptions guiding contemporary critical pedagogy. In her discussion, Lather attempts to unsettle the certainties underlying the totalizing categories of the kind of critical pedagogy advocated by McLaren.

Lather points out the historical tensions between feminist and critical pedagogy and argues that what is enacted in the modernist assumptions of critical pedagogy is a kind of "masculinist voice"-one of certainty, abstraction, and universalism. In opposition to this stance, Lather advocates a questioning stance of multiplicity of knowledges, heterogeneity, and the uncertain. Using Alison Jones's account of the complexities she saw in the teaching of her course on feminist theory in education as a counterexample, Lather argues for a more open, nonreductive praxis in opposition to the traditional certainties of what she calls the "masculinist voice" of critical pedagogy.

Feminists today write from a much more complex place than they did in the heady days of the late 1960s and early 1970s. In terms of theory, there is clearly a distinction that needs to be made between ascribed identity - the location we inhabit through the definition of others - and the political stance we have chosen. Women theorists do not necessarily read and write as women; they may write from a purportedly gender-neutral but symbolically male location. And men may write as feminists if they share feminist concerns and goals.

An overemphasis on women's social identity as women can once again present them as the only ones "bearing sex" and deflect from serious attention to the logic or coherence of their thought, attention given without question to male writers. Thus it is important to acknowledge that although "lived experience" may heighten a person's understanding of the exercise of power, it does not inevitably reduce individuals to preexisting identities. Nonetheless, the idea that the personal is political has been a key claim of feminist politics from the beginning.

Although some men are concerned with women's issues and certainly not all women are feminists, these theoretical stances continue to be profoundly gendered. That is, both men and women are concerned with "gender-neutral" issues of politics, culture, science, and economics, but in most cases only women are concerned with what are defined as women's issues or with feminist theory. If theory presents complicated questions of identity and power, the social world presents a starker landscape. Globally, patriarchy is alive and well. Men throughout the world continue to control politics and the economy while girls and women are disadvantaged and exploited in a variety of ways.

Although in the metropolitan countries white middle-class women have gained access to higher education and the professions, most women throughout the world continue to labour under traditional male dominance and control. Racism and its historical consequences continue to shape most societies, and men continue to hold most positions of political and economic power worldwide. Education is an important sphere in the struggle for equity and gender justice, and here feminist educational theorists can contribute a great deal. In the broadest sense, feminists are in alliance with other movements for justice and equality throughout the world and the fight for gender equity is part of a wider struggle for social justice.

Feminist educational thinkers thus call for alliances for shared political goals while continuing to articulate our own interests as feminists. The essays in this collection suggest a variety of feminist engagements with male-authored theory. Rather than rejecting patriarchal philosophy and male-dominated political movements because they are flawed, the feminist educational theorists represented here have attempted to achieve a critical engagement with male theorists-not dismissing them because of their limited vision, but engaging and subverting them for feminist goals.

STUART HALL AND CULTURAL STUDIES

It is quite implausible to retrace the vast and diverse spectrum of Stuart Hall's theoretical work in any detailed or coherent fashion. Perhaps, for this reason, a good friend in the United Kingdom spurned this project, muttering "only an American would be so audacious as to write a paper on Stuart Hall!" Indeed, it is an enormous task. Apart from coauthored and edited volumes, Hall's writings are found as chapters or journal articles, making it sometimes difficult to access his work.

Although I shall draw on a range of essays by Hall to illustrate important points, I want to take what he calls the five "theoretical turns" as a central template. I am referring to his reflections given in a talk at the international "Cultural Studies Now and in the Future" conference, published in Cultural Studies, edited by Lawrence Grossberg, Cody Nelson, and Paula Treichler (1992a). In this chapter, Hall reflects on his own involvement in, and the evolution of, cultural studies as well as various theoretical issues. This seems a useful way to begin to reflect upon the man and the "field." (Many cultural studies scholars would resist this term.)

"The search for beginnings is tempting but illusory," writes Hall. What has become known as British cultural studies grew out of the work of men such as Hall, Richard Hoggart, and Raymond Williams as well as others, already doing the work before "it" was named Stuart Hall recalls, "I sometimes feel like a tableau vivant, a spirit of the past resurrected, laying claim to the authority of an origin. After all, didn't cultural studies emerge somewhere at that moment when I first met Raymond Williams, or in the glance I exchanged with Richard Hoggart? In that moment, cultural studies were born; it emerged full grown from the head!"

While cognizant of this "grandfather narrative", Hall rejects being positioned in cultural studies metanarrative. Influenced by the work of structuralists such as Roland Barthes and Claude Levi-Strauss in France and Raymond Williams and Richard Hoggart in the United Kingdom, cultural studies produced a rupture with the kinds of sociological thinking of the 1960s. This "cultural turn" gave rise to "a new interdisciplinary field of study organized around culture as a privileged concept-'cultural studies.'"

A postgraduate research center, the Center for Contemporary Cultural Studies (CCCS), was established during this time at the University of Birmingham. It was first directed by Richard Hoggart, who at that time was professor of modern English literature. Cultural studies has always been interdisciplinary and has researched, challenged, and broadened understandings in, among other disciplines, popular culture, media studies, film studies, communication, ethnography, anthropology, and sociology. It has drawn from many areas, including sociological analyses, Marxist thought, French semiotics, poststructuralism, feminism, and psychoanalytic theory, all the while, Hall (1997a) explains, "radically rethink[ing] the articulation between the material and the cultural or symbolic factors in social analysis.

This is the intellectual point of reference from which 'cultural studies' took its point of departure". "What was the bibliography of a cultural studies thesis?" asked Hall, reflecting on the years at the Center for Contemporary Cultural Studies. "Nobody knew". Many scholars, well-known to education, have been associated with this interdisciplinary early work: Paul Gilroy, Paul Willis, and, importantly for understanding the evolution of the CCCS, many feminist scholars: Hazel Carby, Pratibha Parmar, Rebecca O'Rourke, and Chris Weedon. In sum, cultural studies emerged out of a plethora of histories, disciplines, methodologies, methods, questions and issues.

During the fifties and sixties, mainstream British sociology was "militantly empiricist and quantitative", relying heavily on traditional-functionalist American sociological models. Such reified theories lacked the explanatory power to deal with "culture" in the new, dynamic ways being conceptualized by scholars at the CCCS, who were interested in studying communicative practices, institutions, ideological beliefs, and the arts. They were also interested in debating the agenda of the New Left while examining the wider social, economic, political, and historical processes that affected cultural practices in the local and global contexts of informational and multinational capitalistic systems.

Now, culture was being conceptualized as a process, a set of practices, the production and exchange of meanings, or representations between members of a society. (For example, language is a privileged system of representation.) Human beings were seen as socially "regulated" by these meanings through the norms and codes that we live by and adhere to in any given culture. That is to say, participants in a culture make sense of or understand events around them in similar ways.

Hall explains, "Every social activity or institution generates and requires its own distinctive world of meanings and practices - its own culture.... Every social practice has cultural or discursive conditions of existence. Social practices, in so far as they depend on meaning for their operation and effects take place within discourse, are 'discursive'" (225-26; emphasis in the original). Culture, here, was no longer being addressed as merely "a way of life" or "shared values of a group or society," as conventional anthropological and sociological definitions might portray it.

One might imagine that the early years at the Center for Contemporary Cultural Studies marked a time of great theoretical growth and innovation. In the seventies and eighties, extraordinary work was produced by Hall and his colleagues as they clustered in different working groups (history group, media group, race and politics group, Tel Quel, etc.) and made their working papers available in a number of publications. However, Hall describes these years of intellectual stretching as a time of "theoretical noise" with "a great deal of bad feeling, argument, unstable anxieties and angry silences". He chronicles some of this theoretical work and struggles in various accounts.

Hall evokes the biblical story of Jacob who wrestled with a man (the angel of the Lord) until "the breaking of the day" to emphasize the necessary struggle with theory that he and others underwent during this time. As he writes, "the only theory worth having is that which you have to fight off, not that which you speak with profound fluency. I remember looking at [Althusser's] idea of "theoretical practice" in Reading Capital and thinking, 'I've gone as far in this book as it is proper to go.' I felt, I will not give an inch to this profound misreading, this super-structuralist mistranslation, of classical Marxism unless he beats me down, unless he defeats me in the spirit. He'll have to march over me to convince me. I warred with him, to the death".

Graeme Turner (1990) explains that Hall has been a "conduit" for British scholars in interpreting European theory, much of which had not been translated in English; Turner also sees Hall as currently performing this function in the United States. In his talk at the cultural studies conference in Illinois in 1992, Hall outlined five key theoretical moments or "theoretical turns" at the CCCS:

> First, the opening of the question of the personal as political and its consequences for changing the object of study in cultural studies, was completely revolutionary in a theoretical and practical way. Second, the radical expansion of the notion of power, which had hitherto been very much developed within the framework of the notion of the public, the public domain, with the effect that we could not use the term power - so key to the earlier problematic of hegemony - in the same way. Third, the centrality of questions of gender and sexuality to the understanding of power itself. Fourth, the opening of many of the questions that we thought we had abolished around the dangerous area of the subjective and the subject, which lodged those questions at the center of cultural studies as a theoretical practice. Fifth, the "re-opening" of the closed frontier between social theory and the theory of the unconscious-psychoanalysis. It's hard to describe the import of the opening of that new continent in cultural studies.

These themes exemplify a rethinking of many "classical" modernist theorists' ideas (e.g., Karl Marx, Antonio Gramsci, Jürgen Habermas, Ferdinand de Saussure). Scholars at the CCCS stretched through what Hall calls "Semiotics 1," structuralist notions of language, linguistics, and semiotics, where "the subject is left as an empty space". After engaging with psychoanalytic models, they were able to critique the inadequacies in these earlier models of semiotics, language, film theory, and the like with a more dynamic "Semiotics 2." The French intellectuals (especially Michel Foucault and Jacques Lacan) influenced Hall's theorizing of the encoding/decoding process in analyzing how viewers respond to media and text, greatly influencing film studies in general.

Hall explained that Marxism was not a central project on their cultural studies agenda, but that it raised fundamental issues regarding class relationships, questions of power, exploitation, politics, and ideology. Thus, Hall and others found themselves working "within shouting distance of Marxism, working against

Marxism, working with it, working to try to develop Marxism". However, some leftists nostalgically yearned for the kinds of analyses from which the CCCS moved as its scholars expanded theoretical notions through engaging with psychoanalytic and postmodern ideas (e.g., Jacques Derrida, Julia Kristeva, Lacan and Foucault), allowing them to re-theorize subjectivity, identity, language, discursivity, and power.

Much criticism, not so much of Hall, but of cultural studies in general has focused precisely on this shift, and importantly from the Left. Carole Stabile believes that with postmodernism, consumption has overtaken production and class struggle has become an "obsolete concept". Robert McChesney chides the field for having "fallen from Stuart Hall's brilliant 1979 conception of the market and its relation to class inequality". Aijaz Ahmad, senior fellow at the Center for Contemporary Studies, Nehru Memorial Museum and Library, New Delhi, reminds us that cultural studies emerged out of concerns for the poor, dispossessed, and underprivileged in society.

Its forefathers were imprisoned for their ideas. For Ahmad, "a few of them [British cultural studies scholars] got sucked into the storm of French post-structuralism as it swept the British Isles. Much work that is now done in British cultural studies strikes me as being distributed between those earlier kinds of commitments and the later kinds of obscurity". Another powerful criticism of cultural studies relates to relevance, a concern addressed by Hall in his talk at the 1990 Illinois cultural studies conference. "Against the urgency of people dying in the streets what in God's name is the point of cultural studies?" Hall asked.

He used the contemporary example of AIDS, a complex political site, to raise questions about the concrete meanings of theoretical and intellectual work: "Anyone who is into cultural studies seriously as an intellectual practice must feel, on their pulse, its ephemerality, its insubstantiality, of how little it registers, how little it changes anything or gets anybody to do anything. If you don't feel that as one tension in the work you are doing, theory has let you off the hook". Here Hall underscores the necessity of rootedness in praxis, that political work and intellectual work are connected and integrated.

He seems aware of this prevalent criticism, emphasizing engaged, political work: "I come back to the difficulty of instituting a genuine cultural and critical practice, which is intended to produce some kind of organic intellectual political work, which doesn't not try to inscribe itself in the overarching meta-narrative of achieved knowledges, within institutions". However, as others have observed in some circles, cultural studies as a discipline has become in vogue, professionalized, and depoliticized despite its history of critical praxis. Canadian feminist Ann Wilson remarks that "academics doing this work begin to look like the late twentieth century's academic version of the fop strolling down the mall: an attempt to stage oneself as hip".

Hall himself chides the "rapid institutionalisation" and the "theoretical fluency" of cultural studies, especially in the North American context. Wilson correctly relates this current vogue to issues of funding. Earlier, I mentioned the grand narrative of "Britishness." The CCCS may be clothed in a spatial and cultural hegemony. Handel Kashope Wright critiques the "centrism" of the Center for Contemporary Cultural Studies.

Through the use of international examples from Africa, Asia, and non-Anglo-phone Europe, he relocates the origins of cultural studies as multiplicitous, noting, "The ubiquitous assertions that Birmingham is the inaugural cultural studies institution implies that wherever cultural studies is to be found in the world today, it migrated there from Birmingham. This is an ironically imperialistic development for a discourse concerned with the inclusion of the subaltern in literary, historical, sociological and cultural analysis".

Similar to Wright, but from a feminist perspective, Wilson acknowledges the problem that cultural studies are rooted in interpretive practices informed by Marxism and structuralism, "potentially another permutation of a European intellectual tradition which has not accommodated the interests of women, particularly women from non-European cultures". She criticizes that some cultural studies work replicates the historical privilege of universities as the domains of the elite. She critiques the "blindness to its own inscription of relations of power." For Wilson, the inadequate attention to power relations raises a question for a feminist: "is it possible to discuss gender within cultural studies?" Despite the political origins of cultural studies, its academics are complicit in perpetuating ivory tower notions of power and privilege.

FEMINISMS AND CULTURAL STUDIES

The five theoretical turns named by Hal! have been historically feminist questions. For example, the well-known slogan "The personal is political," as Angela Davis explains was a phrase emanating out of the early activist moments of the second-wave twentieth-century women's movement, exposing the masculinist ideological separation of public and private spheres. Women began speaking publicly about issues previously regarded "as a fact of private life to be shielded at all costs from scrutiny in the public sphere".

Dorothy Hobson's 1992 ethnographic work at the CCCS, for example, on the role of radio and television programs in the daily lives of working-class housewives, is a fine example of retheorizing this "private" sphere. She examines the TV and radio programs that housewives "select," programs regulated by patriarchal and productive relations of what constitute "masculine" and "feminine" activities and interests. Indeed, feminism had a great impact on the theoretical ideas at the CCCS. Hall recalls its advent: "It is not known generally how and where feminism first broke in. I use the metaphor deliberately: As a thief in the night, it broke in, interrupted, made an unseemly noise, seized the time, crapped on the table of cultural studies." I find this biblical metaphor curious.

Is Hall comparing feminism, this "thief in the night" to a time of judgment and of blessing as in the New Testament? Clearly, the metaphor evokes the notion of the "boys at the Center being taken off guard" as Wilson explains, and that they were compelled to examine their own investment in power and privilege, and the male-centeredness of their theories. Now they were faced with a retheorizing of such concepts as power and hegemony to include patriarchy. For anyone to jump on a table and "crap" on it signifies that she has been trying to be heard in vain for too long. Ann Wilson argues that although Hall claims to use the metaphor deliberately, "it marks a certain degree of ambivalence"- or at least discomfort. As Alice Walker writes, "societies all over the world fear woman's critique".

Wilson takes issue with the suggestion that feminism sneaked into the academy like "Cat Woman" ready to steal intellectual property. Reflecting on her own experience and that of many other feminist scholars, she protests that they were there, almost as a drone, in classes, taught by men, and expected to "enter into that universal position of 'man.'" "So, as a feminist," she writes, "I don't feel as if I picked the locks of the academy and entered in the middle of the night: I, like most other women academics whom I know, have been in the academy for a long time, as students and teachers.

Rather than as Cat Woman entering the academy, I feel as if I have been a bit of a drone working in the foundry to refashion intellectual critical tools with, until relatively recently, little recognition of the work. This may seem like quibbling about metaphors, but what is at stake is the historical account". "The exclusion of women and their points of view is not just a political omission and a moral blind spot but constitutes an epistemological deficit as well," stresses Seyla Benhabib. Hall admits the difficulty of remaining theoretically open.

He describes it as "a painful exercise as feminist insistence that patriarchy and gender be put on the table caused a profound re-thinking of models and of concepts (e.g., production, reproduction, Gramscian and Althusserian conceptions of hegemony). He reflects, "In one area after another of the Centre's work feminism has sent certainties and orthodoxies back to the drawing-board". Although Hall does not mention race in the five theoretical turns, much of the

CCCS's work during the early years theorized race. For example, under Hall's directorship, scholars such as Hazel Carby, Errol Lawrence, Paul Gilroy, and Pratibha Parmar contributed to the well-known volume The Empire Strikes Back: Race and Racism in 70s Britain.

Like Hall earlier, Gilroy deflates any romantic notions of this collaborative effort: "We were always divided by 'racial' and gender differences and it was unusual to be able to work together at all". Graeme Turner critiques Hall's autobiographical omissions in an acclaimed earlier volume edited by Hall entitled, Policing the Crisis: Mugging, the State, and Law and Order: "In this book, Hall's own background (West Indian) must have played a part in recovering the issue of race as one of concern to cultural studies: surprisingly, perhaps, issues of race and empire have not been at the forefront of his published work over the years".

This might be an unfair criticism, since it has been a rather recent phenomenon that men have vulnerably named themselves in their work. More recently Hall has invoked his cultural background. How do these five theoretical turns outlined by Hall relate to black feminist issues? Gender and power are theorized differently from black and white subject positions, as black feminists remind white and male theorists. So often, these theorists take an "add-on" or even parallelist approach. In The Empire Strikes Back, Hazel Carby advocates the importance of black female specificity, arguing her points through examples of the family, patriarchy, and reproduction as concepts grounded in white feminist history.

She writes, "The experience of Black women does not enter the parameters of parallelism". Regarding feminist/ psychoanalytic theories mentioned earlier, British black feminist film theorist Lola Young argues that they are inadequate, often not identifying race as a specific problematic related to gender.

She refers to Mary Anne Doane's 1991 "Dark Continents" as an example of white feminist ambivalence regarding the use of psychoanalytic theory in discussing race. In the

Americas, the personal is and has always been political for black women, whose personal lives have been violated in particular ways. Consider reproductive rights: Marsha Tyson Darling argues that white male patriarchy has established a legacy of property interests using black women. She demonstrates that black women are targeted in black magazines such as Essence and Ebony for the sale of the birth control methods Depo Provera and Norplant.

2

Teenage and Media Practice

Publication of North Carolina's first statewide survey of adolescent sexual behaviour revealed that a majority of Tar Heel teens were engaging in sex while in high school, and many were becoming sexually active in middle school. One out of six teens who took part in the 1994 National Youth Risk Behaviour Survey said they had lost their virginity by age 13. Nearly three quarters of the 2,439 students surveyed reported having engaged in intercourse by the 12th grade. And despite their growing awareness that condoms were the best defense against contracting HIV and other sexually transmitted diseases, nearly half of these young people reported they did not use them.

In fact, one third of the sexually active students reported they used no birth control at all. In line with national statistics, the study results pointed to a hard reality: All adolescents are vulnerable when it comes to risky sexual behaviour. It was against this backdrop that the qualitative study reported here was launched. The study was guided by the premise that if we can figure out how adolescents with different personal and social identities and sociocultural backgrounds select, interact, and apply media matter in their everyday lives, we will be able to do a better job of reaching them with media messages that they will listen to and act on.

Key questions included: What role does the mass media play in national trends of early sexual intercourse, unplanned teenage pregnancies, and out-of-wedlock births? How do mass media images and messages about love, sex, and relationships interact with what teens learn at home, in school, and from their friends? How do teens assimilate through media practice what they learn about sexuality in the course of their everyday lives?

In previous empirical work on adolescents' room culture we had found that many teens draw heavily from media images and storylines as they wrestle with who they are and where they fit in the world. Working from a developmental perspective that recognized identity formation as a key task of adolescence, we devised a model that explained how adolescents' media practice revolved around identity. Drawing on sociogenetic theories of development, we asserted that media practice could only be understood in context.

It was with the embodied knowledge acquired through "lived through experience," Steele and Brown reasoned, that teens "build on and transform the shared sociocultural knowledge available through the media". However, in these earlier studies we had not looked more broadly to see how media practice intersected with the everyday activities and systems of social interactions that make up teens' everyday lives. Our understanding of Lived Experience was theoretically rather than empirically driven.

This study takes the next step and considers the dialectic give-and-take between teens and media in the context of their everyday lives. For most adolescents, that context includes interactions with family in various configurations and with school and friend or peer networks. Church and job affiliations also play prominent roles in some adolescents' lives, but they seem to follow from family and peer influences. Consequently, they were not included among the domains studied.

The study complements two mass communication research streams: content analyses of sexual content in the mass media and media effects research focusing on teenagers. (Effects studies on adolescent sexuality are rare.) Researchers have done a good job of chronicling the kinds and amount of sexual media content available to teens, but knowing what teens can access is not the same as knowing how they use or make sense of what's available. Also, most content analyses focus on a single medium, even though most teens interact with multiple media on a daily basis. Television has received the most research attention, even though magazines, music, and movies become increasingly important sources of information about sex and ways to be as teens grow older.

In hopes of remedying some of these problems, this study considered how teens weave sexual media content drawn from all of the major media into their identities through media practice. The study was grounded in the belief that the mass media constitute a rich and diverse tool kit of sexual scripts and role models that teens use as they explore the possible selves they might become. Special attention was paid to what occurs when teens' media practices intersect with the influences of family, friends, and school.

The study was a qualitative, multi-method investigation designed like a funnel-wide at the top (in terms of numbers of participants and areas of inquiry) to generate a broad understanding of teens' media practices, and narrower in focus at the bottom to explore emerging themes in greater depth. The first phase consisted of eight focused group discussions in which a total of 51 teens participated. A subset of these teens, one to three from each focus group, kept written or tape-recorded media journals and then participated in a room tour or in-depth interview.

In addition to being suited to the grounded theory approach recommended by Glaser & Strauss, the triangulated data-gathering structure created an opportunity to compare how the teens interacted and what they had to say in a group setting with their behaviour and expressions in the one-on-one context of room tours and in-depth interviews. Beginning the inquiry with focus groups made it possible to tap into the wide array of ideas and information that emerged as the teens interacted with one another and with the discussion moderator.

The goal of the focus groups was to get teens talking about sexuality, operationalized as love, sex, and relationships, in an informal, relaxed setting that would simulate their everyday talk and clarify the socially-constructed meanings they shared. The self-account media journals kept by participants afforded an additional vantage point from which to explore the dialogic tension between group loyalties and individual attitudes, values, and beliefs.

Recruitment strategy was guided by three objectives:

1. To involve both younger and older teens so that developmental differences could be considered. Rather than screen participants by age, I elected to rely on rank in school as the admittedly rough cut between younger (enrolled in middle school) and older (enrolled in high school) teens.
2. To oversample teens more likely to engage in risky sexual behaviour (e.g., intercourse at a young age, unprotected sex, or sex with multiple partners).
3. To include teens who frequently are underrepresented in studies of adolescent sexuality due to recruitment and retention problems and the challenges of getting parental consent.

Black teens, school dropouts, teens who have left home and are living on their own, and teens who use drugs and/or alcohol frequently fall into categories 2 and 3. Focus group teens were recruited through naturally-occurring friend groups (Anderson and Drexel) and organisations that worked with the populations of interest: a county-wide adolescent parenting program designed to help teenage mothers complete high school without getting pregnant again (Teen Mothers), a recreation center serving a predominantly Black neighborhood (Spencer), and a downtown teen center (City Space) that catered to young people looking for a place to hang out and be with friends after school and on weekends. Most of the teens lived in a Southeastern town of about 40,000; a few lived in adjoining communities.

Recruitment flyers were explicit about the topics of discussion and monetary incentives. For example, the headline on a flyer designed to recruit middle school teens read: "TEENS! Get paid $15 for talking about the media and how it fits with your life!" The text gave additional details about the study and invited teens to "participate in a group discussion about what the media have to do with your opinions about love, sex and relationships." Twenty-four males and 27 females participated in the focus groups. About half of the teens were in middle school; half were in high school.

A few of the high-school-aged teens had dropped out of high school but were attending a Graduate Equivalency Degree (GED) program offered by a nearby community college. One teen had completed high school. The focus groups with middle school teens were same sex and, with one exception, same race. Informed consent was obtained from teens and parents or guardians in two phases: first to participate in a focus group and, subsequently, to keep a media journal and participate in a room tour or in-depth interview.

Although this approach necessitated tracking down consent forms twice, it gave teens and their parents a clear choice about participating in the second study phase. Fact sheets about the project invited parents to call the investigator if they had questions, and courtesy visits; were made to the homes of teens who did not have telephones or who wanted someone to talk with a parent or guardian about the teen's interest in participating.

Phone calls placed the morning of or day before each focus group reminded teens to come, and care was taken to hold the focus groups at times and in places convenient to the teens. When they arrived, the teens filled out a face sheet containing demographic questions and a brief media questionnaire detailing the media they liked best and how much time they spent with various types of media. After some informal talk about media preferences, two music videos-Blackstone's "I Don't Want To Say Goodbye" and TLC's "Creep"-were previewed to jump start discussion about sexual media content.

The videos were selected because they were popular (on MTV's top 10 playlist) and provocative but noncontroversial in their treatment of sexual relationships. In addition, both videos featured Black artists. Studies of TV viewing patterns have indicated that White viewers will watch shows featuring Black actors, but Black viewers are less likely to watch shows with only White actors and actresses.

Moderators followed a loosely-structured discussion guide to ensure consistency across groups, but they were encouraged to pursue related topics as they arose. Actual discussion times ranged from about 60 - 90 minutes. Snacks were served, and the journal-keeping/room tour phases of the study were explained toward the end of each session. Each teenager received $15 in cash for participating in the focus group. Each focus group was tape-recorded, and I took notes during or immediately following each session. Tapes were dubbed, then transcribed by experienced transcriptionists. I reviewed all transcripts for accuracy. When questions arose, I replayed the original audio-tape and consulted my notes to figure out what was actually said.

Each journal-keeper was supplied with a small tape recorder or boombox and two audiotapes, as well as a personal "journal kit" containing a notebook, coloured pen, scissors, and glue stick to encourage active participation. I personally delivered a kit to each participating teen's home in order to get a glimpse of the home environment and to demonstrate my interest in the teen as a person. Journal keepers were expected to spend 15 minutes a day for 7 days recording or writing down commentary about what they saw and heard in the media and how it related to what they had learned about love, sex, and relationships at home, in school, and from their friends.

Daily prompts were designed to keep journal-keepers focused on the topic of sexuality, operationalized as "love, sex, and relationships." The teens were encouraged to clip out and comment on advertisements, headlines, and pictures about love, sex, and relationships found in their favorite magazines. They were also encouraged to write down or tape-record the lyrics to songs they particularly liked. A $20 incentive was offered for keeping a journal.

The final stage of data-gathering involved talking in greater depth with teens about what they had said or written in their journals and accompanying them on self-narrated tours of their bedrooms. The room tours gave teens an opportunity to talk about the significance of their favorite things. The teens were asked to pay particular attention to room decorations and memorabilia that pointed to their sense of who they were, what they valued, and the kind of life they wanted to lead. Participants who preferred to be interviewed elsewhere were given that option. Several of the high-school-aged teens chose to be interviewed in a local coffee shop. Teens were paid an additional $20 for participating in a room interview. The incentive payment plan was explained in straightforward language (e.g., you "will be paid for...") in both parents' and teens' informed consent forms.

Validity - assurance that the research actually illuminates constructs of interest-is always a concern, regardless of research method. In qualitative studies, the structure of the inquiry is one test of validity. In this case, the triangulation of data, such as looking for corroboration of inferences from the multiple perspectives of focused group discussions, media journals, and one-on-one interviews, was used to substantiate findings.

ANALYSIS

Data analysis began with the writing of my first field notes and continues to this day. During the information seeking phase of the project, I tried to stay close to the data by replaying audiotapes, re-reading transcripts and field notes, and studying what the teens chose to include in their media journals. By continually contrasting what study participants were saying with emerging themes and patterns, I was able to adjust working hypotheses and identify questions that merited further probing.

Tentative theories were put to the test of teens' scrutiny during each subsequent round of data gathering. Using this constant comparative approach advocated by Glaser and Strauss, the scope of inquiry was narrowed gradually until saturation, the point when variation is accounted for and understood, was reached. Morse defines saturation as the test of adequacy in qualitative research.

Redundancy is another term for the same thing; in other words, the point when additional data provide no new results. This same method of comparison continues to guide consideration of the data as I write accounts of my findings. Because of the vast amount of data generated - more than 30 hours of tape-recorded material, 13 paper journals, and several hundred pages of verbatim transcripts-I decided to use a computerized data analysis program, NUD-IST, to help me systematically make sense of this complex material.

The program facilitated both theory-driven, hierarchical coding and more intuitive, discovery-driven coding. Systematically coding the material helped me understand what "were there," what concepts, theories, and supporting evidence were embedded in the data. Using the two coding modes in combination made it easier to be methodical and thorough. Each transcript was coded separately, then coding notations were merged through whole data set reports. I also used the program's report function to maintain a chronological coding log that served as another check on my subjectivity.

A review of progressive coding reports make it possible for anyone who wishes to retrace the analytical judgments made, thereby strengthening the reliability or trustworthiness of findings. Because the Adolescents' Media Practice Model structures this report, a brief description of the model may be useful to the reader before considering results. The model is based on the notion that teens' interactions with media are part of the dialectical process of becoming that characterizes human existence.

For adolescents, this process is wrapped up in forging a cohesive sense of self and figuring out where one fits in the world. Informed by Johnson's conceptualisation of the production, circulation, and consumption of cultural texts, the model was drawn as a circuit to highlight the connections between teens' identity work and their media practices, (e.g., the everyday activities and routines of media consumption). The model was based on the premise that teens' sense of who they are shapes their encounters with media, and those encounters in turn shape their sense of themselves, including their sexual selves.

Five key components were specified in the initial presentation of the model. The intention was to represent a seamless process in which Identity, Selection, Interaction, and Application interact against the backdrop or within the parameters of Lived Experience. Lived Experience is a sociogenetic construct that accounts for the complex ways in which race, class, gender, lifestage, and countless other variables differentiate one person's experience of day-to-day occurrences from another person's. Conceived as the situated reality of individuals and groups, the term was placed above the circuit to suggest the role of Lived Experience as ground for the entire circuit.

The media components of the model were defined as follows: (a) Selection: the act of choosing among media-related alternatives; (b) Interaction: the cognitive, affective, and/or behavioral engagement with media that produces cultural meanings; and (c) Application: the ways in which teens make media active in their everyday lives. Illustrative examples or attributes of the three media-related components were positioned along the perimeter of the circuit. They were Motivation, Attention, Interpretation, Evaluation, Incorporation, and Appropriation. In a more recent version of the model, Resistance was substituted for Appropriation.

According to the model, teens' media practices should be understood as integral parts of the continuous process of cultural production and reproduction, including the production and reproduction of sexual norms. Typical adolescents interact with media all day long. They wake up to the radio, talk with friends at school about yesterday's episode of their favorite TV show, and then flip through TV channels or the latest issue of their favorite magazine while relaxing after school.

Teens' selectivity in making media choices, their creative interpretations of media content, and the varied ways they actively use media in their everyday lives are the essential elements of media practice. But rather than focus on these moments of practice, this analysis considers how teens' media practices intersect with other major influences on teen sexuality-namely those of the family, friends, and school-through social relations. Data presented were generated in 1995.

IDENTITY AND LIVED EXPERIENCE

A primary challenge of adolescence is self-definition. Teens work at defining the "real me," including the "sexual me," as they prepare for entry into the adult world. Whereas 50 years ago a teen's family, friends, school, and church probably were the primary influences on his or her attitudes, values, and beliefs about sexuality, today's teens have access to a fifth powerful influence - the ubiquitous mass media. Reaching worldwide, the media bring teens compelling images of sexuality that range from the predictability of a television soap opera or country-western ballad to the unpredictability of an independent filmmaker or recording artist. These media windows on the world are part of teens' Lived Experience.

Not unlike adults at social functions, teens look for people or situations "like them" in the media. When they find people or story lines that resonate with their lives, they pay attention. For example, the everyday challenges of being a teenager sparked Lindsey's interest in the television show, My So Called Life.

Well, it's my only favorite show... I like it because it is about a 15 year old girl and her life. It tells her thoughts and feelings about things. She has problems like most teenagers do. She is faced with guns, violence, drinking, drugs, sex, and school. It is a good show because it is so close in relation to teens nowadays. It shows good ways to handle our problems and fears.

The "credibility factor" was a standard many teens applied to media content. For example, Tenita (16, Black, Teen

Mother) wrote in her journal that she liked to watch soap operas.

> Their always someone fallin' in love or havin' a baby. Soap Operas' is nothing like everyday life. Their relationships are so fairy tale like they get divorce and get back together. That doesn't happen much in everyday life. Sex on the other hand is about like everyday life. They have sex a lot and it is so romantic. I like to watch soap opera's, even though I can't see them since I am in school.

Even though she recognized the fairy tale nature of soap opera story lines, Tenita was unable to apply the same critical standard to soap sex. Did this view of sex as romantic make it easier for her to have intercourse at age 14 with a guy she hardly knew who was five years her senior? A similar naivete (or was it bravado?) was expressed by one of the Spencer boys, during the group discussion about favorite TV shows.

> What they doin' on TV anti videos is really based on real life, ya know. What you see in movies like really happened, ya know? It depends on what kind of movie you watch... right? If you watch the Real Stories of the Highway Patrol, they showin', they really showin' what happened in real life... they try to base the show on their actions in real life...

In the preceding examples, the teens' judgments about credibility hinge on abstract world views that have been acquired over their entire lifetimes. In order for media content to be believable, it must correspond with what they know of the world through lived experience. Ethnicity also affects Selection. Black teens showed a marked preference for media featuring Black actors, performers, and content. For example, six Black teens but no White teens listed Jason's Lyric, a love story about a Black couple, as their first or second favorite movie. The preference for Black performers by Black teens was even more evident in their listings of favorite musicians.

All of the performers they liked were Black even though their musical styles ranged from rhythm and blues (R&B) to rap to jazz. Similar demarcations were seen with magazines.

For instance, the White middle school girls all listed YM or Seventeen as their favorite magazines. Both are edited for a mainstream, predominantly White audience. None of the Black girls read these magazines. Instead, they listed Black hair magazines (Black Hair, Braids) and Ebony (beauty and fashion), Jet (current events), and Word Up (music) as their favorites.

Gender differences were also apparent in media preferences. Black artists or musical groups such as Mary J. Blige, Brandi, and Salt 'N' Pepa were listed by several of the Black females, but none of the Black males. Similarly, White musicians never were listed as boys' favorites, only girls'. Gender cross-overs were more frequent with television shows, particularly the popular docu-dramas that have come into vogue. For example, Seinfeld was fairly popular with White boys and girls, as were Ellen and Home Improvement. None of these shows appeared in the Black teens' rankings of favorite shows.

Differences in developmental level also affect media preferences. Several of the younger (middle school) White boys listed Forrest Gump as a favorite movie, and they also liked the slapstick humor of Jim Carey's Ace Ventura and Dumb and Dumber. Mask, another comedy featuring Carey and an improbable plot, appeared four times, a favorite of both Black and White teens. None of these movies showed up as best shows for high-school-aged teens, suggesting that the storylines were less appealing to more mature audiences. For early adolescents, however, actor Carey got it just right: the dumber, the better. In his journal, Karl, then in seventh grade, explained the appeal of "dumb" this way:

Anyway, um, I really like this movie [Dumb and Dumber]. I thought it was very funny. There were several dumb humor parts, and that's the kind of humor I like. I find it very easy to watch this because there are very sarcastic parts and they did some stupid things. I thought the movie was hysterical. The plot was pretty good, too.

Sometimes, however, teens can't find role models to whom they can relate. Tanya (13, Black female) critiqued the television show 90210 for not being "true to life," a phrase that approximates the notion of Lived Experience:

> I used to watch 90210 till I was like, this is not real! I wanted it to be closer to the way things really are! How many of us parents will let us go spend the night at our boyfriend's house, and have us drivin' they cars way up and down the streets. I mean, some people' parents do that, but not mine! I mean, shoot, have boyfriends here and there, and talk to your parents about every little thing you do, and have them perfectly understand and never put you on punishment for nothin' you do? These kids, I mean, they in jail and their parents don't ground them or nothin'!
>
> It's like, they just let them go off and do what they wanna do! "Sure, honey, you want to borrow my car to go there'?" I hate to think! Shoot! They're gonna put me on lockdown. Shoot! Nobody watches that show no more, I don't think.

Tanya's perception that nobody watched 90210 anymore was based on her Lived Experience as a Black teen from a lower income home. It is not surprising that the exploits of an essentially all-White cast of affluent teens living in Beverly Hills struck her as "stupid." Jade, 16, a Black teenage mother, watched TV talk shows from dawn to dusk when she had a day off from school and work because that was the one place she saw other Black teens whose situations paralleled her own. But even on talk shows she rarely found reinforcement for her goal of completing high school and attending business school.

> I don't see anybody in my position on the media, except for negatives. They don't show nobody, you know, tryin' to go to school and get good grades 'n stuff... And usually when I see the talk shows, it's people talking against me, and stuff like that.

Historically, American researchers have seen exposure; a term used to indicate time [spent] with media, as the key to media effects. This is problematic, however, because measures of exposure tell us nothing about the context of viewing/ listening or the amount of attention paid to the sexual components of media content. Close examination in this study of teens' engagement with media produced an understanding that posits a syncretic and holistic definition of Interaction, one that includes emotional, psychological, and physical dimensions.

The teens' responses to the video stimuli used in the focus groups help to illustrate this point. Both videos told stories about heterosexual relationships: Blackstreet from a male perspective, TLC from a female perspective. The Blackstreet video told a "break up and make up" story (as one of the teens labeled it) by juxtaposing saccharin lyrics with spicy visuals that encouraged erotic readings.

Against the backdrop of the smooth, lazy harmonies associated with R & B, the story is told through the juxtaposition of sepia-tinted flashbacks of childhood scenes with cuts of the unfolding narrative and cuts of the group singing. In contrast, the TLC video features an upbeat, hip-hop tempo and the blatant eroticism of what might be characterized as a postmodern belly dance. Bare stomachs, undulating hips, and satin pajamas stirred up by off-camera wind machines combine to weave a sultry spell punctuated by the staccato refrain of a trumpet.

Between-group differences in Interaction were evident already during the showing of the music videos. They were drawn along lines of race, gender, and developmental stage. The middle school White girls squealed and squirmed when confronted with the videos' in-your-face sexuality, while the middle school Black girls giggled and danced. The middle school boys, Black and White, watched mostly in silence but then alternated between being silly and strutting their macho stuff during the discussion that followed.

The older teens moaned and groaned at the very thought of watching music videos, then yawned with disdain at Blackstreet's rhythm and blues' style or puzzled over the suggestive language and images used in the videos, especially the narratively-complex Blackstreet production. Differences were equally pronounced when the teens started talking about the videos. No group spoke with one voice, but there was a tendency in all of the groups to build on shared perceptions. As they responded to the moderator's questioning, the teens adjusted their understanding of what took place in the videos and moved toward consensus about what they had seen and heard.

This consensus on content or form held up across groups, supporting the view that even "open" media texts allow only so much room for creative interpretation. Lively contestations within groups over the meaning of certain actions, lyrics, gestures, scenes, and sequences again underscored the importance of development and lived experience in media practice. The tendency of groups to seek common understandings was illustrated by the Spencer boys as they related the storyline of the Blackstreet video. "There were these dudes standin' on the stoop," said Tyrone, 14, launching the story. "They were sayin'..." "`Bout some, ah, girl," continued Arizona, 14.

"Yeah, they um, one of 'em, this girl, they was sayin'... shit, like play games. Like one day she not in the mood and the next day she try to get off... and that's about it," interpreted Smittie, 14. Then, Tyrone summed up: "Oh, um... These people, they were urn, I think they broke up or somethin'. Then they got back together when he gave her a ring with a Hershey's kiss on it. And they showed these little kids, and the little boy gave the girl one." Individual-level differences in comprehension and interpretation also were apparent. In some cases, individual teens missed entirely the "preferred" or producer-intended meaning of the videos.

For example, most of the Drexel boys were convinced that Blackstone's lead singer Riley wanted to "have sex," but when the moderator pressed them to make clear why they thought this the boys had to struggle to make sense of the flashbacks used throughout the video. Their confusion may have resulted from a lack of familiarity with production techniques, or it may have stemmed from inexperience with the sexual behaviour pictured or suggested.

For example, several groups had difficulty discerning what the "Creep" video really was about. "That's all I see was dancin' in rows, thas' all. I don't get the point of that creep part, whatever that is," volunteered Smittie, 14, during the Spencer boys' discussion. The responses of the 3-member Riverside High School group were even more naive, demonstrating again how interpreting or understanding media content is linked to experience. Andrew: Well, I think both of them sort of dealt with problems in relationships, or, I don't know, because like even though we couldn't tell what was going on in the second one, just the word "creep" implies that it wasn't like something necessarily fun that they were doing, you know? Like there was some tension.

Mod: What do you mean?

Jonathan: Well, if you are going to call somebody a creep or if you are calling yourself creep or if you are using the word creep in general sort of means that you are either mad at the other person, or, you know. I don't know, it just doesn't seem like a very positive word.

When the Adolescents' Media Practice Model (Steele & Brown, 1995) was introduced, two types of Application, appropriation and incorporation, were specified. The forms were so intertwined, however, that it was difficult to explicate where one ended and the other began. In the initial formulation, Appropriation was seen as an active "taking" from the media that was expressed through room culture and the conscious modelling of media roles and behaviors.

Incorporation, in contrast, was seen as a more subconscious embodiment of the ideologies and cultural styles embedded in media content. However, reviewers argued that these were really one and the same activity. Upon closer examination of teens' media practices in this study, two types of appropriation have been discerned. One serves the function of social reproduction, the business of reproducing societal norms and making them look natural. Without knowing it, Jonathan, 18, explicated incorporation quite effectively:

Yeah, I feel like even though I disagree with a lot of things that are on TV, it still does affect me. It's kind of like what you see on TV, you kind of assume is normal, you know? You see this sit-com of like the normal family, and they are doing things, they are kind of saying that this type of like behaviour is normal... It's kind of like when you are little and you see your parents, they are kind of like this model of like what you are supposed to do. So, you like copy that, whether consciously or not. So it's kind of like that.

The other type of application takes the form of resistance, teens' practice of using media to open up a space for combating the status quo. Teens who feel marginalized, a category that can include ethnic minorities, lesbians, gays, nerds, drug users, and school leavers, frequently seek out media and story lines that glamorize the very things mainstream society frowns upon. Black teens' enthusiastic embrace of rap music is a familiar example of teens using media to fight what they perceive to be the wrongs of the dominant culture. In this study, it was the City Scape teens that used alternative media to resist what they didn't like about the world around them.

Many of the City Scape teens named as favorites High Times, a magazine dedicated to "chronicling the subculture of marijuana growing and harvesting" and movies like Pulp Fiction (graphically violent and sexually explicit in the tradition of film noir) and Flashback (the storyline centers around mind-altering drugs). Some of them were drawn to hard rock and heavy metal music. What is it about the pounding drums, angry bass, grating guitars, and screaming vocals characteristic of these genres that some teens find appealing? Arnett (1996) says that individual "metalheads" listen for different reasons, but that "most of all there is the ideology of it, the ideology of alienation.

To metalheads, heavy metal performers represent a rare authenticity in a corrupt world, and the ideology of alienation gives metalheads a way of making sense of that world". Peter, 18, was a teen who gravitated toward heavy metal because of its raw power, its authenticity. He liked bass mostly for the sensation. "It just like shakes the house," he said, describing how "you could feel the air" being forced out of the speakers by heavy bass instrumentals. His embrace of the methalheads' existential ennui seemed to fit Arnett's (1996) claim: "It is not merely a diversion, but something that both shapes and reflects their view of the world and of themselves". In view of these findings, the model has been revised to include incorporation and resistance to illustrate Application.

The gratifications teens seek when they select different media (Motivation) have a major impact on Application. If a teenager is looking for sexual information to apply in everyday situations, chances are good that the sexual information he or she finds will be "incorporated" in exactly this way. Elizabeth (13, White, Anderson Middle School), for example, was clear about how she applied material gleaned from YM, one of her "more favorite magazines":

Inside you can read about almost anything that's going on in lots of people's lives. They tell you about how to deal with lots of different situations such as being overweight, your friends not liking you, family problems, or they always give lots of information about love.

Although she reads her horoscope simply for pleasure, Elizabeth reads the Romance section of YM with an eye to positioning her boyfriend on a personal/social acceptability scale.

There's one section called Say Anything. I like to read this because it's all about embarrassing moments. I like to read those because it makes me realize how good of a day I had! Another section that I like is called Romance. It's all about the sweet things that different guys have done for girls. This is good because then you can add qualities to your dream boyfriend, or realize how good you got it since he does all that kind of stuff.

If anyone discounts the importance of teen relationships, Elizabeth's observation should dispel their doubts: "What they [adults] don't realize is these are our practices for when we get older. I think they should be taken very seriously..." Less accepting of the romantic script promulgated by teen girls' magazines, Meredith, 18 (White, City Space), sharply criticized that script even as she made it explicit. She used it to reinforce her own resistance, a move that exemplifies Application as Resistance. When asked during her interview/journal to describe the image of young women projected by Seventeen magazines, she responded:

> I think that, you know, it's a little like probably rich girl, and she has moral values, and you have to go out, probably do good in school, and you have got to have a boyfriend, and you, you know, can't do drugs or try alcohol, you know, and you can't smoke cigarettes, you know. You can't do this or that, or this or that. And it's, but it's, you know, like a 12-year-old girl gets that and she thinks that that has to be her life. You know, she has to like go to school, meet some guy, get married, have kids, you know, and have a career at the same time. And it's just like, it doesn't really give people a chance to think for themselves. [It's] some kind of a brainwashing thing.

Ironically, even though Meredith was sharply critical of mainstream media messages and was keeping company with an alternative crowd during the period of the study, she nevertheless confessed to wanting to live out the mainstream script, not in the present, but in 5 or 10 years.

> Most of the people I know and myself included would say that of everyone that I hang out with, I am one of the most likely people to end up married with kids and a little house with a white picket fence and just completely happy that way, you know, and having it last just because of the way I am.

Her words suggest how difficult it is to escape the pull of the dominant ideology, particularly when one is part of the privileged class (White, middle class) that reproduces it through the schools, courts, mass media, and other institutions that are part of the apparatus of power. Imagine the impact of these same institutions and the dominant ideology that guides their actions on teens who see themselves as not fitting the accepted scripts.

Sexuality, like the self, is a social construction subject to a variety of competing influences. The peer group is an important source of sexual values, prescriptions, and social comparisons, as is the school, where adolescents spend from one third to as much as one half of their waking hours on an average school day. Parents, too, are important. As Harter (1990) points out, "Parental expectations, evaluations, and exhortations also play a major role and may well conflict with the values of the peer culture".

Although initially conceived as discrete identifiers, it became clear as the study unfolded that the terms family, friends, and school hold multiple meanings for teens. In addition, activities in all three spheres were intertwined, as evidenced by Arizona's (14, Black male) account of a conversation with his mother. "She was tellin' me about sex!... and them boys was tellin' me about it too," he related. "Did they tell you the same thing?" the moderator asked. "Naw, my mama was tellin' me not to do it... All the boys was tellin' me to jump on it!"

The family traditionally has been viewed as the primary socialisation agent in a child's life, the teacher of the culture and its unwritten rules. Recent work on teen vulnerability and resiliency suggests that strong or close family ties are one predictor of a teen's ability to get through adolescence without siring a child, landing in jail, developing a drug habit, or dropping out of school.

Of course, the challenge for researchers is to agree on what constitutes strong, close, family, and risky behaviour, all terms with contested definitions. Of particular interest in the context of this study was whether teens who came from troubled families relied more heavily than other teens on media for sexual information or role models. The data provided no definitive answers but did make it clear that everyday family dynamics influence teens' media practices as well as their outlooks on life.

Arizona, for example, shared a house with eight brothers. Still talking about his mama's warning that he'd better have "safe sex or no sex," Arizona told his focus group peers: "My daddy told me before he left, he said, 'Don't do nothin' I wouldn't do!'.. So I can do anything, you know what I'm sayin'? Cuz my daddy do anything!" Although physically absent, his father's attitude toward women and sex undoubtedly affected Arizona's interpretation of media narratives about sex (Interaction) and his subsequent Incorporation of those narratives into his own life.

Matt (13, White), in contrast, was a member of what typically is cast as the all-American family. However, despite living with two parents (mother and stepfather) and two sisters in a middle class home, television sometimes played the role of parental stand-in, particularly when it came to learning about sexual relationships. The following excerpt from his tape-recorded journal provides a good example of how the influences of the family and the mass media intersect, producing a "multivoicedness" that characterizes much of what we say, think, and feel.

Matt always made explicit in his journal at least two voices by reading the written journal instructions aloud, into the taperecorder, then responding to the prompt in his own words. When responding to a prompt about what he wanted for himself as a sexual human being, Matt replied:

Okay. I'd like at one time to get married and have children. I guess I'd like to, umm, ahh, have sex. I don't know if I will wait until I'm married. Of course, we would all like to, but if that is possible.... Yeah, okay. I will move on. I really hope my mom doesn't listen to this. Umm, which she better not. She won't.

Prompt: Talk about what you've learned from your parents and other family members about love, sex and relationships.

Matt: Not much. It's not exactly a dinner table discussion, unfortunately. Well, not unfortunately. You always hear that it should be from your school and stuff. I talk more with my sister than anything, and I haven't enough. Okay, let's move on. I'm sorry. I'm mumbling on and on.

Prompt: Have you ever talked with your mother, father. Oh... by observing the way they act?

Matt: Not really. Umm, can't really relate to a 40-year-old at this moment.

It is instructive to note the interplay of voices when just Matt was speaking. First, he gave voice to dominant society's preferred sexual script, the one third-graders chant to taunt one another: "First comes love, then comes marriage, then comes Suzie with a baby carriage." Then, he appropriated the message encapsulated in the music, movies, and TV sitcoms he liked: "I guess I'd like to, umm, ahh, have sex. I don't know if I will wait until I'm married."

Matt's "inner voice" or conscience interrupted the media message that sex outside of marriage is acceptable with a midstream "mm, ahh," apparently triggered by fear that his mother might hear his doubts about waiting for marriage to have sex. Then, her voice and possibly that of his minister and friends are heard: "Of course, we would all like to..." Several teens attested to the adverse effect of being given too little autonomy or trust by parents. Jade, 16, for one, said her parents' refusal to let her even sit on the front steps with her boyfriend caused her to start seeing him in the park and eventually led to her skipping school and spending time during the day at his empty (of adults) house. Now she has a six-month-old daughter.

Even though Jade, like many of her peers, wanted freedom from parental rules, she nevertheless acknowledged that her parents did have some influence on her media practices. For example, when Jade got pregnant during her junior year in high school, her mother gave her a copy of People magazine that featured a cover story titled, "Babies Who Have Babies." "I think it was a joke," Jade wrote in her journal. "But I don't know. I went ahead and read the article."

Shawn, one of the Drexel Middle School boys, complained to his focus group peers, "I don't even getta watch what I wanna watch... my mom comes in and is flickin' the channels." Earlier, when talking about the almost voyeristic enjoyment they derived from watching the bikini-clad females in the television show Bay Watch, he and his buddies indicated that they kept their visual appetites hidden, at least from their parents.

Important as parents or other significant adults are in the lives of most teenagers, adolescence remains a time when young people reach out to their age-mates to explore who they are and what to expect from the world. Throughout adolescence, teens gather information about same-sex and opposite-sex relationships from their peers. Scholars from various disciplines have helped us understand where ideas about who to love and how it feels to be in love originate in their explorations of motivated models, cultural models, and the development of feeling norms. Teens' media practices help explain how those models and norms become enculturated and shape desire.

Within the context of close friendships and wider circles of friends, teens use the media both as something to do and as something to consume. "[W]e need to realize that people no longer learn primarily through verbal instruction in this culture, but through pictures and images, which get directly at fantasy and desire and feed the hunger for stimulation and excitement" although teens spend a lot of time alone with their music, often in the safe haven of their bedrooms or cars, it would be a mistake to think that teens' love for music is a solitary pleasure.

When the moderator asked some of the City Scape teens whether listening to music was "kind of a one-on-one thing," the reply was: "No, man! Most of the time it's like in the van just sitting around with a bunch of friends just driving around with a bunch of friends. Sometimes, it's alone, but either way it's phat!" Echoing this theme of music being a connector to friends even if listening alone, Peter, 18, gave this account:

I'm talking in this thing [tape recorder] as I'm driving along, cuz I'm listenin' to a song right now. I'm not sure who it is, but it sounds really cool, and really quiet, and really, uh, I don't know what the word for it is. Aaah, I'm just thinkin' about that girl that I know, that I was talkin' to on the Internet, becuz this is like.... it kind of reminds me of her in a way... the stuff that she listens to and everything [voice rising], you know? And the stuff that she was playin' in the background when we were talkin' on the phone was kind of like this sort of stuff. I don't know.

It's just so hard to find somebody who has the same interests, and then I do, and she's like 18 hours away by car.

Peter's comments demonstrate how intertwined the various aspects of media practice are. In this case, he is drawn to the music (Selection) and continues listening to it (Attention) as he drives because of his interest in the girl (Motivation) he met on the Internet. She, in turn, had described (or identified) herself to him by the music she liked.

During the study design phase of the project, I conceptualized school as the shorthand for sex education classes. However, the equation was faulty. School holds far more complex meanings for most teens, and they learn more about sex in the hallways than in the classroom. Among the several objections study teens voiced about school-based sex education programs was the heavy emphasis on disease, redundancy from one year to the next, avoidance of topics the teacher might find embarrassing or objectionable, and a tendency to speak about sexual relationships in scientific instead of humanistic terms. Elizabeth summed it up when she observed in her journal, "We've had so many sex-ed classes, but I don't think they help any... because... all they teach is basically body parts. Nobody really cares about what's inside of them."

Hungry for information about how to develop and sustain relationships, teens instead get information about self-esteem and how to say "no." When invited toward the end of the in-depth interviews and in the last-day journal prompt to ask questions about anything that was on their minds, the middle school boys, in particular, made it clear that there were plenty of things they wanted to know about sex but weren't learning in school. Jamie raised these questions:

1. Can a girl get pregnent all of the time or just at a certain stage?
2. Can any non-diseased couple get herpies or warts by sex?
3. Is there protection for a male and/or female that prevents everything including pregnency?

The questions above, posed by an eighth-grade boy, underscore the vast amount of work that needs to be done if we want adolescents to learn what they need to know to prevent pregnancy and avoid STDs before they become sexually active. Because the scope of the study was intentionally broad and relied on qualitative research methods, its contribution to the literature does not lie in hypothesis-driven findings about what approach to promoting healthy sexuality will work best under what circumstances.

Rather, its contribution is to offer (a) a new way of understanding the relationship between teenage sexuality and the mass media, and (b) evidence that the influence of media is inextricably meshed with the contexts of teens' everyday lives. Although I use the term theory with trepidation, the study contributes to mass media theory by refining the Adolescents' Media Practice Model introduced by Steele and Brown in 1995. It does so by more carefully explicating the media components of the model-Selection, Interaction, and Application-and by considering Lived Experience from the perspective of ethnicity, gender, and developmental level.

The study also makes a contribution by putting its emphasis on media practice rather than on media content or media effects, the traditional foci of mass media research. Although sexual media content must certainly be factored into discussions of teens, sex, and media, the evidence in this study suggests we must look beyond content to how it is used, understood, appropriated, or resisted by teens immersed in the ups and downs of everyday life. Teens are active users of media, and their media practices depend to a large extent on their lived experience, the concrete, on-the-ground ways they have experienced the world on a day-to-day basis. Teens respond to media from where they are and from what they know of life.

Unfortunately, some teens don't often see "people like them" or lives "like theirs" in the media. When they do see or hear people and storylines they can relate to, the data suggest these teens may be influenced more than peers who see images of themselves all the time. Somehow, regardless of race, class, gender, intelligence, or any other personal quality that distinguished one from another, the study teens bought into the idea of the American dream (e.g., education, job, house, and family). Even teens highly critical of the dominant ideology or teenage mothers who had jeopardized their chances of achieving the dream still aspired to many of its tenets.

The discrepancies between teens' media preferences, interactions, and applications according to race, class, gender, and developmental phase underscore a major limitation of the study. It was cross-sectional. A longitudinal study of teens from pre-adolescence (ages 10 - 11) to early adolescence (12 - 14) through mid- (15 - 17) to late-adolescence (18 - 19) is needed if we want to consider more fully the role of the developmental phase in teens' media practices.

Similarly, more cross-disciplinary research is called for. One reviewer made this observation about an earlier draft: "The findings themselves echo what professional sexuality educators and surveyors have been reporting for seventy years." If this is so, it is high time mass communications researchers joined the conversation. Cat, 18, spoke for a lot of teens when she summed up her feelings:

I wish we could be flat out. I mean like honest about it. You know'? Cuz it's like everyone wants to hide their sexuality and the fact that people have sex. And they say they don't want to expose kids to it because it's such a horrible thing. You know, it's like, oh god. You know? And it's like your period is just a dirty thing that you can't discuss in front of people, or it's like, it's not natural. And I wish when I was a kid someone could have just said, "This is sex. This is the way it is, and this is how we do it. This is what is going to happen to you. You're gonna get your period. It's gonna hurt. You're gonna have to do this about it, you know?

This is what makes you pregnant," and let that just be it. And not do it in such a way that made me feel so paranoid about it, and so embarrassed because I wanted to know what was going on, you know? Cuz I couldn't talk to my mom, cuz all my mom did was give me books, and I couldn't talk to my teachers.

3

Femininity and the Modernisation

In a striking critique of modern society, Michel Foucault has argued that the rise of parliamentary institutions and of new conceptions of political liberty was accompanied by a darker countermovement, by the emergence of a new and unprecedented discipline directed against the body. More is required of the body now than mere political allegiance or the appropriation of the products of its labour: The new discipline invades the body and seeks to regulate its very forces and operations, the economy and efficiency of its movements.

The disciplinary practices Foucault describes are tied to peculiarly modern forms of the army, the school, the hospital, the prison, and the manufactory; the aim of these disciplines is to increase the utility of the body, to augment its forces:

What was then being formed was a policy of coercions that act upon the body, a calculated manipulation of its elements, its gestures, its behaviour. The human body was entering a machinery of power that explores it, breaks it down and rearranges it. A "political anatomy," which was also a "mechanics of power," was being born; it defined how one may have a hold over others' bodies, not only so that they may do what one wishes, but so that they may operate as one wishes, with the techniques, the speed and the efficiency that one determines. Thus, discipline produces subjected and practiced bodies, "docile" bodies.

The production of "docile bodies" requires that an uninterrupted coercion be directed to the very processes of bodily activity, not just their result; this "microphysics of power" fragments and partitions the body's time, its space, and its movements. The student, then, is enclosed within a classroom and assigned to a desk he cannot leave; his ranking in the class can be read off the position of his desk in the serially ordered and segmented space of the classroom itself. Foucault tells us that "Jean-Baptiste de la Salle dreamt of a classroom in which the spatial distribution might provide a whole series of distinctions at once, according to the pupil's progress, worth, character, application, cleanliness, and parents' fortune." The student must sit upright, feet upon the floor, head erect; he may not slouch or fidget; his animate body is brought into a fixed correlation with the inanimate desk.

The minute breakdown of gestures and movements required of soldiers at drill is far more relentless:

> Bring the weapon forward. In three stages, raise the rifle with the right hand, bringing it close to the body so as to hold it perpendicular with the right knee, the end of the barrel at eye level, grasping it by striking it with the right hand, the arm held close to the body at waist height. At the second stage, bring the rifle in front of you with the left hand, the barrel in the middle between the two eyes, vertical, the right hand grasping it at the small of the butt, the arm outstretched, the triggerguard resting on the first finger, the left hand at the height of the notch, the thumb lying along the barrel against the moulding. At the third stage....

These "body-object articulations" of the soldier and his weapon, the student and his desk, effect a "coercive link with the apparatus of production." We are far indeed from older forms of control that "demanded of the body only signs or products, forms of expression or the result of labour."

The body's time, in these regimes of power, is as rigidly controlled as its space: The factory whistle and the school bell mark a division of time into discrete and segmented units that regulate the various activities of the day. The following timetable, similar in spirit to the ordering of my grammar school classroom, was suggested for French "coles mutuelles" of the early nineteenth century:

> 8:45 entrance of the monitor, 8:52 the monitor's summons, 8:56 entrance of the children and prayer, 9:00 the children go to their benches, 9:04 first slate, 9:08 end of dictation, 9:12 second slate, etc.

Control this rigid and precise cannot be maintained without a minute and relentless surveillance.

Jeremy Bentham's design for the Panopticon, a model prison, captures for Foucault the essence of the disciplinary society. At the periphery of the Panopticon, a circular structure; at the center, a tower with wide windows that open onto the inner side of the ring. The structure on the periphery is divided into cells, each with two windows, one facing the windows of the tower, the other facing the outside, allowing an effect of backlighting to make any figure visible within the cell. "All that is needed, then, is to place a supervisor in a central tower and to shut up in each cell a madman, a patient, a condemned man, a worker or a schoolboy."

Each inmate is alone, shut off from effective communication with his fellows, but constantly visible from the tower. The effect of this is "to induce in the inmate a state of conscious and permanent visibility that assures the automatic functioning of power"; each becomes to himself his own jailer. This "state of conscious and permanent visibility" is a sign that the tight, disciplinary control of the body has gotten a hold on the mind as well. In the perpetual self-surveillance of the inmate lies the genesis of the celebrated "individualism" and heightened self-consciousness which are hallmarks of modern times. For Foucault, the structure and effects of the Panopticon resonate throughout society: Is it surprising that "prisons resemble factories, schools, barracks, hospitals, which all resemble prisons?"

Foucault account in Discipline and Punish of the disciplinary practices that produce the "docile bodies" of modernity is a genuine tour de force, incorporating a rich theoretical account of the ways in which instrumental reason takes hold of the body with a mass of historical detail. But Foucault treats the body throughout as if it were one, as if the bodily experiences of men and women did not differ and as if men and women bore the same relationship to the characteristic institutions of modern life.

Where is the account of the disciplinary practices that engender the "docile bodies" of women, bodies more docile than the bodies of men? Women, like men, are subject to many of the same disciplinary practices Foucault describes. But he is blind to those disciplines that produce a modality of embodiment that is peculiarly feminine. To overlook the for.ns of subjection that engender the feminine body is to perpetuate the silence and powerlessness of those upon whom these disciplines have been imposed. Hence, even though a liberatory note is sounded in Foucault's critique of power, his analysis as a whole reproduces that sexism which is endemic throughout Western political theory.

We are born male or female, but not masculine or feminine. Femininity is an artifice, an achievement, "a mode of enacting and reenacting received gender norms which surface as so many styles of the flesh." In what follows, I shall examine those disciplinary practices that produce a body which in gesture and appearance is recognizably feminine. I consider three categories of such practices: those that aim to produce a body of a certain size and general configuration; those that bring forth from this body a specific repertoire of gestures, postures, and movements; and those directed toward the display of this body as an ornamented surface. I shall examine the nature of these disciplines, how they are imposed, and by whom. I shall probe the effects of the imposition of such discipline on female identity and subjectivity. In the final section I shall argue that these disciplinary practices must be understood in the light of the modernisation of patriarchal domination, a modernisation that unfolds historically according to the general pattern described by Foucault.

Styles of the female figure vary over time and across cultures: they reflect cultural obsessions and preoccupations in ways that are still poorly understood. Today, massiveness, power, or abundance in a woman's body is met with distaste. The current body of fashion is taut, small-breasted, narrowhipped, and of a slimness bordering on emaciation; it is a silhouette that seems more appropriate to an adolescent boy or a newly pubescent girl than to an adult woman. Since ordinary women have normally quite different dimensions, they must of course diet.

Mass-circulation women's magazines run articles on dieting in virtually every issue. The Ladies' Home Journal of February 1986 carries a "Fat-Burning Exercise Guide," while Mademoiselle offers to "Help Stamp out Cellulite" with "Six Sleek-Down Strategies." After the diet-busting Christmas holidays and later, before summer bikini season, the titles of these features become shriller and more arresting. The reader is now addressed in the imperative mode: Jump into shape for summer! Shed ugly winter fat with the all-new Grapefruit Diet! More women than men visit diet doctors, while women greatly outnumber men in self-help groups such as Weight Watchers and Overeaters Anonymous-in the case of the latter, by well over 90 percent.

Dieting disciplines the body's hungers: Appetite must be monitored at all times and governed by an iron will. Since the innocent need of the organism for food will not be denied, the body becomes one's enemy, an alien being bent on thwarting the disciplinary project. Anorexia nervosa, which has now assumed epidemic proportions, is to women of the late twentieth century what hysteria was to women of an earlier day: the crystallisation in a pathological mode of a widespread cultural obsession.

A survey taken recently at UCLA is astounding: Of 260 students interviewed, 27.3 percent of the women but only 5.8 percent of men said they were "terrified" of getting fat: 28.7 percent of women and only 7.5 percent of men said they were obsessed or "totally preoccupied" with food. The body images of women and men are strikingly different as well: 35 percent of women but only 12.5 percent of men said they felt fat though other people told them they were thin. Women in the survey wanted to weigh ten pounds less than their average weight; men felt they were within a pound of their ideal weight.

A total of 5.9 percent of women and no men met the psychiatric criteria for anorexia or bulimia. Dieting is one discipline imposed upon a body subject to the "tyranny of slenderness"; exercise is another. Since men as well as women exercise, it is not always easy in the case of women to distinguish what is done for the sake of physical fitness from what is done in obedience to the requirements of femininity. Men as well as women lift weights, do yoga, calisthenics, and aerobics, though "jazzercise" is a largely female pursuit.

Men and women alike engage themselves with a variety of machines, each designed to call forth from the body a different exertion: There are Nautilus machines, rowing machines, ordinary and motorized exercycles, portable hip and leg cycles, belt massagers, trampolines; treadmills, arm and leg pulleys. However, given the widespread female obsession with weight, one suspect that many women are working out with these apparatuses in the health club or at the gym with a different aim in mind and in quite a different spirit than the men.

But there are classes of exercises meant for women alone, these designed not to firm or to reduce the body's size overall, but to resculpture its various parts on the current model. M. J. Saffon, "international beauty expert," assures us that his twelve basic facial exercises can erase frown lines, smooth the forehead, raise hollow checks, banish crow's feet, and tighten the muscles under the chin.

There are exercises to build the breasts and exercises to banish "cellulite," said by "figure consultants" to be a special type of female fat. There is "spot-reducing," an umbrella term that covers dozens of punishing exercises designed to reduce "problem areas" like thick ankles or "saddlebag" thighs. The very idea of "spot-reducing" is both scientifically unsound and cruel, for it raises expectations in women that can never be realized: The pattern in which fat is deposited or removed is known to be genetically determined.

It is not only her natural appetite or unreconstructed contours that pose a danger to women: The very expressions of her face can subvert the disciplinary project of bodily perfection. An expressive face lines and creases more readily than an inexpressive one. Hence, if women are unable to suppress strong emotions, they can at least learn to inhibit the tendency of the face to register them. Sophia Loren recommends a unique solution to this problem: A piece of tape applied to the forehead or between the brows will tug at the skin when one frowns and act as a reminder to relax the face. The tape is to be worn whenever a woman is home alone.

There are significant gender differences in gesture, posture, movement, and general bodily comportment: Women are far more restricted than men in their manner of movement and in their lived spatiality. In her classic paper on the subject, Iris Young observes that a space seems to surround women in imagination which they are hesitant to move beyond: This manifests itself both in a reluctance to reach, stretch, and extend the body to meet resistances of matter in motion-as in sport or in the performance of physical tasks - and in a typically constricted posture and general style of movement.

Woman's space is not a field in which her bodily intentionality can be freely realized but an enclosure in which she feels herself positioned and by which she is confined. The "loose woman" violates these norms: Her looseness is manifest not only in her morals, but in her manner of speech, and quite literally in the free and easy way she moves. In an extraordinary series of over two thousand photographs, many candid shots taken in the street, the German photographer Marianne Wex has documented differences in typical masculine and feminine body posture.

Women sit waiting for trains with arms close to the body, hands folded together in their laps, toes pointing straight ahead or turned inward, and legs pressed together. The women in these photographs make themselves small and narrow, harmless; they seem tense; they take up little space. Men, on the other hand, expand into the available space; they sit with legs far apart and arms flung out at some distance from the body. Most common in these sitting male figures is what Wex calls the "proferring position": the men sit with legs thrown wide apart, crotch visible, feet pointing outward, often with an arm and casually dangling hand resting comfortably on an open, spread thigh.

In proportion to total body size, a man's stride is longer than a woman's. The man has more spring and rhythm to his step; he walks with toes pointed outward, holds his arms at a greater distance from his body, and swings them farther; he tends to point the whole hand in the direction he is moving. The woman holds her arms closer to her body, palms against her sides; her walk is circumspect. If she has subjected herself to the additional constraint of high-heeled shoes, her body is thrown forward and off-balance: The struggle to walk under these conditions shortens her stride still more.

But women's movement is subjected to a still finer discipline. Feminine faces, as well as bodies, are trained to the expression of deference. Under male scrutiny, women will avert their eyes or cast them downward; the female gaze is trained to abandon its claim to the sovereign status of seer. The "nice" girl learns to avoid the bold and unfettered staring of the "loose" woman who looks at whatever and whomever she pleases. Women are trained to smile more than men, too.

In the economy of smiles, as elsewhere, there is evidence that women are exploited, for they give more than they receive in return; in a smile elicitation study, one researcher found that the rate of smile return by women was 93 percent, by men only 67 percent. In many typical women's jobs, graciousness, deference, and the readiness to serve are part of the work; this requires the worker to fix a smile on her face for a good part of the working day, whatever her inner state. The economy of touching is out of balance, too: men touch women more often and on more parts of the body than women touch men: female secretaries, factory workers, and waitresses report that such liberties are taken routinely with their bodies.

Feminine movement, gesture, and posture must exhibit not only constriction, but grace as well, and certain eroticism restrained by modesty:

All three. Here is field for the operation for a whole new training: A woman must stand with stomach pulled in, shoulders thrown slightly back, and chest out, this to display her bosom to maximum advantage. While she must walk in the confined fashion appropriate to women, her movements must, at the same time, be combined with a subtle but provocative hip-roll. But too much display is taboo: Women in short, low-cut dresses are told to avoid bending over at all, but if they must, great care must be taken to avoid an unseemly display of breast or rump. From time to time, fashion magazines offer quite precise instructions on the proper way of getting in and out of cars.

These instructions combine all three imperatives of women's movement: A woman must not allow her arms and legs to flail about in all directions; she must try to manage her movements with the appearance of grace - no small accomplishment when one is climbing out of the back seat of a Fiat - and she is well advised to use the opportunity for a certain display of leg.

All the movements we have described so far are self-movements; they arise from within the woman's own body. But in a way that normally goes unnoticed, males in couples may literally steer a woman everywhere she goes: down the street, around corners, into elevators, through doorways, into her chair at the dinner table, around the dance-floor. The man's movement "is not necessarily heavy and pushy or physical in an ugly way; it is light and gentle but firm in the way of the most confident equestrians with the best trained horses."

We have examined some of the disciplinary practices a woman must master in pursuit of a body of the right size and shape that also displays the proper styles of feminine motility.

But woman's body is an ornamented surface too, and there is much discipline involved in this production as well. Here, especially in the application of make-up and the selection of clothes, art and discipline converge, though, as I shall argue, there is less art involved than one might suppose.

A woman's skin must be soft, supple, hairless, and smooth; ideally, it should betray no sign of wear, experience, age, or deep thought. Hair must be removed not only from the face but from large surfaces of the body as well, from legs and thighs, an operation accomplished by shaving, buffing with fine sandpaper, or foul-smelling depilatories. With the new high-leg bathing suits and leotards, a substantial amount of pubic hair must be removed too. The removal of facial hair can be more specialized. Eyebrows are plucked out by the roots with a tweezer. Hot wax is sometimes poured onto the mustache and cheeks and then ripped away when it cools.

The woman who wants a more permanent result may try electrolysis: This involves the killing of a hair root by the passage of an electric current down a needle which has been inserted into its base. The procedure is painful and expensive. The development of what one "beauty expert" calls "good skin-care habits" requires not only attention to health, the avoidance of strong facial expressions, and the performance of facial exercises, but the regular use of skin-care preparations, many to be applied oftener than once a day: cleansing lotions (ordinary soap and water "upsets the skin's acid and alkaline balance"), washoff cleansers (milder than cleansing lotions), astringents, toners, make-up removers, night creams, nourishing creams, eye creams, moisturizers, skin balancers, body lotions, hand creams, lip pomades, suntan lotions, sun screens, facial masks.

Provision of the proper facial mask is complex: There are sulfur masks for pimples; hot or oil masks for dry areas; also cold masks for dry areas; tightening masks; conditioning masks; peeling masks; cleansing masks made of herbs, cornmeal, or almonds; mud packs. Black women may wish to use "fade creams" to "even skin tone." Skin-care preparations are never just sloshed onto the skin, but applied according to precise rules: Eye cream is dabbed on gently in movements toward, never away from, the nose; cleansing cream is applied in outward directions only, straight across the forehead, the upper lip, and the chin, never up but straight down the nose and up and out on the cheeks.

The normalizing discourse of modern medicine is enlisted by the cosmetics industry to gain credibility for its claims. Dr. Christiaan Barnard lends his enormous prestige to the Glycel line of "cellular treatment activators"; these contain "glycosphingolipids" that can "make older skin behave and look like younger skin." The Clinique computer at any Clinique counter will select a combination of preparations just right for you.

Ultima II contains "procollagen" in its anti-aging eye cream that "provides hydration" to "demoralizing lines." "Biotherm" eye cream dramatically improves the "biomechanical properties of the skin." The Park Avenue clinic of Dr. Zizmor, "chief of dermatology at one of New York's leading hospitals," offers not only medical treatment such as dermabrasion and chemical peeling but "total deep skin cleansing" as well.

Really good skin-care habits require the use of a variety of aids and devices: facial steamers; faucet filters to collect impurities in the water; borax to soften it; a humidifier for the bedroom; electric massagers; backbrushes; complexion brushes; loofahs; pumice stones; blackhead removers. I will not detail the implements or techniques involved in the manicure or pedicure.

The ordinary circumstances of life as well as a wide variety of activities cause a crisis in skin-care and require a stepping up of the regimen as well as an additional laying on of preparations. Skin-care discipline requires a specialized knowledge: A woman must know what to do if she has been skiing, taking medication, doing vigorous exercise, boating, or swimming in chlorinated pools; if she has been exposed to pollution, heated rooms, cold, sun, harsh weather, the pressurized cabins on airplanes, saunas or steam rooms, fatigue or stress.

Like the schoolchild or prisoner, the woman mastering good skin-care habits is put on a timetable: Georgette Klinger requires that a shorter or longer period of attention be paid to the complexion at least four times a day. Hair-care, like skin-care, requires a similar investment of time, the use of a wide variety of preparations, the mastery of a set of techniques and again, the acquisition of a specialized knowledge. The crown and pinnacle of good hair care and skin care is, of course, the arrangement of the hair and the application of cosmetics.

Here the regimen of hair care, skin care, manicure, and pedicure is recapitulated in another mode. A woman must learn the proper manipulation of a large number of devices-the blow dryer, styling brush, curling iron, hot curlers, wire curlers, eye-liner, lipliner, lipstick brush, eyelash curler, mascara brush-and the correct manner of application of a wide variety of products-foundation, toner, covering stick, mascara, eye shadow, eye gloss, blusher, lipstick, rouge, lip gloss, hair dye, hair rinse, hair lightener, hair "relaxer," etc.

In the language of fashion magazines and cosmetic ads, making up is typically portrayed as an aesthetic activity in which a woman can express her individuality. In reality, while cosmetic styles change every decade or so and while some variation in make-up is permitted depending on the occasion, making up the face is, in fact, a highly stylized activity that gives little rein to self-expression.

Painting the face is not like painting a picture; at best, it might be described as painting the same picture over and over again with minor variations. Little latitude is permitted in what is considered appropriate make-up for the office and for most social occasions; indeed, the woman who uses cosmetics in a genuinely novel and imaginative way is liable to be seen not as an artist but as an eccentric. Furthermore, since a properly -madeup face is, if not a card of entree, at least a badge of acceptability in most social and professional contexts, the woman who chooses not to wear cos metics at all faces sanctions of a sort which will never be applied to someone who chooses not to paint a watercolour.

Are we dealing in all this merely with sexual difference? Scarcely. The disciplinary practices I have described are part of the process by which the ideal body of femininity - and hence the feminine body-subject-is constructed; in doing this, they produce a "practiced and subjected" body, i.e., a body on which an inferior status has been inscribed. A woman's face must be made up, that is to say, made over, and so must her body: she is ten pounds overweight; her lips must be made more kissable; her complexion dewier; her eyes more mysterious.

The "art" of make-up is the art of disguise, but this presupposes that a woman's face, unpainted, is defective. Soap and water, a shave, and routine attention to hygiene may be enough for him; for her they are not. The strategy of much beauty-related advertising is to suggest to women that their bodies are deficient, but even without such more or less explicit teaching, the media images of perfect female beauty which bombard us daily leave no doubt in the minds of most women that they fail to measure up.

The technologies of femininity are taken up and practiced by women against the background of a pervasive sense of bodily deficiency: This accounts for what is often their compulsive or even ritualistic character. The disciplinary project of femininity is a "set-up": It requires such radical and extensive measures of bodily transformation that virtually every woman who gives herself to it is destined in some degree to fail. Thus, a measure of shame is added to a woman's sense that the body she inhabits is deficient: she ought to take better care of herself; she might after all have jogged that last mile.

Many women are without the time or resources to provide themselves with even the minimum of what such a regimen requires, e.g., a decent diet. Here is an additional source of shame for poor women who must bear what our society regards as the more general shame of poverty. The burdens poor women bear in this regard are not merely psychological, since conformity to the prevailing standards of bodily acceptability is a known factor in economic mobility.

The larger disciplines that construct a "feminine" body out of a female one are by no means race- or class-specific. There is little evidence that women of colour or working-class women are in general less committed to the incarnation of an ideal femininity than their more privileged sisters. This is not to deny the many ways in which factors of race, class, locality, ethnicity, or personal taste can be expressed within the kinds of practices I have described.

The rising young corporate executive may buy her cosmetics at BergdorfGoodman while the counter-server at McDonald's gets hers at the K-Mart; the one may join an expensive "upscale" health club, while the other may have to make do with the $9.49 GFX Body-Flex II Home-Gym advertised in the National Enquirer: Both are aiming at the same general result. In the regime of institutionalized heterosexuality woman must make herself "object and prey" for the man: It is for him that these eyes are limpid pools, this cheek baby-smooth.

In contemporary patriarchal culture, a panoptical male connoisseur resides within the consciousness of most women: They stand perpetually before his gaze and under his judgment. Woman lives her body as seen by another, by an anonymous patriarchal Other. We are often told that "women dress for other women." There is some truth in this: Who but someone engaged in a project similar to my own can appreciate the panache with which I bring it off? But women know for whom this game is played: They know that a pretty young woman is likelier to become a flight attendant than a plain one and that a well-preserved older woman has a better chance of holding onto her husband than one who has "let herself go."

Here it might be objected that performance for another in no way signals the inferiority of the performer to the one for whom the performance is intended: The actor, for example, depends on his audience but is in no way inferior to it; he is not demeaned by his dependency. While femininity is surely something enacted, the analogy to theater breaks down in a number of ways.

First, as I argued earlier, the self-determination we think of as requisite to an artistic career is lacking here: Femininity as spectacle is something in which virtually every woman is required to participate. Second, the precise nature of the criteria by which women are judged, not only the inescapability of judgment itself, reflects gross imbalances in the social power of the sexes that do not mark the relationship of artists and their audiences.

An aesthetic of femininity, for example, that mandates fragility and a lack of muscular strength produces female bodies that can offer little resistance to physical abuse, and the physical abuse of women by men, as we know, is widespread. It is true that the current fitness movement has permitted women to develop more muscular strength and endurance than was heretofore allowed; indeed, images of women have begun to appear in the mass media that seem to eroticize this new muscularity. But a woman may by no means develop more muscular strength than her partner; the bride who would tenderly carry her groom across the threshold is a figure of comedy, not romance.

Under the current "tyranny of slenderness" women are forbidden to become large or massive; they must take up as little space as possible. The very contours a woman's body takes on as she matures - the fuller breasts and rounded hips - have become distasteful. The body by which a woman feels herself judged and which by rigorous discipline she must try to assume is the body of early adolescence, slight and unformed, a body lacking flesh or substance, a body in whose very contours the image of immaturity has been inscribed.

The requirement that a woman maintain a smooth and hairless skin carries further the theme of inexperience, for an infantilized face must accompany her infantilized body, a face that never ages or furrows its brow in thought. The face of the ideally feminine woman must never display the marks of character, wisdom, and experience that we so admire in men.

To succeed in the provision of a beautiful or sexy body gains a woman attention and some admiration but little real respect and rarely any social power. A woman's effort to master feminine body discipline will lack importance just because she does it: Her activity partakes of the general depreciation of everything female. In spite of unrelenting pressure to "make the most of what they have," women are ridiculed and dismissed for the triviality of their interest in such "trivial" things as clothes and make-up.

Further, the narrow identification of woman with sexuality and the body in a society that has for centuries displayed profound suspicion toward both does little to raise her status. Even the most adored female bodies complain routinely of their situation in ways that reveal an implicit understanding that there is something demeaning in the kind of attention they receive. Marilyn Monroe, Elizabeth Taylor, and Farrah Fawcett have all wanted passionately to become actressesartists and not just "sex objects."

But it is perhaps in their more restricted motility and comportment that the inferiorisation of women's bodies is most evident: Women's typical body language, a language of relative tension and constriction, is understood to be a language of subordination when it is enacted by men in male status hierarchies. In groups of men, those with higher status typically assume looser and more relaxed postures: The boss lounges comfortably behind the desk while the applicant sits tense and rigid on the edge of his seat.

Higher-status individuals may touch their subordinates more than they themselves get touched; they initiate more eye contact and are smiled at by their inferiors more than they are observed to smile in return. What is announced in the comportment of superiors is confidence and ease, especially ease of access to the Other.

Female constraint in posture and movement is no doubt overdetermined: The fact that women tend to sit and stand with legs, feet, and knees close or touching may well be a coded declaration of sexual circumspection in a society that still maintains a double standard, or an effort, albeit unconscious, to guard the genital area. In the latter case, a woman's tight and constricted posture must be seen as the expression of her need to ward off real or symbolic sexual attack. Whatever proportions must be assigned in the final display to fear or deference, one thing is clear: Woman's body language speaks eloquently, though silently, of her subordinate status in a hierarchy of gender.

If what we have described is a genuine discipline-a "system of micropower that is essentially non-egalitarian and asymmetrical"-who then are the disciplinarians? Who is the top sergeant in the disciplinary regime of femininity? Historically, the law has had some responsibility for enforcement: In times gone by, for example, individuals who appeared in public in the clothes of the other sex could be arrested. While cross-dressers are still liable to some harassment, the kind of discipline we are considering is not the business of the police or the courts.

Parents and teachers, of course, have extensive influence, admonishing girls to be demure and ladylike, to "smile pretty," to sit with their legs together. The influence of the media is pervasive, too, constructing as it does not do an image of the female body as spectacle, nor can we ignore the role played by "beauty experts" or by emblematic public personages such as Jane Fonda and Lynn Redgrave. But none of these individuals - the skin-care consultant, the parent, and the policeman - does in fact wield the kind of authority that is typically invested in those who manage more straightforward disciplinary institutions.

The disciplinary power that inscribes femininity in the female body is everywhere and it is nowhere; the disciplinarian is everyone and yet no one in particular. Women regarded as overweight, for example, report that they are regularly admonished to diet, sometimes by people they scarcely know. These intrusions are often softened by reference to the natural prettiness just waiting to emerge: "People have always said that I had a beautiful face and 'if you'd only lose weight you'd be really beautiful.'" Here, "people"-friends and casual acquaintances alike - act to enforce prevailing standards of body size.

Foucault tends to identify the imposition of discipline upon the body with the operation of specific institutions, e.g., the school, the factory, the prison. To do this, however, however, is to overlook the extent to which discipline can be institutionally unbound as well as institutionally bound. The anonymity of disciplinary power and its wide dispersion have consequences which are crucial to a proper understanding of the subordination of women.

The absence of a formal institutional structure and of authorities invested with the power to carry out institutional directives creates the impression that the production of femininity is either entirely voluntary or natural. The several senses of "discipline" are instructive here. On the one hand, discipline is something imposed on subjects of an "essentially inegalitarian and asymmetrical" system of authority. Schoolchildren, convicts, and draftees are subject to discipline in this sense. But discipline can be sought voluntarily as well, as, for example, when an individual seeks initiation into the spiritual discipline of Zen Buddhism.

Discipline can, of course, be both at once: The volunteer may seek the physical and occupational training offered by the army without the army's ceasing in any way to be the instrument by which he and other members of his class are kept in disciplined subjection. Feminine bodily discipline has this dual character: On the one hand, no one is marched off for electrolysis at the end of a rifle, nor can we fail to appreciate the initiative and ingenuity displayed by countless women in an attempt to master the rituals of beauty. Nevertheless, insofar as the disciplinary practices of femininity produce a "subjected and practiced," an inferiorized, body, they must be understood as aspects of a far larger discipline, an oppressive and inegalitarian system of sexual subordination.

This system aims at turning women into the docile and compliant companions of men just as surely as the army aims to turn its raw recruits into soldiers. Now the transformation of oneself into a properly feminine body may be any or all of the following: a rite of passage into adulthood; the adoption and celebration of a particular aesthetic; a way of announcing one's economic level and social status; a way to triumph over other women in the competition for men or jobs; or an opportunity for massive narcissistic indulgence. The social construction of the feminine body is all these things, but it is at base discipline, too, and discipline of the inegalitarian sort.

The absence of formally identifiable disciplinarians and of a public schedule of sanctions serves only to disguise the extent to which the imperative to be "feminine" serves the interest of domination. This is a lie in which all concur: Making up is merely artful play; one's first pair of high-heeled shoes is an innocent part of growing up and not the modern equivalent of foot-binding. Why aren't all women feminists? In modern industrial societies, women are not kept in line by fear of retaliatory male violence; their victimisation is not that of the South African black.

Nor will it suffice to say that a false consciousness engendered in women by patriarchal ideology is at the basis of female subordination. This is not to deny the fact that women are often subject to gross male violence or that woman and men alike are ideologically mystified by the dominant gender arrangements. What I wish to suggest instead is that an adequate understanding of women's oppression will require an appreciation of the extent to which not only women's lives but their very subjectivities are structured within an ensemble of systematically duplicitous practices.

The feminine discipline of the body is a case in point: The practices which construct this body have an overt aim and character far removed, indeed radically distinct, from their covert function. In this regard, the system of gender subordination, like the wage-bargain under capitalism, illustrates in its own way the ancient tension, between what is and what appears: The phenomenal forms in which it is manifested are often quite different from the real relations which form its deeper structure.

The lack of formal public sanctions does not mean that a woman who is unable or unwilling to submit herself to the appropriate body discipline will face no sanctions at all. On the contrary, she faces a very severe sanction indeed in a world dominated by men: the refusal of male patronage. For the heterosexual woman, this may mean the loss of a badly needed intimacy; for both heterosexual women and lesbians, it may well mean the refusal of a decent livelihood.

As noted earlier, women punish themselves too for the failure to conform. The growing literature on women's body size is filled with wrenching confessions of shame from the overweight:

I felt clumsy and huge. I felt that I would knock over furniture, bump into things, tip over chairs, not fit into vw's, especially when people were trying to crowd into the back seat. I felt like I was taking over the whole room.... I felt disgusting and like a slob. In the summer I felt hot and sweaty and I knew people saw my sweat as evidence that I was too fat.

I feel so terrible about the way I look that I cut off connection with my body. I operate from the neck up. I do not look in mirrors. I do not want to spend time buying clothes. I do not want to spend time with make-up because it's painful for me to look at myself.

I can no longer bear to look at myself. Whenever I have to stand in front of a mirror to comb my hair I tie a large towel around my neck. Even at night I slip my nightgown on before I take off my blouse and pants. But all this has only made it worse and worse. It's been so long since I've really looked at my body.

The depth of these women's shame is a measure of the extent to which all women have internalized patriarchal standards of bodily acceptability. A fuller examination of what is meant here by "internalisation" may shed light on a question posed earlier: Why isn't every woman a feminist?

Something is "internalized" when it gets incorporated into the structure of the self. By "structure of the self" I refer to those modes of perception and of self-perception which allow a self to distinguish itself both from other selves and from things which are not selves. I have described elsewhere how a generalized male witness comes to structure woman's consciousness of herself as a bodily being. This, then, is one meaning of "internalisation."

The sense of oneself as a distinct and valuable individual is tied not only to the sense of how one is perceived, but also to what one knows, especially to what one knows how to do; this is a second sense of "internalisation."Whatever its ultimate effect, discipline can provide the individual upon whom it is imposed with a sense of mastery as well as a secure sense of identity. There is a certain contradiction here: While its imposition may promote a larger disempowerment, discipline may bring with it a certain development of a person's powers.

Women, then, like other skilled individuals, have a stake in the perpetuation of their skills, whatever it may have cost to acquire them and quite apart from the question whether, as a gender, they would have been better off had they never had to acquire them in the first place. Hence, feminism, especially a genuinely radical feminism that questions the patriarchal construction of the female body, threatens women with a certain deskilling, something people normally resist: Beyond this, it calls into question that aspect of personal identity which is tied to the development of a sense of competence.

Resistance from this source may be joined by a reluctance to part with the rewards of compliance; further, many women will resist the abandonment of an aesthetic that defines what they take to be beautiful. But there is still another source of resistance, one more subtle perhaps, but tied once again to questions of identity and internalisation. To have a body felt to be "feminine" - a body socially constructed through the appropriate practices-is in most cases crucial to a woman's sense of herself as female and, since persons currently can be only as male or female, to her sense of herself as an existing individual.

To possess such a body may also be essential to her sense of herself as a sexually desiring and desirable subject. Hence, any political project which aims to dismantle the machinery that turns a female body into a feminine one may well be apprehended by a woman as something that threatens her with desexualisation, if not outright annihilation. The categories of masculinity and femininity do more than assist in the construction of personal identities; they are critical elements in our informal social ontology.

This may account to some degree for the otherwise puzzling phenomenon of homophobia and for the revulsion felt by many at the sight of female bodybuilders; neither the homosexual nor the muscular woman can be assimilated easily into the categories that structure everyday life. The radical feminist critique of femininity, then, may pose a threat not only to a woman's sense of her own identity and desirability but to the very structure of her social universe.

Of course, many women are feminists, favoring a program of political and economic reform in the struggle to gain equality with men. But many "reform" or liberal feminists, indeed, many orthodox Marxists, are committed to the idea that the preservation of a woman's femininity is quite compatible with her struggle for liberation. These thinkers have rejected a normative femininity based upon the notion of "separate spheres" and the traditional sexual division of labour while accepting at the same time conventional standards of feminine body display. If my analysis is correct, such feminism is incoherent.

Foucault has argued that modern bourgeois democracy is deeply flawed in that it seeks political rights for individuals constituted as unfree by a variety of disciplinary micropowers that lie beyond the realm of what is ordinarily defined as the "political.""The man described for us whom we are invited to free," he says, "is already in himself the effect of subjection much more profound than himself." If, as I have argued, female subjectivity is constituted in any significant measure in and through the disciplinary practices that construct the feminine body, what Foucault says here of "man" is perhaps even truer of "woman."

Marxists have maintained from the first the inadequacy of a purely liberal feminism: We have reached the same conclusion through a different route, casting doubt at the same time on the adequacy of traditional Marxist prescriptions for women's liberation as well. Liberals call for equal rights for women, traditional Marxists for the entry of women into production on an equal footing with men, the socialisation of housework and proletarian revolution: neither calls for the deconstruction of the categories of masculinity and femininity. Femininity as a certain "style of the flesh" will have to be surpassed in the direction of something quite different, not masculinity, which is in many ways only its mirror opposite, but a radical and as yet unimagined transformation of the female body.

Foucault has argued that the transition from traditional to modern societies has been characterized by a profound transformation in the exercise of power, by what he calls "a reversal of the political axis of individualisation." In older authoritarian systems, power was embodied in the person of the monarch and exercised upon a largely anonymous body of subjects; violation of the law was seen as an insult to the royal individual. While the methods employed to enforce compliance in the past were often quite brutal, involving gross assaults against the body, power in such a system operated in a haphazard and discontinuous fashion; much in the social totality lay beyond its reach.

By contrast, modern society has seen the emergence of increasingly invasive apparatuses of power: These exercise a far more restrictive social and psychological control than was heretofore possible. In modern societies, effects of power "circulate through progressively finer channels, gaining access to individuals themselves, to their bodies, their gestures and all their daily actions." Power now seeks to transform the minds of those individuals who might be tempted to resist it, not merely to punish or imprison their bodies. This requires two things: a finer control of the body's time and its movements - a control that cannot be achieved without ceaseless surveillance and a better understanding of the specific person, of the genesis and nature of his "case."

The power these new apparatuses seek to exercise requires a new knowledge of the individual: Modern psychology and sociology are born. Whether the new modes of control have charge of correction, production, education, or the provision of welfare, they resemble one another; they exercise power in a bureaucratic mode-faceless, centralized, and pervasive. A reversal has occurred: Power has now become anonymous, while the project of control has brought into being a new individuality. In fact, Foucault believes that the operation of power constitutes the very subjectivity of the subject. Here, the image of the Panopticon returns: Knowing that he may be observed from the tower at any time, the inmate takes over the job of policing himself.

The gaze which is inscribed in the very structure of the disciplinary institution is internalized by the inmate: Modern tech nologies of behaviour are thus oriented toward the production of isolated and self-policing subjects. Women have their own experience of the modernisation of power, one which begins later but follows in many respects the course outlined by Foucault. In important ways, a woman's behaviour is less regulated now than it was in the past. She has more mobility and is less confined to domestic space. She enjoys what to previous generations would have been an unimaginable sexual liberty.

Divorce, access to paid work outside the home, and the increasing secularisation of modern life has loosened the hold over her of the traditional family and, in spite of the current fundamentalist revival, of the church. Power in these institutions was wielded by individuals known to her. Husbands and fathers enforced patriarchal authority in the family. As in the ancien regime a woman's body was subject to sanctions if she disobeyed.

Not Foucault's royal individual but the Divine Individual decreed that her desire be always "unto her husband," while the person of the priest made known to her God's more specific intentions concerning her place and duties. In the days when civil and ecclesiastical authority was still conjoined, individuals formally invested with power were charged with the correction of recalcitrant women whom the family had somehow failed to constrain. By contrast, the disciplinary power that is increasingly charged with the production of a properly embodied femininity is dispersed and anonymous; there are no individuals formally empowered to wield it; it is, as we have seen, invested in everyone and in no one in particular.

This disciplinary power is peculiarly modern: It does not rely upon violent or public sanctions, nor does it seek to restrain the freedom of the female body to move from place to place. For all that, its invasion of the body is well-nigh total: The female body enters "a machinery of power that explores it, breaks it down and rearranges it." The disciplinary techniques through which the "docile bodies" of women are constructed aim at a regulation which is perpetual and exhaustive-a regulation of the body's size and contours, its appetite, posture, gestures, and general comportment in space and the appearance of each of its visible parts.

As modern industrial societies change and as women themselves offer resistance to patriarchy, older forms of domination are eroded. But new forms arise, spread, and become consolidated. Women are no longer required to be chaste or modest, to restrict their sphere of activity to the home, or even to realize their properly feminine destiny in maternity: Normative femininity is coming more and more to be centered on woman's body-not its duties and obligations or even its capacity to bear children, but its sexuality, more precisely, its presumed heterosexuality and its appearance.

There is, of course, nothing new in women's preoccupation with youth and beauty. What is new is the growing power of the image in a society increasingly oriented toward the visual media. Images of normative femininity, it might be ventured, have replaced the religiously oriented tracts of the past. New too is the spread of this discipline to all classes of women and its deployment throughout the life cycle. What was formerly the speciality of the aristocrat or courtesan is now the routine obligation of every woman, be she a grandmother or a barely pubescent girl.

To subject oneself to the new disciplinary power is to be up-to-date, to be "with-it"; as I have argued, it is presented to us in ways that are regularly disguised. It is fully compatible with the current need for women's wage labour, the cult of youth and fitness, and the need of advanced capitalism to maintain high levels of consumption. Further, it represents a saving in the economy of enforcement: Since it is women themselves who practice this discipline on and against their own bodies, men get off scot-free.

The woman who checks her make-up half a dozen times a day to see if her foundation has caked or her mascara run, who worries that the wind or rain may spoil her hairdo, who looks frequently to see if her stockings have bagged at the ankle, or who, feeling fat, monitors everything she eats, has become, just as surely as the inmate of Panopticon, a self-policing subject, a self committed to a relentless self-surveillance. This self-surveillance is a form of obedience to patriarchy.

It is also the reflection in woman's consciousness of the fact that she is under surveillance in ways that he is not, that whatever else she may become, she is importantly a body designed to please or to excite. There has been induced in many women, then, in Foucault's words, "a state of conscious and permanent visibility that assures the automatic functioning of power." Since the standards of female bodily acceptability are impossible fully to realize, requiring as they do a virtual transcendence of nature, a woman may live much of her life with a pervasive feeling of bodily deficiency. Hence, a tighter control of the body has gained a new kind of hold over the mind.

Foucault often writes as if power constitutes the very individuals upon whom it operates:

The individual is not to be conceived as a sort of elementary nucleus, a primitive atom, a multiple and inert material on which power comes to fasten or against which it happens to strike.... In fact, it is already one of the prime effects of power that certain bodies, certain gestures, certain discourses, certain desires, come to be identified and constituted as individuals.

Nevertheless, if individuals were wholly constituted by the power/knowledge regime Foucault describes, it would make no sense to speak of resistance to discipline at all. Foucault seems sometimes on the verge of depriving us of a vocabulary in which to conceptualize the nature and meaning of those periodic refusals of control which, just as much as the imposition of control, mark the course of human history.

Peter Dews accuses Foucault of lacking a theory of the "libidinal body," i.e., the body upon which discipline is imposed and whose bedrock impulse toward spontaneity and pleasure might perhaps become the locus of resistance. Do women's "libidinal" bodies, then, not rebel against the pain, constriction, tedium, semistarvation, and constant self-surveillance to which they are currently condemned? Certainly they do, but the rebellion is put down every time a woman picks up her eyebrow tweezers or embarks upon a new diet. The harshness of a regimen alone does not guarantee its rejection, for hardships can be endured if they are thought to be necessary or inevitable.

While "nature," in the form of a "libidinal" body, may not be the origin of a revolt against "culture," domination and the discipline it requires are never imposed without some cost. Historically, the forms and occasions of resistance are manifold. Sometimes, instances of resistance appear to spring from the introduction of new and conflicting factors into the lives of the dominated: The juxtaposition of old and new and the resulting incoherence or "contradiction" may make submission to the old ways seem increasingly unnecessary.

In the present instance, what may be a major factor in the relentless and escalating objectification of women's bodies-namely, women's growing independence-produces in many women a sense of incoherence that calls into question the meaning and necessity of the current discipline? As women (albeit a small minority of women) begin to realize an unprecedented political, economic, and sexual self-determination, they fall ever more completely under the dominating gaze of patriarchy. It is this paradox, not the "libidinal body," that produces, here and there, pockets of resistance.

In the current political climate, there is no reason to anticipate either widespread resistance to currently fashionable modes of feminine embodiment or joyous experimentation with new "styles of the flesh"; moreover, such novelties would face profound opposition from material and psychological sources identified earlier in this chapter. In spite of this, a number of oppositional discourses and practices have appeared in recent years.

An increasing number of women are "pumping iron," a few with little concern for the limits of body development imposed by current canons of femininity. Women in radical lesbian communities have also rejected hegemonic images of femininity and are struggling to develop a new female aesthetic. A striking feature of such communities is the extent to which they have overcome the oppressive identification of female beauty and desirability with youth: Here, the physical features of aging-"character" lines and graying hair - not only do not diminish a woman's attractiveness, they may even enhance it.

A popular literature of resistance is growing, some of it analytical and reflective, like Kim Chernin The Obsession, some oriented toward practical self-help, like Marcia Hutchinson recent Transforming Body Image: Learning to Love the Body You Have. This literature reflects a mood akin in some ways to that other and earlier mood of quiet desperation to which Betty Friedan gave voice in The Feminine Mystique.

Nor should we forget that a massbased women's movement is in place in this country, which has begun a critical questioning of the meaning of femininity, if not yet in this, then in other domains of life. We women cannot begin the re-vision of our own bodies until we learn to read the cultural messages we inscribe upon them daily and until we come to see that even when the mastery of the disciplines of femininity produce a triumphant result, we are still only women.

4

Theorising the Female Spectator

In his lecture on "Femininity," Freud forcefully inscribes the absence of the female spectator of theory in his notorious statement, "to those of you who are women this will not apply-you are yourselves the problem." Simultaneous with this exclusion operated upon the female members of his audience, he invokes, as a rather strange prop, a poem by Heine. Introduced by Freud's claim concerning the importance and elusiveness of his topic-"Throughout history people have knocked their heads against the riddle of the nature of femininity"-are four lines of Heine's poem:

Heads in hieroglyphic bonnets,

Heads in turbans and black birettas,

Heads in wigs and thousand other Wretched, sweating heads of humans

The effects of the appeal to this poem are subject to the work of overdetermination Freud isolated in the text of the dream. The sheer proliferation of heads and hats (and hence, through a metonymic slippage, minds), which are presumed to have confronted this intimidating riddle before Freud, confers on his discourse the weight of an intellectual history, of a tradition of interrogation.

Furthermore, the image of hieroglyphics strengthens the association made between femininity and the enigmatic, the undecipherable, that which is "other." And yet Freud practices a slight deception here, concealing what is elided by removing the lines from their context, castrating, as it were, the stanza. For the question over which Heine's heads brood is not the same as Freud's-it is not "What is Woman?," but instead, "what signifies Man?" The quote is taken from the seventh section (entitled "Questions") of the second cycle of The North Sea. The full stanza, presented as the words of "a young man,/His breast full of sorrow, his head full of doubt," reads as follows:

> O solve me the riddle of life,
>
> The teasingly time-old riddle,
>
> Over which many heads already have brooded,
>
> Heads in hats of hieroglyphics,
>
> Turbaned heads and heads in black skull-caps,
>
> Heads in perrukes and a thousand other
>
> Poor, perspiring human heads-
>
> Tell me, what signifies Man?
>
> Whence does he come? Whither does he go?
>
> Who lives up there upon golden stars?

The question in Freud's text is thus a disguise and a displacement of that other question, which in the pretext is both humanistic and theological. The claim to investigate an otherness is a pretense, haunted by the mirror-effect by means of which the question of the woman reflects only the man's own ontological doubts. Yet what interests me most in this intertextual misrepresentation is that the riddle of femininity is initiated from the beginning in Freud's text as a question in masquerade. But I will return to the issue of masquerade later.

More pertinently, as far as the cinema is concerned, it is not accidental that Freud's eviction of the female spectator/auditor is copresent with the invocation of a hieroglyphic language. The woman, the enigma, the hieroglyphic, the picture, the image-the metonymic chain connects with another: the cinema, the theatre of pictures, a writing in images of the woman but not for her. For she is the problem.

The semantic valence attributed to a hieroglyphic language is two-edged. In fact, there is a sense in which the term is inhabited by a contradiction. On the one hand, the hieroglyphic is summoned, particularly when it merges with a discourse on the woman, to connote an indecipherable language, a signifying system which denies its own function by failing to signify anything to the uninitiated, to those who do not hold the key. In this sense, the hieroglyphic, like the woman, harbors a mystery, an inaccessible though desirable otherness.

On the other hand, the hieroglyphic is the most readable of languages. Its immediacy, its accessibility are functions of its status as a pictorial language, a writing in images. For the image is theorized in terms of certain closeness, the lack of a distance or gap between sign and referent. Given its iconic characteristics, the relationship between signifier and signified is understood as less arbitrary in imagistic systems of representation than in language "proper." The intimacy of signifier and signified in the iconic sign negates the distance which defines phonetic language.

And it is the absence of this crucial distance or gap which also, simultaneously, specifies both the hieroglyphic and the female. This is precisely why Freud evicted the woman from his lecture on femininity. Too close to herself, entangled in her own enigma, she could not step back, could not achieve the necessary distance of a second look.

Thus, while the hieroglyphic is an indecipherable or at least enigmatic language, it is also and at the same time potentially the most universally understandable, comprehensible, and appropriable of signs. And the woman shares this contradictory status. But it is here that the analogy slips. For hieroglyphic languages are not perfectly iconic. They would not achieve the status of languages if they were-due to what Todorov and Ducrot refer to as a certain non-generalizability of the iconic sign:

Now it is the impossibility of generalizing this principle of representation that has introduced even into fundamentally morphemographic writing systems such as Chinese, Egyptian, and Sumerian, the phonographic principle. We might almost conclude that every logography [the graphic system of language notation] grows out of the impossibility of a generalized iconic representation; proper nouns and abstract notions (including inflections) are then the ones that will be noted phonetically.

The iconic system of representation is inherently deficient-it cannot disengage itself from the "real," from the concrete; it lacks the gap necessary for gencralizability (for Saussure, this is the idea that, "Signs which are arbitrary realize better than others the ideal of the semiotic process."). The woman, too, is defined by such an insufficiency. My insistence upon the congruence between certain theories of the image and theories of femininity is an attempt to dissect the episteme which assigns to the woman a special place in cinematic representation while denying her access to that system.

The cinematic apparatus inherits a theory of the image which is not conceived outside of sexual specifications. And historically, there has always been a certain imbrication of the cinematic image and the representation of the woman. The woman's relation to the camera and the scopic regime is quite different from that of the male. As Noel Burch points out, the early silent cinema, through its insistent inscription of scenarios of voyeurism, conceives of its spectator's viewing pleasure in terms of that of the Peeping Tom, behind the screen, reduplicating the spectator's position in relation to the woman as screen.

Spectatorial desire, in contemporary film theory, is generally delineated as either voyeurism or fetishism, as precisely a pleasure in seeing what is prohibited in relation to the female body. The image orchestrates a gaze, a limit, and its pleasurable transgression. The woman's beauty, her very desirability, becomes a function of certain practices of imaging-framing, lighting, camera movement, and angle. She is thus, as Laura Mulvey has pointed out, more closely associated with the surface of the image than its illusory depths, its constructed three-dimensional space which the man is destined to inhabit and hence control.

In Now Voyager, for instance, a single image signals the momentous transformation of the Bette Davis character from ugly spinster aunt to glamorous single woman. Charles Affron describes the specifically cinematic aspect of this operation as a "stroke of genius':

> The radical shadow bisecting the face in white/dark/white strata creates a visual phenomenon quite distinct from the makeup transformation of lipstick and plucked eyebrows.... This shot does not reveal what we commonly call acting, especially after the most recent exhibition of that activity, but the sense of face belongs to a plastique pertinent to the camera. The viewer is allowed a different perceptual referent, a chance to come down from the nerve-jarring, first sequence and to use his eyes anew.

A "plastique pertinent to the camera" constitutes the woman not only as the image of desire but as the desirous image-one which the devoted cinephile can cherish and embrace. To "have" the cinema is, in some sense, to "have"the woman. But Now Voyager is, in Affron's terms, a "tear-jerker," in others, a "woman's picture," that is, a film purportedly produced for a female audience. What, then, of the female spectator? What can one say about her desire in relation to this process of imaging? It would seem that what the cinematic institution has in common with Freud's gesture is the eviction of the female spectator from a discourse purportedly about her (the cinema, psychoanalysis)-one which, in fact, narrativizes her again and again.

A LASS BUT NOT A LACK

Theories of female spectatorship are thus rare, and when they are produced, seem inevitably to confront certain blockages in conceptualisation. The difficulties in thinking female spectatorship demand consideration. After all, even if it is admitted that the woman is frequently the object of the voyeuristic or fetishistic gaze in the cinema, what is there to prevent her from reversing the relation and appropriating the gaze for her own pleasure?

Precisely the fact that the reversal itself remains locked within the same logic. The male striptease, the gigolo-both inevitably signify the mechanism of reversal itself, constituting themselves as aberrations whose acknowledgment simply reinforces the dominant system of aligning sexual difference with a subject/object dichotomy. And an essential attribute of that dominant system is the matching of male subjectivity with the agency of the look.

The supportive binary opposition at work here is not only that utilized by Laura Mulvey - an opposition between passivity and activity, but perhaps more importantly, an opposition between proximity and distance in relation to the image. It is in this sense that the very logic behind the structure of the gaze demands a sexual division. While the distance between image and signified (or even referent) is theorized as minimal, if not nonexistent, that between the film and the spectator must be maintained, even measured. One need only think of Noel Burch's mapping of spectatorship as a perfect distance from the screen (two times the width of the image) - a point in space from which the filmic discourse is most accessible.

But the most explicit representation of this opposition between proximity and distance is contained in Christian Metz's analysis of voyeuristic desire in terms of a kind of social hierarchy of the senses: "It is no accident that the main socially acceptable arts are based on the senses at a distance, and that those which depend on the senses of contact are often regarded as 'minor' arts (= culinary arts, art of perfumes, etc.)." The voyeur, according to Metz, must maintain a distance between himself and the image - the cinephile needs the gap which represents for him the very distance be tween desire and its object. In this sense, voyeurism is theorized as a type of metadesire:

If it is true of all desire that it depends on the infinite pursuit of its absent object, voyeuristic desire, along with certain forms of sadism, is the only desire whose principle of distance symbolically and spatially evokes this fundamental rent. Yet even this status as metadesire does not fully characterize the cinema for it is a feature shared by other arts as well (painting, theatre, opera, etc.). Metz thus adds another reinscription of this necessary distance.

What specifies the cinema is a further reduplication of the lack which prompts desire. The cinema is characterized by an illusory sensory plenitude (there is "so much to see") and yet haunted by the absence of those very objects which are there to be seen. Absence is an absolute and irrecoverable distance. In other words, Noel Burch is quite right in aligning spectatorial desire with a certain spatial configuration. The viewer must not sit either too close or too far from the screen. The result of both would be the same-he would lose the image of his desire.

It is precisely this opposition between proximity and distance, control of the image and its loss, which locates the possibilities of spectatorship within the problematic of sexual difference. For the female spectator there is a certain overpresence of the image-she is the image. Given the closeness of this relationship, the female spectator's desire can be described only in terms of a kind of narcissism-the female look demands a becoming. It thus appears to negate the very distance or gap specified by Metz and Burch as the essential precondition for voyeurism.

From this perspective, it is important to note the constant recurrence of the motif of proximity in feminist theorist (especially those labeled "new French feminisms") which purport to describe a feminine specificity. For Luce Irigaray, female anatomy is readable as a constant relation of the self to itself, as an autoeroticism based on the embrace of the two lips which allow the woman to touch herself without mediation.

Furthermore, the very notion of property, and hence possession of something which can be constituted as other, is antithetical to the woman: "Nearness however, is not foreign to woman, nearness so close that any identification of one or the other, and therefore any form of property, is impossible. Woman enjoys a closeness with the other that is so near she cannot possess it any more than she can possess herself." Or, in the case of female madness or delirium, "women do not manage to articulate their madness: they suffer it directly in their body." The distance necessary to detach the signifiers of madness from the body in the construction of even a discourse which exceeds the boundaries of sense is lacking. In the words of Helène Cixous, "More so than men who are coaxed toward social success, toward sublimation, women are body."

This theme of the overwhelming presence-to-itself of the female body is elaborated by Sarah Kofman and Michèle Montrelay as well. Kofman describes how Freudian psychoanalysis outlines a scenario whereby the subject's passage from the mother to the father is simultaneous with a passage from the senses to reason, nostalgia for the mother henceforth signifying a longing for a different positioning in relation to the sensory or the somatic, and the degree of civilisation measured by the very distance from the body. Similarly, Montrelay argues that while the male has the possibility of displacing the first object of desire (the mother), the female must become that object of desire:

> Recovering her as maternal body (and also as phallus), the woman can no longer repress, "lose," the first stake of representation.... From now on, anxiety, tied to the presence of this body, can only be insistent, continuous. This body, so close, which she has to occupy, is an object in excess which must be "lost," that is to say, repressed, in order to be symbolised.

This body so close, so excessive, prevents the woman from assuming a position similar to the man's in relation to signifying systems. For she is haunted by the loss of a loss, the lack of that lack so essential for the realisation of the ideals of semiotic systems. Female specificity is thus theorized in terms of spatial proximity. In opposition to this "closeness" to the body, a spatial distance in the male's relation to his body rapidly becomes a temporal distance in the service of knowledge.

This is presented quite explicitly in Freud's analysis of the construction of the "subject supposed to know." The knowledge involved here is a knowledge of sexual difference as it is organized in relation to the structure of the look, turning on the visibility of the penis. For the little girl in Freud's description, seeing and knowing are simultaneous-there is no temporal gap between them. In "Some Psychological Consequences of the Anatomical Distinction Between the Sexes," Freud claims that the girl, upon seeing the penis for the first time, makes her judgment and her decision in a flash. She has seen it and knows that she is without it and wants to have it." In the lecture on "Femininity" Freud repeats this gesture, merging perception and intellec tion: "They [girls] at once notice the difference and, it must be admitted, its significance too."

The little boy, on the other hand, does not share this immediacy of understanding. When he first sees the woman's genitals he "begins by showing irresolution and lack of interest; he sees nothing or disowns what he has seen, he softens it down or looks about for expedients for bringing it into line with his expectations." A second event, the threat of castration, is necessary to prompt a rereading of the image, endowing it with a meaning in relation to the boy's own subjectivity.

It is in the distance between the look and the threat that the boy's relation to knowledge of sexual difference is formulated. The boy, unlike the girl in Freud's description, is capable of a revision of earlier events, a retrospective understanding which invests the events with a significance which is in no way linked to an immediacy of sight. This gap between the visible and the knowable, the very possibility of disowning what is seen, prepares the ground for fetishism. In a sense, the male spectator is destined to be a fetishist, balancing knowledge and belief.

The female, on the other hand, must find it extremely difficult, if not impossible, to assume the position of fetishist. That body which is so close continually reminds her of the castration which cannot be "fetishized away." The lack of a distance between seeing and understanding, the mode of judging "in a flash," is conducive to what might be termed as "overidentification" with the image. The association of tears and "wet wasted afternoons" (in Molly Haskell's words) with genres specified as feminine (the soap opera, the "woman's picture") points very precisely to this type of overidentirication, this abolition of a distance, in short, this inability to fetishize. The woman is constructed differently in relation to processes of looking. For Irigaray, this dichotomy between distance and proximity is described as the fact that:

> The masculine can partly look at itself, speculate about itself, represent itself and describe itself for what it is, whilst the feminine can try to speak to itself through a new language, but cannot describe itself from outside or in formal terms, except by identifying itself with the masculine, thus by losing itself. Irigaray goes even further: the woman always has a problematic relation to the visible, to form, to structures of seeing. She is much more comfortable with, closer to, the sense of touch.

The pervasiveness, in theories of the feminine, of descriptions of such a claustrophobic closeness, a deficiency in relation to structures of seeing and the visible, must clearly have consequences for attempts to theorize female spectatorship. And, in fact, the result is a tendency to view the female spectator as the site of an oscillation between a feminine position and a masculine position, invoking the metaphor of the transvestite.

Given the structures of cinematic narrative, the woman who identifies with a female character must adopt a passive or masochistic position, while identification with the active hero necessarily entails an acceptance of what Laura Mulvey refers to as a certain "masculinisation" of spectatorship: "As desire is given cultural materiality in a text, for women (from childhood onwards) trans-sex identification is a habit that very easily becomes second Nature. However, this Nature does not sit easily and shifts restlessly in its borrowed transvestite clothes."

The transvestite wears clothes which signify a different sexuality, a sexuality which, for the woman, allows a mastery over the image and the very possibility of attaching the gaze to desire. Clothes make the man, as they say. Perhaps this explains the ease with which women can slip into male clothing. As both Freud and Cixous point out, the woman seems to be more bisexual than the man. A scene from Cukor Adams Rib graphically demonstrates this ease of female transvestism.

As Katharine Hepburn asks the jury to imagine the sex role reversal of the three major characters involved in the case, there are three dissolves linking each of the characters successively to shots in which they are dressed in the clothes of the opposite sex. What characterizes the sequence is the marked facility of the transformation of the two women into men in contradistinction to a certain resistance in the case of the man. The acceptability of the female reversal is quite distinctly opposed to the male reversal which seems capable of representation only in terms of farce. Male transvestism is an occasion for laughter; female transvestism only another occasion for desire.

Thus, while the male is locked into sexual identity, the female can at least pretend that she is other-in fact; sexual mobility would seem to be a distinguishing feature of femininity in its cultural construction. Hence, transvestism would be fully recuperable. The idea seems to be this: it is understandable that women would want to be men, for everyone wants to be elsewhere than in the feminine position. What is not understandable within the given terms is why a woman might flaunt her femininity, produce her as an excess of femininity, in other words, foreground the masquerade.

Masquerade is not as recuperable as transvestism precisely because it constitutes an acknowledgement that it is femininity itself which is constructed as mask - as the decorative layer which conceals a nonidentity. For Joan Riviere, the first to theorize the concept, the masquerade of femininity is a kind of reaction-formation against the woman's trans-sex identification, her transvestism. After assuming the position of the subject of discourse rather than its object, the intellectual woman whom Riviere analyzes felt compelled to compensate for this theft of masculinity by overdoing the gestures of feminine flirtation.

Womanliness therefore could be assumed and worn as a mask, both to hide the possession of masculinity and to avert the reprisals expected if she was found to possess it-much as a thief will turn out his pockets and ask to be searched to prove that he has not the stolen goods. The reader may now ask how I define womanliness or where I draw the line between genuine womanliness and the masquerade. My suggestion is not, however, that there is any such difference; whether radical or superficial, they are the same thing.

The masquerade, in flaunting femininity, holds it at a distance. Womanliness is a mask which can be worn or removed. The masquerade's resistance to patriarchal positioning would therefore lie in its denial of the production of femininity as closeness, as presence-to-itself, as, precisely, imagistic. The transvestite adopts the sexuality of the other-the woman becomes a man in order to attain the necessary distance from the image. Masquerade, on the other hand, involves a realignment of femininity, the recovery, or more accurately, simulation, of the missing gap or distance.

To masquerade is to manufacture a lack in the form of a certain distance between oneself and one's image. If, as Moustafa Safouan points out, "to wish to include in oneself as an object the cause of the desire of the Other is a formula for the structure of hysteria," then masquerade is antihysterical for it works to effect a separation between the cause of desire and oneself. In Montrelay's words, "the woman uses her own body as a disguise." The very fact that we can speak of a woman "using" her sex or "using" her body for particular gains is highly significant-it is not that a man cannot use his body in this way but that he doesn't have to. The masquerade doubles representation; it is constituted by a hyperbolisation of the accoutrements of femininity.

Apropos of a recent performance by Marlene Dietrich, Sylvia Bovenschen claims, "we are watching a woman demonstrate the representation of a woman's body." This type of masquerade, an excess of femininity, is aligned with the femme fatale and, as Montrelay explains, is necessarily regarded by men as evil incarnate: "It is this evil which scandalises whenever woman plays out her sex in order to evade the word and the law. Each time she subverts a law or a word which relies on the predominantly masculine structure of the look."

By destabilizing the image, the masquerade confounds this masculine structure of the look. It effects a defamiliarisation of female iconography. Nevertheless, the preceding account simply specifies masquerade as a type of representation which carries a threat, disarticulating male systems of viewing. Yet, it specifies nothing with respect to female spectatorship. What might it mean to masquerade as spectator? To assume the mask in order to see in a different way?

MEN SELDOM MAKE PASSES AT GIRLS WHO WEAR GLASSES

The first scene in Now Voyager depicts the Bette Davis character as repressed, unattractive, and undesirable or, in her own words, as the spinster aunt of the family. ("Every family has one.") She has heavy eyebrows, keeps her hair bound tightly in a bun, and wears glasses, a drab dress, and heavy shoes. By the time of the shot discussed earlier, signalling her transformation into beauty, the glasses have disappeared, along with the other signifiers of unattractiveness. Between these two moments there is a scene in which the doctor who cures her actually confiscates her glasses (as a part of the cure).

The woman who wears glasses constitutes one of the most intense visual cliches of the cinema. The image is a heavily marked condensation of motifs concerned with repressed sexuality, knowledge, visibility and vision, intellectuality, and desire. The woman with glasses signifies simultaneously intellectuality and undesirability; but the moment she removes her glasses (a moment which, it seems, must almost always be shown and which is itself linked with a certain sensual quality), she is transformed into spectacle, the very picture of desire.

Now, it must be remembered that the cliche is a heavily loaded moment of signification, a social knot of meaning. It is characterized by an effect of ease and naturalness. Yet, the cliche has a binding power so strong that it indicates a precise moment of ideological danger or threat-in this case, the woman's appropriation of the gaze. Glasses worn by a woman in the cinema do not generally signify a deficiency in seeing but an active looking, or even simply the fact of seeing as opposed to being seen. The intellectual woman looks and analyzes, and in usurping the gaze she poses a threat to an entire system of representation.

It is as if the woman had forcefully moved to the other side of the specular. The overdetermination of the image of the woman with glasses, its status as a cliche, is a crucial aspect of the cinematic alignment of structures of seeing and being seen with sexual difference. The cliche, in assuming an immediacy of understanding, acts as a mechanism for the naturalisation of sexual difference. But the figure of the woman with glasses is only an extreme moment of a more generalized logic. There is always a certain excessiveness, a difficulty associated with women who appropriate the gaze, who insist upon looking.

Linda Williams has demonstrated how, in the genre of the horror film, the woman's active looking is ultimately punished. And what she sees, the monster is only a mirror of her-both woman and monster are freakish in their difference-defined by either "too much" or "too little." Just as the dominant narrative cinema repetitively inscribes scenarios of voyeurism, internalizing or narrativizing the film-spectator relationship, taboos in seeing are insistently formulated in relation to the female spectator as well. The man with binoculars is countered by the woman with glasses.

The gaze must be dissociated from mastery. In Leave Her to Heaven, the female protagonist's excessive desire and overpossessiveness are signaled from the very beginning of the film by her intense and sustained stare at the major male character, a stranger she first encounters on a train. The discomfort her look causes is graphically depicted. The Gene Tierney character is ultimately revealed to be the epitome of evil-killing her husband's crippled younger brother, her unborn child, and ultimately herself in an attempt to brand her cousin as a murderess in order to ensure her husband's future fidelity.

In Humoresque, Joan Crawford's problematic status is a result of her continual attempts to assume the position of spectator-fixing John Garfield with her gaze. Her transformation from spectator to spectacle is signified repetitively by the gesture of removing her glasses. Rosa, the character played by Bette Davis in Beyond the Forest, walks to the station every day simply to watch the train departing for Chicago. Her fascination with the train is a fascination with its phallic power to transport her to "another place."

This character is also specified as having a "good eye"-she can shoot both pool and guns. In all three films the woman is constructed as the site of an excessive and dangerous desire. This desire mobilizes extreme efforts of containment and unveils the sadistic aspect of narrative. In all three films the woman dies. As Claire Johnston points out, death is the "location of all impossible signs," and films demonstrate that the woman as subject of the gaze is clearly an impossible sign. There is a perverse rewriting of this logic of the gaze in Dark Victory, where the woman's story achieves heroic and tragic proportions not only in blindness, but in a blindness which mimes sight-when the woman pretends to be able to see.

THE CENSORSHIP OF THE FEMALE GAZE

This process of narrativizing the negation of the female gaze in the classical Hollywood cinema finds its perfect encapsulation in a still photograph taken in 1948 by Robert Doisneau, Un Regard Oblique. Just as the Hollywood narratives discussed above purport to center a female protagonist, the photograph appears to give a certain prominence to a woman's look. Yet, both the title of the photograph and its organisation of space indicate that the real site of scopophiliac power is on the margins of the frame.

The man is not centered; in fact, he occupies a very narrow space on the extreme right of the picture. Nevertheless, it is his gaze which defines the problematic of the photographs: it is his gaze which effectively erases that of the woman. Indeed, as subject of the gaze, the woman looks intently.

But not only is the object of her look concealed from the spectator, her gaze is encased by the two poles defining the masculine axis of vision. Fascinated by nothing visible - a blankness or void for the spectator - unanchored by a "sight" (there is nothing "proper" to her vision-save, perhaps, the mirror), the female gaze is left free-floating, vulnerable to subjection.

The faint reflection in the shop window of only the frame of the picture at which she is looking serves merely to rearticulate, en abwme the emptiness of her gaze, the absence of her desire in representation. On the other hand, the object of the male gaze is fully present, there for the spectator. The fetishistic representation of the nude female body, fully in view, insures a masculinisation of the spectatorial position. The woman's look is literally outside the triangle which traces complicity between the man, the nude, and the spectator. The feminine presence in the photograph, despite a diegetic centering of the female subject of the gaze, is taken over by the picture as object.

And, as if to doubly "frame" her in the act of looking, the painting situates its female figure as a spectator (although it is not clear whether she is looking at herself in a mirror or peering through a door or window). While this drama of seeing is played out at the surface of the photograph, its deep space is activated by several young boys, out-of-focus, in front of a belt shop.The opposition out-of-focus/in-focus reinforces the supposed clarity accorded to the representation of the woman's "non-vision."

Furthermore, since this out-of-focus area constitutes the precise literal center of the image, it also demonstrates how the photograph makes figurative the operation of centering-draining the actual center point of significance in order to deposit meaning on the margins. The male gaze is centered, in control-although it is exercised from the periphery.

The spectator's pleasure is thus produced through the framing/negation of the female gaze. The woman is there as the butt of a joke-a "dirty joke" which, as Freud has demonstrated, is always constructed at the expense of a woman. In order for a dirty joke to emerge in its specificity in Freud's description, the object of desire - the woman - must be absent and a third person (another man) must be present as witness to the joke-"so that gradually, in place of the woman, the onlooker, now the listener, becomes the person to whom the smut is addressed."

The terms of the photograph's address as joke once again ensure a masculinisation of the place of the spectator. The operation of the dirty joke is also inextricably linked by Freud to scopophilia and the exposure of the female body:

Smut is like an exposure of the sexually different person to whom it is directed. By the utterance of the obscene words it compels the person who is assailed to imagine the part of the body or the procedure in question and shows her that the assailant is himself imagining it. It cannot be doubted that the desire to see what is sexual exposed is the original motive of smut.

From this perspective, the photograph lays bare the very mechanics of the joke through its depiction of sexual exposure and a surreptitious act of seeing (and desiring). Freud's description of the joke-work appears to constitute a perfect analysis of the photograph's orchestration of the gaze. There is a "voice-off" of the photographic discourse, however-a component of the image which is beyond the frame of this little scenario of voyeurism. On the far left-hand side of the photograph, behind the wall holding the painting of the nude, is the barely detectable painting of a woman imaged differently, in darkness-out of sight for the male, blocked by his fetish.

Yet, to point to this almost invisible alternative in imaging is also only to reveal once again the analyst's own perpetual desire to find a not-seen that might break the hold of representation. Or to laugh last. There is a sense in which the photograph's delineation of a sexual politics of looking is almost uncanny. But, to counteract the very possibility of such a perception, the language of the art critic effects a naturalisation of this joke on the woman.

The art-critical reception of the picture emphasizes a natural but at the same time "imaginative" relation between photography and life, ultimately subordinating any formal relations to a referential ground: "Doisneau's lines move from right to left, directed by the man's glance; the woman's gaze creates a line of energy like a hole in space.... The creation of these relationships from life itself is imagination in photography." "Life itself," then, presents the material for an "artistic" organisation of vision along the lines of sexual difference.

Furthermore, the critic would have us believe that chance events and arbitrary clicks of the shutter cannot be the agents of a generalized sexism because they are particular, unique- "Kertesz and Doisneau depend entirely upon our recognition that they were present at the instant of the unique intersection of events." Realism seems always to reside in the streets and, indeed, the out-of-focus boys across the street, at the center of the photograph, appear to act as a guarantee of the "chance" nature of the event, its arbitrariness, in short - its realism.

Thus, in the discourse of the art critic the photograph, in capturing a moment, does not construct it; the camera finds a naturally given series of subject and object posi tions. What the critic does not consider are the conditions of reception of photography as an art form, its situation within a much larger network of representation. What is it that makes the photograph not only readable but pleasurable-at the expense of the woman? The critic does not ask what makes the photograph a negotiable item in a market of signification.

THE MISSING LOOK

The photograph displays insistently, in microcosm, the structure of the cinematic inscription of a sexual differentiation in modes of looking. Its process of framing the female gaze repeats that of the cinematic narratives described above, from Leave Her to Heaven to Dark Victory. Films play out scenarios of looking in order to outline the terms of their own understanding. And given the divergence between masculine and feminine scenarios, those terms would seem to be explicitly negotiated as markers of sexual difference.

Both the theory of the image and its apparatus, the cinema, produce a position for the female spectator - a position which is ultimately untenable because it lacks the attribute of distance so necessary for an adequate reading of the image. The entire elaboration of femininity as a closeness, a nearness, as present-to-itself is not the definition of an essence but the delineation of a place culturally assigned to the woman. Above and beyond a simple adoption of the masculine position in relation to the cinematic sign, the female spectator is given two options: the masochism of overidentification or the narcissism entailed in becoming one's own object of desire, in assuming the image in the most radical way.

The effectivity of masquerade lies precisely in its potential to manufacture a distance from the image, to generate a problematic within which the image is manipulable, producible, and readable by the woman. Doisneau's photograph is not readable by the female spectator-it can give her pleasure only in masochism. In order to "get" the joke, she must once again assume the position of transvestite.

It is quite tempting to foreclose entirely the possibility of female spectatorship, to repeat at the levei of theory the gesture of the photograph, given the history of a cinema which relies so heavily on voyeurism, fetishism, and identification with an ego ideal conceivable only in masculine terms. And, in fact, there has been a tendency to theorize femininity and hence the feminine gaze as repressed, and in its repression somehow irretrievable, the enigma constituted by Freud's question.

Yet, as Michel Foucault has demonstrated, the repressive hypothesis on its own entails a very limited and simplistic notion of the working of power. The "no" of the father, the prohibition, is its only technique. In theories of repression there is no sense of the productiveness and positivity of power. Femininity is produced very precisely as a position within a network of power relations. And the growing insistence upon the elaboration of a theory of female spectatorship is indicative of the crucial necessity of understanding that position in order to dislocate it.

5

Fashion and Image

For the past decade, Madonna Louise Ciccone has been a highly influential pop culture icon and the center of a storm of controversy. She is the best-selling and most discussed female singer in popular music, one of the most prominent stars of music video, an aspiring movie actress, and, most of all, a superstar of pop culture. For her fans, she is the ultimate pop icon, the image of fashion and identity, which produced legions of Madonna wannabees who slavishly imitated her fashion statements. For her detractors, she is the ultimate in crass commercialism and media manipulation, the epitome of banal consumerism run rampant in media culture.

Madonna has thus become a site of contestation and controversy, adored and abhorred by audiences, critics, and academics alike. Most of the polemics, however, are contentious, of an either/or and pro or con nature, and they fail to grasp the many sides of the Madonna phenomenon. While some celebrate her as a subversive cultural revolutionary, others attack her as antifeminist, or as irredeemably trashy and vulgar. Against such one-sided interpretations, however, I argue that "Madonna" is a site of genuine contradiction that must be articulated and appraised to adequately interpret her images, works, and their effects.

My argument is that Madonna's images and reception highlights the social constructedness of identity, fashion, and sexuality. By exploding boundaries established by dominant gender, sexual, and fashion codes, she encourages experimentation, change, and production of one's individual identity. Yet by privileging the creation of image, looks, fashion, and style in the production of identity, Madonna reinforces the norms of the consumer society which offers the possibilities of a new commodity "self" through consumption and the products of the fashion industry.

Grasping this contradiction is the key to Madonna's effects and to interrogating the conditions under which the multiplicity of discourses on Madonna, and contradictory readings and evaluations, are produced. Madonna pushes the most sensitive buttons of sexuality, gender, race, and class, offering challenging and provocative images and cultural artifacts, as well as ones that reinforce dominant conventions.

FASHION AND IDENTITY

Madonna is interesting for cultural studies because her work, popularity, and influence reveal important features of the nature and function of fashion and identity in the contemporary world. Fashion offers models and material for constructing identity. Traditional societies had relatively fixed social roles and sumptuary codes, so that clothes and one's appearance instantly denoted one's social class, profession, and status. Identity in traditional societies was usually fixed by birth, marriage, and accomplishment, and the available repertoire of roles was tightly constricted. Gender roles were especially rigid, while work and status were tightly circumscribed by established social codes and an obdurate system of status ascription.

During the medieval period, identities in Western Europe were especially circumscribed and rules even dictated what members of different classes could or could not wear. Modern societies eliminated rigid codes of dress and fashion, and beginning around 1700 changing fashions of apparel and appearance began proliferating. Although a capitalist market dictated that only certain classes could afford the most expensive attire, which signified social privilege and power, in the aftermath of the French Revolution, fashion was democratized in countries which carried through a democratic revolution, so that anyone who could afford certain clothes and make-up could wear and display what they wished (whereas previously, sumptuary laws forbade members of certain classes from dressing and appearing like the ruling elites).

Modernity also offered new possibilities for constructing personal identities. Modern societies made it possible for individuals to produce - within certain limits - their own identities and to experience identity crises. Already in the eighteenth century, the philosopher David Hume formulated the problem of personal identity, of what constituted one's true selfhood, even suggesting that there was no substantial or transcendental self. The issue became an obsession with Rousseau, Kierkegaard, and many other Europeans who experienced rapid change, the breakdown of traditional societies, and the emergence of modernity.

In modernity, fashion is an important constituent of one's identity, helping to determine how one is perceived and accepted. Fashion offers choices of clothes, style, and image through which one could produce an individual identity. In a sense, fashion is a constituent feature of modernity, interpreted as an era of history marked by perpetual innovation, by the destruction of the old and the creation of the new. Fashion itself is predicated on producing ever new tastes, styles, dress, and practices. Fashion perpetuates a restless, modern personality, always seeking what is new and admired, while avoiding what is old and passe.

Fashion and modernity go hand in hand to produce modern personalities who seek their identities in constantly new and trendy clothes, looks, attitudes, and style, and who are fearful of being out-of-date or unfashionable. Of course, fashion in modern societies was limited by gender codes, economic realities, and the force of social conformity which continued to dictate what one could or could not wear, and what one could or could not be. Fashion in modernity itself underwent complex stages of historical development, though by the beginning of the twentieth century, modern fashion rationalized clothing and cosmetics, and mass markets began to make changes in fashion open to mass consumption.

Yet fashion codes continued to be relatively fixed for some classes and regions. Documentary footage from the U.S. in the 1950s shown in the 1982 ABC documentary Heroes of Rock and other sources, depicted parents, teachers and other arbiters of good taste attempting to dictate proper and improper fashion, thus policing the codes of fashion and identity. Crossing gender codes in fashion was for centuries a good way to mark oneself as a social outcast or even to land in jail or a mental institution.

The 1960s exhibited a massive attempt to overthrow the cultural codes of the past and fashion became an important element of the construction of new identities, along with sex, drugs, and rock and roll, phenomena also involved in the changing fashions of the day. In the 1960s, "antifashion" in clothes and attire became fashionable and the subversion and overthrowing of cultural codes became a norm. So-called fashion subversion continued to be in vogue during the following decades, and the fashion industry allowed new flexibility and marketed an everchanging array of new styles and looks.

By means of such fashion moves, individuals could quickly produce their own identities through resisting dominant fashion codes and producing their own fashion statements, or using dominant styles in their own ways. One of Stuart Ewen's students provides interesting testimony concerning how it was possible to produce one's own style against dominant fashion codes:

> I went to Catholic school for twelve years. In grammar school, I wore a uniform for eight years. I used to try to rebel against this in little ways, such as not wearing the tie I was supposed to, or by wearing the wrong type of collar.... It was a way of finding me a little freedom, a way of fighting the system in a small way.

Indeed, Madonna herself tells in an early interview how she expressed adolescent rebellion through fashion from the time she was a young girl, indicating she and her girlfriend dressed extravagantly:

> Only because we knew that our parents didn't like it. We thought it was fun. We got dressed to the nines. We got bras and stuffed them so our breasts were over - large and wore really tight sweaters - we were sweater-girl floozies. We wore tons of lipstick and really badly applied makeup and huge beauty marks and did our hair up like Tammy Wynette.

During this period, media culture became a particularly potent source of cultural fashions, providing models for appearance, behaviour, and style. The long-haired and unconventionally dressed rock stars of the 1960s and the 1970s influenced changes in styles of hair, dress, and behaviour, while their sometimes rebellious attitudes sanctioned social revolt, as when Bob Dylan proclaimed that "The Times They are A'Changing," or that change was "Blowing in the Wind." Groups like The Beatles, The Rolling Stones, Jefferson Airplane, and performers like Janis Joplin or Jimi Hendrix sanctioned countercultural revolt and the appropriation of new styles of dress, behaviour, and attitudes.

The association of rock culture with long hair, social rebellion, and non conformity in fashion continued through the 1970s with successive waves of heavy metal rock, punk, and new wave attaining popularity. More conservative television programming, films, and pop music by contrast provided mainstream models for youth. During the past two decades, cultural conservatives have been reacting strongly against 1960s radicalism and fashion, and youth culture and fashion have become battlefields between traditionalist conservatives and cultural radicals, attempting to overturn traditional gender roles, fashion codes, and values and behaviour. Thus, fashion and social identities are themselves part of a process of social struggle and conflict between opposing models and ideologies.

Conservatives have their fashion models and style, as do subcultural rebels. Political struggles thus are partly played out in fashion wars as well as elections and political debate.

High school in particular is a period in which young people construct their identities, attempting to "become someone". High school has been a terrain of contradiction and struggle for the past decades. While some parents and teachers attempt to instill traditional values and ideas, youth culture is often in opposition to conservative culture.

Although the 1980s was a predominantly conservative period with the election of Ronald Reagan and a "right turn" in U.S. culture, the images from popular music figures sometimes cut across the conservative grain. Michael Jackson, Prince, Boy George, and other rock groups undermined traditional gender divisions and promoted polymorphic sexuality. Cyndi Lauper revelled in offbeat kookiness, while Pee Wee Herman engaged in silly and infantile behaviour to the delight of his young (and older) audiences. Throwing off decades of cool sophistication, maturity, respectability, and taste, Pee Wee made it OK to be silly and weird, or at least different.

THE MADONNA PHENOMENON

It was in this period during the 1980s, in which youth identities were being renegotiated in a conservative era that Madonna first came to prominence. Her early music videos and concert performances transgressed traditional fashion boundaries and she engaged in overt sexual behaviour and titillation, subverting the boundaries of "proper" female behaviour. Thus, from the beginning Madonna was one of the most outrageous female icons among the repertoire of circulating images sanctioned by the culture industries.

Although there were no doubt many more far out and subversive figures than Madonna, their images and messages did not circulate through mainstream culture and thus did not have the efficacy of the popular. The early Madonna sanctioned rebellion, nonconformity, individuality, and experimentation with fashion and lifestyles. Madonna's constant change of image and identity promoted experimentation and the creation of one's own fashion and style. Her sometimes dramatic shifts in image and style suggested that identity was a construct, that it was something that one produced, and that it could be modified at will. The way that Madonna deployed fashion in the construction of her identity made it clear that one's appearance and image helps produce what one is, or at least how one is perceived and related to.

Thus, Madonna problematized identity and revealed its constructedness and alterability. Madonna was successively a dancer, musician, model, singer, music video star, movie and stage actress, "America's most successful businesswoman," and a pop superstar who excelled in marketing her image and selling her goods. Consciously grafting her own image, she moved from being a boy toy, material girl, and ambitious blonde, to artiste of music videos, films, and concerts.

Her music shifted from disco and bubblegum rock, to personal statements and melodic torch singing, to (with the aid of her music videos) pop modernism. Madonna's hair changed from dirty blonde to platinum blonde, to black, brunette, redhead, and multifarious variations thereof. Her body changed from soft and sensuous to glamorous and svelte to hard and muscular sex machine to futuristic technobody. Her clothes and fashion changed from flashy trash, to haute couture, to far-out techno-couture, to lesbian S. & M. fashion, to postmodern pastiche of all and every fashion style. New images and a new identity for all occasions and epochs.

As it turns out, Madonna's fashion moves generally caught shifts in cultural style and taste, and thus achieved the status of the popular, providing fashion models and material for appropriation by her vast and varied audiences. Consequently, to properly grasp the Madonna phenomenon, one must perceive her marketing strategies, the ways that she sold successive images and incorporated various audiences, and the mechanisms through which she herself became a pop superstar. Madonna is one of the greatest PR machines in history and she has hired top agents, publicists, and "creative" personnel to market her and produce her images.

From the beginning her every move was surrounded by publicity and year after year Madonna references in media culture have proliferated. Indeed, a Nexis data-base search for "Madonna and pop" references from the decade from 1984 to 1993 indicated over 20,000 citations! "Madonna" is her publicity and image and the "Madonna phenomenon" is thus importantly a successful marketing and publicity story.

While there are certain continuities in Madonna's development which I will explicate, there are also at least three distinct periods that can be (roughly) equated to shifts in her music production, her deployment of fashion and sexuality, and the construction of her image. I will accordingly delineate these periods to articulate the contours of what has become known as the "Madonna phenomenon." My focus will be on Madonna's images and cultural production, their impact on their audiences, and her cultural effects over the past decade.

Although I deploy the standard methods of cultural studies featuring textual analysis and reception of texts by audiences, I argue that a generally neglected component of cultural studies-political economy and the production of culture-is an important key to the Madonna phenomenon. For Madonna's success is largely a marketing success and her music, videos, other products, and image are triumphs of extremely successful production and marketing strategies-though she has had her marketing and critical failures, mainly her films. Madonna has made the right connections, has worked with talented music and video producers, has a phalanx of professional business managers and publicists, and has for the most part brilliantly produced her own image and sold it successfully to her audiences.

In 1983, Madonna released her first album, Madonna, and two of the songs ("Lucky Star" and "Holiday") became major hits. Her early music and songs are rather conventional popular dance music aimed at a teenage market. But Madonna was an especially flashy performer and began to attract notice at this point with music videos of her top hits which were featured on MTV, a relatively new channel which was to play a key role in her career. Indeed, Madonna emerged as one of the first MTV superstars, whose music videos quickly sold her image to a vast national audience. From the beginning, Madonna crafted music videos that produced a distinct image which marketed her to various audiences.

One of her early music videos, "Lucky Star," features Madonna as an especially voluptuous sex object, energetic dancer, and innovative fashion trend-setter. The video opens with a black and white sequence with Madonna wearing black sunglasses which she slowly pulls down revealing sultry eyes, intensely focusing on the camera (and viewer). The sunglasses, of course, were symbols of the punk generation, which influenced Madonna during her early 1980s days in New York, and would later become a symbol of the cyberpunk movement as well.

Their deployment suggested that Madonna would reveal something of herself in the video, but that she knew that her performance was an act and that she would maintain her control and subjectivity. The final sequence returns to black and white, depicting Madonna pulling the shades over her eyes as the screen fades to black.

At the end of the brief opening sequence, the screen dissolves to white and a colour sequence shows Madonna dressed totally in black. As the music slowly begins, she writhes in an erotic pose, the camera cuts to a freeze frame of her face, she winks, and the video cuts to Madonna dancing and cavorting with two dancers. The wink, like the opening frame, tells the viewer not to take this too seriously and perhaps to say to women and feminists that although she is presenting herself as the object of the male gaze, as an objectified sexual object, she knows what she is doing, that she is controlling her image. This opens the possibility that Madonna will subvert the very images and frames that she is now exploiting to make herself a lucky star.

Eschewing the narrative frame of most music videos of the day, "Lucky Star" presents a collage of images of Madonna's body. The video shows her energetically dancing, alone or with the two dancers, striking erotic poses, and showing off her body and clothes. It is important to note that the emerging Madonna phenomenon, Madonna as pop megasuperstar, is related to her deployment of music, dance, and image. The music is conventional dance music, but it is good dance music that empowers the audience to dance and exhibit themselves à la Madonna. Indeed, she distinguished herself early on as a dancer in the New York club scene and emerged in her music videos as a spirited performer of her own songs in the form of dance.

Now Madonna might not be a great dancer, but the edits, framing, and movement of her music videos allow her to appear as an attractive image and her dance movements presented her as a free, lively, expressive young woman, using dance to present her as a moving, attractive, and seductive image. In "Lucky Star," Madonna is dressed in a tight and short black skirt with a black leotard underneath. She wears a loose black blouse which lightly covers a black veiled lace body shirt underneath. Around her waist, one sees the famous "unchastity belt"-later marketed by her Boy Toy line of fashion-with a large buckle and chains around the waist. Madonna has a black bow in her hair and a distinctive star earring with smaller crucifix earrings as well. Completing the outfit are black bobby socks and short black boots.

Madonna's fashion at this stage constitutes a subversion of conventional codes and justified wearing any combination of clothes and ornaments that one wished. Of course, Madonna herself became a model of teen fashion and the infamous Madonna "wannabes" slavishly imitated every aspect of her early "flashy trash" clothing and ornamentation. She linked fashion to exhibitionism and aggressive sexuality, connecting fashion revolt with sexual rebellion and the unconventional use of religious symbols like crucifixes. Thus, Madonna legitimated unconventional fashion and sexual behaviour, endearing her to an audience that felt empowered by Madonna's flaunting of traditional standards and codes.

Her other early rock video hit, "Borderline," depicts motifs and strategies that would make Madonna a lucky star. The video narrative images weave two sequences together to illustrate the love song. In colour sequences, Madonna sings, flirts, and seduces a Hispanic youth, while in a black and white sequence an Anglo photographer snaps pictures of her and courts her. In one black and white sequence, she sprays graffiti over lifeless classical sculptures, a modernist gesture of the sort that codes her music videos as transgressors of the codes of high culture, establishing her as a practitioner of pop modernist subversion which breaks rules and attempts innovation, though within the limits of the popular.

In "Borderline," she breaks the taboo of interracial relationships, by depicting her character with a Hispanic youth. While she seems to reject him for the fashion photographer who will make her a star, she rejects the photographer in turn, implying, perhaps, a desire to control her own image, or to pursue her own sexual pleasures. Madonna is already pushing the buttons of sexuality, and going over established pop borderlines, with the lyrics promising a utopia of sexual ecstasy ("You keep on pushing my love over the borderline") and the music has upbeat dancing rhythms which enables Madonna to exhibit her energy and talent as a dancer.

In the video of "Borderline," Madonna wears several different outfits and her hair ranges from dirty and messy blonde in the Hispanic colour sequences to beautifully fashioned glamorous blonde in the black and white sequences. The contrasting video images of the two Madonnas suggests that one's identity is a construct that one can modify or change at will, and indeed Madonna herself was to precisely do this.

In addition, Madonna's offering herself to males of various colours in her music videos (and in reality, if the gossip is true) breaks down racial barriers to sexuality, but is also a clever marketing strategy inviting white, Hispanic, and black youths to fantasize that they too can have or be Madonna. Indeed, it was arguably Madonna's marketing strategy that enabled her to appeal first to white, urban and suburban working-class and middle-class girls who identified with her rebellion and flashy and trashy fashion statements, and then successfully to a wide range of different audiences, pulling in new fans with each successive career move.

Already in her first music videos, Madonna is deploying fashion, sexuality, and the construction of image to present herself both as an alluring sex object and as a transgressor of established borderlines. On one hand, the video validates interracial sex and provides all-too-rare images of Hispanic barrio culture. Yet the two contrasting narrative sequences convey the message that while you might have a good time hanging out with Hispanics, it is the white photographer who will provide the ticket to wealth and success.

But she ends up with the Hispanic youth and the narrative thus valorizes multi-relationships, for the Madonna character continues to see both guys during the narrative sequences, projecting the fantasy image that one can have it all, crossing borderlines from one culture to another, appropriating the pleasures of both cultures and multiple relationships. The video also puts on display the contrasting fashion codes between upper-class culture and Hispanic culture, identifying Anglo culture with high fashion, high art, and luxury. By contrast, Hispanic culture is equated with urban ghettos, blue jeans, pool halls, and less expensive and stylish clothes and ornamentation.

A later Madonna video, "La Isla Bonita," however, utilizes fantasy images of Hispanic fashion as an icon of beauty and romanticism. Such "multiculturalism" and her culturally transgressive moves (i.e. highly explicit sexuality and interracial sexuality) turned out to be highly successful marketing moves that endeared her to large and varied youth audiences. Madonna became a major pop culture figure, however, with the beginning of her concert tours in 1985 and she began consciously marketing her own image and a wide range of fashion accoutrements, which she sold under the Boy Toy label. Already by 1985, the first "Madonna effect" was evident, displaying her powerful impact on her audience:

At concerts her per capita sales of T-shirts and memorabilia are among the highest in rock history. 'She sells more than Springsteen, the Rolling Stones or Duran Duran,' says Dell Furano, the concession merchandiser for her tour. At her San Francisco date, $20 T-shirts sold at the rate of one every six seconds. She began marketing "Madonna-wear," which she described as "sportswear for sexpots." The line included "a $25 lace tank top, a $30 sweatshirt, $20 pants and a medium-priced ($30) tube skirt that can be rolled down for public navel maneuvers."

While an up-scale version of Madonna-wear was also marketed, as were Madonna make-up kits, her image also encouraged thrift-shop down-scale fashion for the Madonna look: wearing underwear outside of skirts, loose t-shirts, cheap bracelets, earrings, chains, and crucifixes also provided appropriate decoration. Indeed, the Madonna look became known as "flash-trash," so that almost any teenage girl could afford to look like Madonna and share her attitudes and styles. Madonna fashion made it possible for teenage girls to produce their own identity, to make their own fashion statements, and to reject standard fashion codes.

During the Virgin Tour, Madonna wore a brightly coloured jacket and tight micro-mini skirt, a sparkly lingerie harness and black lace stockings that stopped at the knee, and an array of ornaments, including crucifixes, a peace medallion, and bracelets. Prancing around in spiked boots, her belly button exposed, Madonna would take off the jacket to reveal a lacy purple shirt and black bra, accenting a lush and accessible sexuality. For the hit song, "Like a Virgin," Madonna appeared in a white wedding dress and screamed "Do you want to marry me" to which the girls and boys both answered, "Yesss!" Thrusting her hips as she sang, "You make me feel like a virgin," she unfolded a belly roll as she intoned, "touched for the very first time."

This highly sexual rendition of the song mocks virginity, but also makes fun of sexuality by ironizing its codes and gestures. Her play with sexual codes reveals sexuality to be a construct, fabricated in part by the images and codes of popular culture, rather than a "natural" phenomenon. It also reveals sexuality to be a field of play, of self-creation and expression, and of desire and pleasure. From the beginning, Madonna would successfully exploit sexuality and would in turn present sexuality as natural, enjoyable, and fun-certainly a healthy attitude in a once puritanical culture.

Madonna wannabees proliferated and she quickly became a model for identity, associating changes in identity with fashion and style changes. Lewis summarizes the early Madonna effect:

> The shopping mall is a site around which female fan participation in female address videos coalesces. 'Madonna is everywhere,' writes one biographer, 'there is even a mall in California that people have nicknamed 'the Madonna mall' because so many girls who shop there try to look just like her.'...In response to the popularity of 'MadonnaStyle,' Macy' s Department Store created a department called 'Madonnaland' devoted to selling the cropped sweaters ($30), cropped pants ($21) and a variety of jewellery accessories such as crucifix earrings and outsize 'pearl' necklaces ($4-59) resembling those worn by Madonna. The department became the location for the mobilisation of Madonna fans in the summer of 1985 when Macy's sponsored a Madonna look-alike contest to coincide with the star's New York concert date.

Madonna's deployment of fashion and sexuality during this early phase is more complex than it appears at first glance. While it is easy to dismiss the early Madonna's posturing as a shameless sex object, boy toy, and material girl who collapses identity into image and style, a closer reading of her music videos produces another picture. For instance, her music video "Material Girl" seems at first glance to be an anthem of Reaganism, which glorifies shallow materialism and celebrates greed and manipulation ("The boy with the cold hard cash/Is always Mr Right...cause I'm just a Material Girl"). On this reading, the song is a replay of Marilyn Monroe's "Diamonds Are a Girl's Best Friend" and is advocating the same calculating and shallow materialist attitudes.

Although Madonna has assumed a Monroe-like look in this video and does deploy some of the fashion and poses of Monroe's 1950s hymn to bourgeois materialism, a closer look at the music video provides some different perspectives. The musical numbers are enframed with a narrative in which a producer looks at the images of Madonna singing and begins courting her. He is casually dressed in a brown work shirt and appears to her as an employee of the studio, yet he asks her out and in the final scene they are seen kissing in an old truck which he had rented for the occasion.

There is thus a tension between the musical numbers which celebrate wealth and materialism, and the narrative which privileges "true love." On one reading, which Madonna herself asserted, the video shows the "material girl" rejecting her wealthy suitors in favour of a poor working boy. When confronted with the critique that she was celebrating crass greed, Madonna responded: "Look at my video that goes with the song. The guy who gets me in the end is the sensitive guy with no money". On this account, Madonna turns down the guys courting her in the music and dance sequences for the poor but sincere guy shown in the "realism" sequences.

A closer reading raises questions, however, as to whether the "poor boy" in the video, played by Keith Carradine, is really "poor" and whether Madonna doesn't actually get a very rich and successful businessman in the video. The narrative images reveal the Carradine character to be a studio mogul who cleverly poses as a sincere poor dude who wins Madonna's heart. Thus, in "Material Girl" Madonna is all things to all people and has it every way: for conservatives of the Reagan years, she is a celebrant of material values, the material girl, who takes the guilt away from sex, greed, and materialism.

For this audience, she is Marilyn Monroe reincarnated, the superpop superstar, the super-ideal male fantasy sex object and female fantasy boy toy icon. But for romantic idealist youth, she is the good girl seeking love, who chooses true love over material temptations. Yet in the music video narrative, she gets both love and a successful guy. Thus, the music video of "Material Girl" arguably deploys modernist aesthetic strategies that put narrative and social codes in tension and that require an active viewer to produce meanings and interpretations from the polysemic text.

The video also expresses elements of Madonna's own philosophy and, arguably, articulates some of her contradictions (i.e. trying to have it all ways). Thus, like modernist art, the music video creates an innovative structure, articulates the artiste's vision, and requires an active reader to decode the possible range of meanings. Moreover, the video "Material Girl" problematizes identity and decouples the link between expensive clothes, wealth, and position. Carradine wears a brown work shirt and pants and this is perfectly alright, the video suggests, indicating that fashion and identity are up to the individual and not societal codes.

Madonna's images and music videos thus legitimate individual choice in appropriating fashion and producing one's image. Yet the most attractive images in the musical production numbers do celebrate high and expensive fashion, diamonds, and other costly ornaments as keys to a successful image and identity. And it could be that the powerful images of wealth and high fashion, reinforced by the musical lyrics, do privilege bourgeois materialism over romance and individual choice in the music video.

A high level of ambiguity, irony, and humor permeates Madonna's work and image. Her use of fashion is humorous and ironic, as are many of her videos and concert acts. The items marketed in her Boy Toy and Slutco lines are often humorous, as are the very titles of the lines themselves. Indeed, the much-maligned term Boy Toy itself is ironic and allows multiple readings. On one level, Madonna is a toy for boys, but on another level boys are toys for her, the Boy Toys are there for her toying around and the unchastity belt comes off at her whim and desire. Indeed, "Material Girl" shows the guys as Madonna's toys and her dance numbers with men during the Virgin Tour concerts present them as her underlings and accessories with whom she toys and dominates.

Crucially, the early Madonna projects in her videos and music an all-too-rare cultural image of a free woman, making her own choices and determining her own life. The early Madonna image of a free spirit floating through life on her own terms is perfectly captured in her role in Susan Seidelman's Desperately Seeking Susan. The message here, consistent with Madonna's other early work, is that one can fundamentally change one's identity by changing one's fashion, appearance, and image. Madonna herself would dramatically exemplify this philosophy in her two succeeding stages in which she radically alters her image and identity.

Indeed, in 1986 alone Madonna metamorphized from the sluttish boy toy in some of her videos, concert performances, and Desperately Seeking Susan to the more sophisticated and serious young woman portrayed in the music video "Live to Tell," her new husband Scan Penn's favorite song and the theme of one of his movies. She then appeared as a short-haired young blonde teenager of "Papa Don't Preach," where the Madonna character decides against abortion when she becomes pregnant.

This music video utilized a narrative and realist form to tell the story of a young woman with a problem whereas another music video from the year, "Open Your Heart," deployed a complex modernist deconstruction in which Madonna problematized the male gaze, appearing as a stripper in a "carousel" porn parlor and dancing off at the end with a young boy, in a Charlie Chaplin outfit, deconstructing oppositions between "sin" and "innocence", adults and youth.

These music videos thus deployed different aesthetic strategies from the traditional narrative form of "Live to Tell" and the gritty realism of "Papa Don't Preach," in which images unproblematically illustrate the lyrics and the lyrics comment on the narrative action, to the deconstructive modernism of "Open Your Heart." Madonna was experimenting with different forms and styles, and in the process constructed a new set of images, and a new identity.

Madonna had arrived. In 1985, her records had sold 16 million singles and albums. She had no. 1 pop hits with "Like a Virgin" and "Crazy for You," and by the time she was 26, Madonna had made seven Top-20 singles in seventeen months (it took Barbra Streisand seventeen years to do the same). Madonna made a successful film debut in Desperately Seeking

Susan and her Virgin Tour established her as one of the hottest figures in pop music. She was featured on the cover of Time magazine and was profiled in People, Newsweek, Rolling Stone, and other popular magazines.

Her first album, Madonna, eventually sold over three million copies and her album Like A Virgin racked up 4.5 million copies in domestic sales, with 2.5 million more worldwide by 1985. Moreover, Madonna knew that she was a superstar and plotted her moves accordingly. Needless to say, Madonna deployed fashion and sexuality to produce the image that would mark her mid-to late 1980s stage, characterized by continued megasuccess as a recording star with best-selling albums and music videos, another successful concert tour ("Who's That Girl?"), a much-discussed and eventually failed marriage with movie actor Scan Penn, and two movies that flopped with critics and audiences (Shanghai Surprise and Who's That Girl?).

The first visible change in image had to do with her weight and body image. The early Madonna was soft and a bit chubby, but rigorous exercise and diet transformed her body. She also changed her hair and fashion styles, utilizing more glamorous haute couture fashion, while frequently changing her hair arrangements. In many photos and in the 1986 film Shanghai Surprise Madonna appeared more and more like Marilyn Monroe with glamorous, wavy, and fluffy blonde hair. She also emulated the look of other classic movie stars like Lana Turner and Marlene Dietrich.

Yet in her rock videos "Cherish" and "Papa Don't Preach," Madonna sported short, cropped blondish hair (à la Jean Seberg in Breathless) and garish platinum blonde hair in the 1987 movie Who's That Girl?, which reprised the figure of the 1930s Hollywood screwball comedy heroine. The song "Like a Prayer" featured Madonna with her natural dark hair and she also appeared in red hair and various shades between light and dark in the videos, photos, and documentary footage of the period from 1986 to the end of the 1980s.

Madonna's 1987 "Who's That Girl?" tour, captured on the video-cassette Ciao Italia!, disclosed her to be twenty pounds lighter and highly athletic. For years, she had been dieting, exercising for hours each day, and even lifting weights to build up her body. The tour featured her energetic dancing, with break-dancer accompaniment, intricate lighting effects, seven or eight costume changes for the star, and dramatic shifts of image and mood throughout the show.

Wearing a skimpy black corset at the start of the show, Madonna played to her sex-kitten image, but then shifted to the romantic sentimental mode of her album True Blue. But after wearing a 1950s prom dress to reflect the innocence of True Blue, she put a black leather jacket over the dress for "Papa Don't Preach," while the words "safe sex" were flashed on a huge screen at the back of the stage. Mocking "Material Girl," Madonna wore a ridiculously tacky outfit and sang the lyrics with a high-pitched Betty Boop twang to ironize the lyrics.

For "La Isla Bonita," she chose a Spanish-style cabaret dress and wore an international melange of clothes in "Holiday", which signalled the celebatory and wholesome attitude she was trying to promote. Eschewing the bawdy sexuality and sexual repartee which marked her earlier Virgin Tour, and that returned in even more extreme forms in the later Blonde Ambition and Girlie Show tours, Madonna is relatively restrained in her deployment of fashion and sexuality during this period, appearing to "mature" in appropriating more traditional images and fashion.

The stage of Madonna's True Blue deployment of more traditional images of women and sexuality, however, undercut her subversiveness as a fashion image and model for young women. Whereas the flash trash of the early Madonna legitimated creating your own fashion statements and mixed and matched cheap attire, Madonna II produced the traditional image of the slender, well-dressed beautiful women, forcing the "wannabees" to go to exercise salons, beauty parlors, and to buy expensive clothing, cosmetics, and jewelry. Indeed, during this period, there was a marked turn to gyms, dieting, and the cultivation of slimness as the ideal for women.

Madonna's image in the fashion magazines also sent out

the message that high and tasteful fashion was back and that flash-trash and antifashion were out. From 1987 to 1989, Madonna thus adopted more traditional fashion and attitudes, and tried to appear more respectful of traditional gender roles. Trying to make her doomed marriage with Scan Penn work, Madonna appeared in romantic love songs videos (True Blue), singing of the joys of devotion, commitment, and true love. Madonna decided to shed the trampy sex kitten look and boy toy image for a more conventional feminine appearance. As Forbes put it:

> She began singing in a deeper, more serious voice, and in a video from her third album wore honey-blonde hair and a demure flowered dress. In July 1987 she got herself on the cover of Cosmopolitan as a glamorous blonde, and in May 1988 she graced the cover of Harper's Bazaar as a prim brunette. Her True Blue' album of that period sold nearly 17 million copies, and she sold more albums among the over-20 crowd than ever.

As noted, Madonna's marketing strategies successively targeted different audiences. While she appealed to young teenage girls in her early work, she quickly incorporated minority audiences with her use of Hispanic and black figures and culture in her videos and stage performances. The True Blue phase incorporated an older audience and perhaps a more conservative one, through her exploitation of more traditional images and types of song. Thus, rather than going for a "lowest common denominator" popularity, Madonna achieved her stardom through successively incorporating different audiences into her orbit.

The effect of Madonna's second phase was thus to legitimate more traditional fashion and images of women. The period was an especially creative one in the field of music video. Her album Like a Prayer revealed her to have matured psychologically and musically. The songs deal with the pain of the breaking up of her marriage with Scan Penn, repressed guilt over her mother's death, conflicts with her father, and the pain and difficulties of growing up.

The music video of the title song brings out religious motifs from Madonna's Catholic upbringing and incorporates a more complex modernist phase in her music video production, which would attract a large academic following. Although in her earlier videos and image construction, Madonna utilized crucifixes as part of her fashion attire, the music video of the track "Like A Prayer" is built primarily around religious images and themes. The video fuses religion and eroticism in a narrative celebrating love, both spiritual and carnal. The refrain, "In the midnight hour, I can feel your power, Just like a prayer, you know I'll take you there," could either refer to religious or sexual ecstasy.

Madonna brings out the latent eroticism in the Catholic religion and uses it for striking aesthetic and moral purposes. She also incorporates the joy and enthusiasm of black gospel music, thus fusing sacred and secular, Catholic and Protestant, themes and images. The video contrasts images of an inside and outside world, where the outside is the site of racial and sexual violence, bigotry, and injustice. The inside world of the church, however, is one of love, community, and goodness-powerful religious messages and images.

The narrative of the "Like a Prayer" video depicts an innocent black man wrongly accused of a crime that the Madonna figure observes. She goes into a church, dreams of making love to the statue of a black saint, and then rescues the innocent black to flamboyant images of gospel singing, burning crosses (representing the evil of Klan bigotry), candles, and other religious iconography. For the dream/fantasy sequence of the video, Madonna wears a black slip which signifies sleep, the oneiric, and eroticism, exploiting the powerful symbolism and aesthetic effects of black.

The imagery promotes integration and harmony between blacks and whites, with Madonna singing with a black choir in a black church, kissing one black man and saving another. The video thus projects a powerful image of goodness and morality, doing the right thing. Yet such are Madonna's contradictions that her use of images undercuts the religious message, as she appears dancing in church in a slip and her erotic behaviour in the church probably goes beyond established boundaries of propriety-indeed Italian television banned the video under pressure from Catholic groups.

But, as always, Madonna profits from her contradictions, appealing both to Catholics gratified to see some eroticism and life injected into its institutions and to see dramatisation of its morality, as well as to lapsed or antiCatholics who are thrilled by subversive images, such as Madonna kissing a black man and dancing in her slip in a church. In the music video of "Express Yourself, which is perhaps the culmination of her second period, Madonna produces a highly complex modernist text that plays with issues of gender, sexuality, and class.

Madonna's forest of symbols unfolds with images of a futuristic city in the air, supported by machinery below, drawing on the iconography of Fritz Lang's modernist film classic Metropolis. Madonna suddenly emerges standing up on a giant swan. Addressing herself to a female subject (a rather rare move), Madonna proclaims: "Come on girls, do you believe in love? Well, I've got something to say about it, and it goes like this." The lyrics of the song affirm self-expression, doing your best in all things ("Don't settle for second best, baby"), and overcoming obstacles to one's goals.

The song employs the imperative mode and Madonna defiantly shouts "Express yourself!" at key junctures in the song. While a verse indicates that "What you need is a big strong hand to lift you to your higher ground," it is clear from the subtext, and the images that accompany the music video, that the "big strong hand" should be your own, and not the typical male helping hand.

Indeed, Madonna is constantly inverting relations of gender power and domination in the video, putting on display the socially constructed images of women, and exhibiting the male fantasies that produce such images of women and sexuality. Utilizing as a frame for the video Lang's Metropolis, Madonna inverts the liberal humanist theme of the film, as Morton argues. Lang's film represents conflicts between workers and capitalists in a futuristic city, as well as between fathers and sons, men and women.

At the end, all conflicts are overcome in naive images of total reconciliation. Madonna's video, by contrast, presents stark and powerful images of the differences between capital and labour, and men and women. Images near the end of the video of two men fighting and of the quasi-violent encounter between Madonna and a male worker suggests the irreconcilability of the opposing interests of class and gender and continual struggle between the classes and sexes as the fate of the human species.

Or, one might read the images of the men fighting as a feminist critique of male violence and brutality - a reading supported by the text as a whole. The video presents a panoply of traditional patriarchal representations of women, beginning with Madonna standing on top of a swan and then representing her holding and becoming a cat, sliding across the floor and licking a plate of milk. In these images, Madonna appropriates traditional feminine images, but then undercuts them by contrasting discordant images of women and assuming the male subject position, showing that all representations of gender are socially constructed and can be assumed and thrown off at will.

The most offensive image, from the standpoint of feminism, Madonna in bondage, can be read as the fantasy of the capitalist male who projects her onto a video screen, in bondage with an iron collar and chains. It is crucial to note that this image is presented as the fantasy of the patriarchal/ capitalist of the video that puts on his monocle to feast his eyes upon Madonna in bondage shown on a video screen. The images here are obviously playing on the concept of cinema constructed by a male gaze, and it suggests that images which objectify women are the projection of males who fantasize women as sex objects. From this perspective, Madonna is putting on display the ways that male fantasy and power objectify women, fantasizing them as in bondage, as animals, as beautiful objects for male lust and domination.

Within this display of male images, however, Madonna suddenly emerges in a suit, with a monocle, and grabs her crotch, signifying her assumption of the male position of power and control. At one point, she rips open the jacket to reveal her breasts and to disclose that the male image is just another social construction, a subject-position that anyone can occupy. By implication, images of women are also subject positions, produced by male power, that women may choose to occupy, or may choose to vacate in favour of male subject positions - or something altogether different.

This deconstructive reading suggests that "Express Yourself puts on display the artificiality of images of gender and suggests that individuals can choose their own images and self-constructions. The lyrics of "Express Yourself" indeed order individuals to produce their own identity and to construct their own selves. And yet, once again, Madonna undercuts her own feminism by displaying herself in traditional fetishized images of women and as appearing as an object for the male gaze, as well as a subject in control of the narrative and the video itself.

There are thus contradictions between Madonna's pop feminism, her deconstruction of dominant images of women, and her replication of precisely these images. Once again, however, Madonna profits from her contradictions, appealing both to feminists and to male viewers like the characters Beavis and Butt-Head who like to ogle female body parts. Thus, her anthem of liberation can be viewed either as a feminist text, or as just another objectification of women's bodies for male pleasure.

BLONDE AMBITION

Thus, the Madonna effects were increasingly contradictory. On one hand, she presents herself as a feminist in control of her life and career, and on the other hand, she presents herself as just another female body to titillate men and provide fashion models for women. During her third period, in the 1990s, she would continue to push the boundaries of sexual representation and to become an icon of sexual liberation. Moreover, she became even more eclectic in her use of fashion and in her image production, drawing on some of her earlier images, which she frequently quoted and sometimes parodied. Madonna also became political during this period, making statements on behalf of AIDS victims, the homeless, saving the rain forests, women's rights, and in 1990 even made a "get out and vote" video, threatening to spank those who refused to vote. In 1992, she supported Bill Clinton for President.

After the break-up of her marriage with Scan Penn in 1989, Madonna continued to explore representations of sexuality and gender, entering upon the stage of her work where she would systematically challenge conventional representations of sexuality. This 1990s phase attracted legions of lesbians and gays, pro-sex feminists and sexual libertarians, and academics who would produce a cottage industry of Madonna readings that attempted to decipher her images and texts. It is quite remarkable the extremes to which Madonna has gone in crossing the boundaries of established norms of sexual representation.

For Madonna has now deployed images of interracial sex, masturbation (in her concert tour), lesbianism, S. & M. sex, and orgies in her work, constantly trying to go beyond the boundaries of the sexually permissible. During the 1990s, Madonna has thus exploited an especially flamboyant deployment of fashion and sexuality, producing a series of complex modernist music videos that expanded the boundaries of the art form and even led MTV to ban one of her productions, "Justify My Love," in 1990 and to rarely play "Erotica" in 1992.

She also produced a book of erotic images, Sex and became herself, as an artifact of pop culture, regularly exhibited in magazines which intersperse interviews or stories with provocative images of Madonna in kiddy-porn poses, drag, or other provocative images. Madonna had obviously developed from young sex object on the move, to mature woman, prepared to control her own destiny and to move music video into new realms of image production.

In her most recent period, marked by a series of highly controversial rock videos, the Blond Ambition tour and the 1991 film of the tour, the 1992 album Erotica and the book Sex, and her 1993 Girlie's Show, Madonna has been recognized as a top pop superstar and even "America's shrewdest businesswoman." Her publicity and marketing machine continued to pump out publicity at a furious rate and the public continued to be fascinated with every detail concerning Madonna's life.

But it was probably her rock videos of the late 1980s and 1990s in which Madonna most notably created wide cultural controversy that attracted the attention of academic critics and cultural theorists. Along with Michael Jackson, she is arguably one of the first rock video superstars and is perhaps the supreme master, or rather mistress, of the form. "Open Your Heart," "Like A Prayer," "Express Yourself," "Justify My Love," and "Vogue" are modernist masterpieces of video art.

Breaking the rules of music videos which deploy expressive images to illustrate the lyrics, Madonna's best music videos contain a multilayered structure of images that require an active viewer to generate the sometimes complex meanings proliferating in the play of the music, lyrics, and images. Or, à la postmodernism, one can simply view her videos as a dazzling stream of images. For, as we shall see, Madonna employs both modernist and postmodernist aesthetic strategies, thus appealing to devotees of both.

Densely crafted feasts of images, her music videos can be enjoyed on several levels by different audiences: teenage girls and boys can process the music and images in different ways according to their own fantasies; more sophisticated music and cultural critics can enjoy grappling with polysemic modernist texts and occasional uses of postmodern strategies; and students of popular culture can attempt to discover why and how Madonna is popular.

Once again, we see how Madonna's "subversive" artistic practices also coalesce with a successful marketing strategy. Thus, Madonna should be interpreted in terms both of her aesthetic practices and her marketing strategies, and her works can thus be read either as works of art, or analyzed as commodities that shrewdly exploit markets. In fact, Madonna is interesting both as an aesthetic and a marketing phenomenon, and a multidimensional reading should interrogate both sides of the Madonna equation.

In the 1990s, Madonna has attempted to produce an identity as an artist. Her rock videos became increasingly complex, or attempted to expand the boundaries of the permissible in terms of male and female gender roles, overt sexuality, parody of religion, and modernist ambiguity. Fashionwise, she sometimes returned to the sexy and flamboyant attire of her early stage, but she mixed it with haute couture, futuristic technofashion, S. & M. chic, and a postmodern pastiche of various fashion styles, subverting oppositions between high and low fashion, much as postmodern art explodes established modernist cultural hierarchies between "high" and "low" culture.

Yet, Madonna deployed the typically modernist strategy of shock in her outlandish use of fashion, sexuality, and religious imagery, especially in her rock videos, which are highly complex cultural texts that allow a multiplicity of readings. If one conceives "postmodern art" to be a fragmented display of disconnected elements in a flat, superficial play of surface without any depth or meaning (as Jameson 1991 and others would have it), most of Madonna's work is emphatically not "postmodern" in this sense. Instead, both her more realist videos and modernist videos convey meanings and messages, though with her more modernist music videos like "Express Yourself," the meanings are often elusive and difficult to grasp.

The modernist strategy of adopting shock techniques have been a constant in Madonna's work and although she deploys camp, irony, and humor, her subject matter and themes are often quite serious. So in a sense, Madonna is more modernist than postmodernist, though her work also embodies postmodern themes and aesthetic strategies. Throughout the Blonde Ambition tour, Madonna played out a deconstructive drama of playing with gender roles, frequently wearing men's clothes, grabbing her crotch, and declaring she was the boss, thus occupying male gender positions. She also had her male dancers wear fake breasts, women's clothes, and submit to her power and control.

The message was that "male" and "female" were social constructs that could be deconstructed and that women could occupy male positions, roles, and behaviour and vice versa. Yet, as I shall argue in the conclusion, Madonna does not subvert relations of domination or offer egalitarian images of relations. Like conservative deconstruction, Madonna puts on display binary oppositions that constitute our culture and society, demonstrates their artificiality, and questions the prioritizing of one of the oppositions over the other, without putting anything new in its place. Thus, she tends to place women, primarily herself, in the position of power and authority which is rigorously exercised over men and women.

To deconstruct traditional gender oppositions and relations of power and domination, Madonna uses irony, humor, and parody to push the sensitive buttons of "masculine" and "feminine" and to provoke reaction to the overthrowing of traditional images and stereotypes and their exchange and mixture in the genders of the future, which would presumably be multiple rather than binary. There was indeed always a strong mixture of irony and satire in Madonna's work from the beginning and her concert performances became increasingly campy, as was the dramatisation of her life on the road in Truth or Dare.

Her performance of "Material Girl" in the Blond Ambition tour, for instance, is pure camp, with Madonna and two female singers sitting on a raised platform in hair-curlers and bathrobes, singing the song with false accents, out of tune and in high-pitched voices. The image puts on display the labour and ridiculous activities that women go through to make themselves "beautiful" and mocks the ideal of the "material girl" (of course, on another level Madonna herself is the extreme example of almost superhuman labour and expense to make herself "beautiful," a contradiction that pervades her work and that I return to in the conclusion).

Her most striking music videos are highly aestheticized, using modernist techniques of the construction of compelling images. The orgy scenes in "Justify My Love" are highly abstract and theatrical and "Vogue" deploys posed images to celebrate pure camp (Strike a pose! Vogue! Vogue!). Indeed, "Vogue" parodies fashion conventions-modeling, posing, photography, and objectification-but reinforces them by identifying voguing with a gay dance phenomenon and then cultural celebrity. On the other hand, the video puts on display the conditions of production of the image by disclosing the poses of fashion and star images and the construction involved in the production of images.

The video opens with parting feathers, signifying camp style and artificiality, and then presents a montage of posed images with her dance troupe assuming fashion poses. Two servants voguing while they clean the house suggests the desirability of image-creation throughout the spheres of everyday life. The frame centers on Madonna who orders "Strike a pose!" and a set of images shows her ensemble obeying. The lyrics sing of escape from everyday life through voguing, transforming oneself into a more desirable image, "You're a superstar, that's what you are!" Voguing, the lyrics suggest, is open to anyone ("It doesn't matter if you're black or white, if you're a boy or a girl") and produces aesthetic self-transcendence for all ("Beauty is where you find it").

But then the static images, derived from the fashion industry, are transposed into the gay dance style documented in Paris isBurning and infused with erotic energy. And finally, Madonna's pantheon of privileged images ("Greta Garbo and Monroe...Bette Davis, Rita Hay worth gave good face") is illustrated by images of Madonna herself striking poses in the guise of the above mentioned celebrities. Madonna has been attacked for "poaching" images and phenomena, like voguing, from gay culture and utilizing its images and style in her work, defused of its original context. She was also attacked by black critics for drawing heavily upon black music in her work and then leaving out references to blacks, or people of colour, in her pantheon of images in "Vogue."

In reference to the first criticism, one could argue that Madonna has done as much as anyone to "normalize" gay and lesbian sexuality in popular media culture, and is indeed idolized by many in the gay and lesbian communities. Likewise, she could respond to her black and other critics of colour that she has done as much as anyone to promote black (and Hispanic) music, dancers, singers, and musicians, while attempting to break down colour lines and barriers between the races. She could also answer that her pantheon in "Vogue" is arguably a gay male pantheon that includes precisely who she cites.

On the other hand, one could also argue that Madonna ultimately privileges whiteness and that the people of colour around her simply highlight her distinctive whiteness. Moreover, her videos and concert performances replicate white superiority and power, showing Madonna totally in control of, overshadowing, and dominating everyone else. In any case, the complexity and sensitivity of issues of race, gender, sexual preference, and class that Madonna takes on demonstrates courage to tackle controversial topics that few popular music figures engage with her consistency and provocativeness.

"Vogue" contains images of corsets and bras and the inside/outside fashion deconstruction that one observes in Madonna's videos and concert performances, in which bras, corsets, and panties are worn outside of blouses, skirts, or suits, suggesting that all fashion is artificial. Her images suggest that corset, bras, and other standard female attire are symbols of women's submission to cultural standards, which might as well be worn outside to make the bondage transparent. On the other hand, these icons of women's oppression to fashion standards are rendered erotic in Madonna's iconography, showing how one can transform signs of oppression into signs of mockery and libidinal enjoyment.

Madonna's modernist deconstruction was disseminated via an aesthetic of shock and excess defined by her fashion, attitude, and behaviour. There were, of course, market reasons why one might adopt such strategies: they create an image, call attention to oneself, and sell. Intense narcissism is ever more visible as a key element in the Madonna phenomenon and one could read the 1990s Madonna as an image factory in which her own image is the meaning of her musical texts and other image productions.

Madonna's continuing to go beyond herself and to push the boundaries of the permissible utilizes modernist aesthetic strategies of excess, shock, spectacle, and theatricality. In the Blonde Ambition tour, Madonna produced a futuristic look, wearing far-out technofashion, suggesting new syntheses of technology and the human. Her blonde hair tied back severely, a microphone unit strapped to her head, and her body adorned with bustiers and futuristic clothes designed by Jean Paul Gaultier; Madonna appears as another species, a new technobody, designer-fashioned for the next century.

The Blonde Ambition show also features male dancers with fake breasts and women dancers with penises, suggesting the emergence of a new species in the technofuture, which subverts previous boundaries between men and women. Grabbing her crotch throughout the show, a defiant Madonna presents herself as an icon of power and sexuality. The dance numbers also exploit far-out fashion and explicit sexuality to constitute her identity as an iconoclastic figure of the transgressor against established conventions. She, like the successful modernist artist, thus establishes new norms by breaking the old ones.

However, her 1992 album Erotica and book Sex indicate that Madonna may be falling into a trap that could render her boring and predictable. The songs in her album and music video "Erotica" deploy some of the same images and blatant sexuality as "Justify My Love" and her earlier sexual provocations, and do not break any new ground. Her book Sex is something of an embarrassment with pictures on shabby paper with an aluminum cover and metal-binding that easily breaks. The pictures of S. & M. in particular are boring and predictable, and the text, supposedly recounting "Madonna's sexual fantasies," is also trite and unerotic. Fashion is deployed in these works to shock and provide libidinal excitement, but by now such imagery is rather commonplace.

But in the best of her music videos, Madonna emerges as a modernist boundary-buster. Her concept of art privileges self-expression, experimentation, pushing the limits of taste, and crossing the borderline into new areas of experience and representation. Madonna has continued to push pop culture beyond previous boundaries and to subvert established rules, conventions, and limits. Her deployment of fashion and sexuality in particular shatters previous rules and conventions and established her identity as an iconoclastic modernist.

On the other hand, so far her modernist moves have been extremely successful from a commercial point of view and Madonna emerges as much as clever businesswoman as artiste. Thus, one must also grasp the "Madonna phenomenon" as a commercial enterprise. In April 1992, it was widely reported that Madonna had signed a $60 million deal with Time-Warner, which would market her albums, music videos, and films, providing her with large royalties, development money, and the opportunity to promote the work of young artists.

Utilizing modernist terminology, Madonna said that she envisaged the contract as an opportunity to produce a group of collaborating artists, that constitute an "artistic think tank" which would be a cross between the Bauhaus, that revolutionized art, architecture, and design in Germany in the 1920s, and Andy Warhol's factory that brought together artists from film, music, painting, fashion, and other contemporary arts in the 1960s and beyond. Forbes reported that during the period 1991/2, Madonna earned $48,000,000, making her; once again, one of the most highly paid performers of the period. Madonna's art, fashion, and identity games have paid and call attention to the fact that media culture is commercial culture that sells cultural commodities to audiences.

THE MODERN AND THE POSTMODERN

Concerning the deployment of fashion and sexuality, Madonna's cumulative message seems to be that you can do, say, and be anything that you want. The construction of one's own identity begins with fashion, with one's "look." Here the fashion message is that you can wear anything that anything goes, that one can construct one's own look out of the materials of one's culture. Madonna's use of fashion as excess, of appearing in the most outlandish and outre costumes imaginable, suggests that fashion is not a rigid code, not a set of rules to which one must conform, but a field of imagination and creativity in which one can construct any image that one wants.

Of course, Madonna's linking of image, fashion, and identity also suggests that it is in one's look, in how one dresses and makes oneself up that identity is anchored-a debatable proposition. But, Madonna intimates, fashion is not enough: one must strike a pose, vogue, develop "attitude," behave in a certain way. Madonna's way is excess, shock, pushing beyond the limits, and always trying to develop something new. The Madonna way is to attract attention through going beyond the bounds of conventional attire and behaviour. Such a position empowers people to dress, act, and be what they want at the same time that it enslaves people in the necessity of developing an image, striking a pose, constructing identity through style, forcing people to worry about how they dress and look and how other people will react to their image.

The Madonna phenomenon thus suggests that in a consumerist promotional culture identity is constructed through image and fashion, involving one's look, pose, and style. Identity is nothing deep as it was in much modern theory that assumed an essential self, or the project of developing an authentic selfhood.

Whereas for Heidegger Selbständigkeit (standing-by-yourself, self-constancy) and Wiederholung (resolute repetition in the face of death of one's fundamental choice of selfhood) constituted authentic selfhood and identity, for Madonna and postmodern identity-construction it is precisely change, constantly redeveloping one's look, and striking outrageous and constantly changing poses that constitutes one's image and identity. Of course, and curiously, Madonna is "authentic" in Heidegger's sense in that she has resolutely adhered to this project now in over a decade of shocking fashion, images, poses, and iconoclastic behaviour, all of which have created and promoted "Madonna."

Moreover, fashion and identity for Madonna are inseparable from her aesthetic practices, from her cultivation of her image in her music videos, films, TV appearances, concerts, and other cultural interventions. Madonna's deployment of fashion and sexuality are structured by an aesthetic of creativity, of producing one's own look and identity. Her practice is linked to an aesthetic of excess and to this day, Madonna continues to go beyond the borders of the permissible, to subvert and transgress established boundaries in fashion and art. In this sense, the putatively postmodern Madonna is enacting a pop modernist aesthetic.

Indeed, more considered and theoretically informed reflection on the Madonna phenomenon may deconstruct, or put in question, certain distinctions between modernism and postmodernism. Many academic discourses fail to adequately conceptualize modernism and describe as "postmodern" quite typical modernist aesthetic strategies, practices, and goals-or they inadequately theorize the "postmodern." Madonna has been theorized as "postmodern" through her deployment of strategies of simulation, pastiche, her implosion of gender, racial, and sexual boundaries, and her use of irony and camp. Yet boundary deconstruction, irony, and camp are arguably modernist strategies and in fact Madonna constantly deploys self-consciously modernist strategies, presenting her work as serious and transgressive art.

In the 1990 Nightline interview and the 1991 film Truth or Dare, Madonna describes her work as "artistic," claiming that she refuses to compromise her artistic integrity. She also indicates that she wants to continue "pushing buttons," being "political," going beyond established boundaries, and creating new and innovative works of art-all self-consciously modernist aesthetic values and goals. Thus, while one might interpret Madonna as "postmodernist" in the light of her uses of Baudrillardian categories of simulation and implosion, one should also be aware of the ways in which Madonna can be read as modernist.

For the most part, theorizing about the "postmodern" is as superficial and one-dimensional as the texts and practices described as postmodern in those terms. A complex and challenging phenomenon like Madonna puts in question and tests one's aesthetic categories and commitments. Yet Madonna does deploy a wide range of aesthetic strategies and so if one's definition of "postmodernism" is a set of cultural practices that combines traditional, modernist, and new postmodernist forms and themes, then Madonna can be interpreted as "postmodern."

However, one should note the extent to which she draws upon classical modernist strategies, images, and forms in her most impressive music videos and concert performances of the past few years. She also has a large repertoire of "realist" music videos in which the images merely illustrate the lyrics of the song and produce realist narratives to accompany the words and music (i.e. "Papa Don't Preach," "Live to Tell," "Oh, Father," "This Used to be My Playground," and "Rain"). And in "Fever," she deploys explicitly postmodern image strategies in which the lyrics of the song, itself a pop song of the 1950s, are flatly intoned over abstract images of a bronzed and electronically contorted Madonna, presenting a flat surface of disconnected images without deeper meaning.

While some have attacked Madonna as being totally antifeminist and a disgrace to women, others have lauded her as the true feminist for our times and as a role model for young women. Camille Paglia, for instance, has celebrated Madonna as "Real Feminist" and an ideal of the strong, independent and successful woman, who successfully affirms her own power and sexuality and defies conventional stereotypes. I too have stressed the extent to which Madonna reverses relations of power and domination and provides strong affirmative images of women.

But one could argue that Madonna merely transposes relations of domination, reversing the roles of men and women, rather than dissolving relations of domination. In her concert performances, her dancers are mere appendages which she dominates and controls, overtly enacting rituals of domination on the stage. In the HBO Blond Ambition tour video of 1990, for example, she is constantly positioning herself in positions of power and control over the male (and female) dancers.

In simulated sex scenes in the tour, Madonna was usually on top and in her infamous masturbation/simulated orgasm scene in "Like A Virgin," the male dancers first fondle Madonna and then disappear as she writhes in an exaggerated orgasm. In response to this critique, one could argue that Madonna is constantly ironizing relations of domination, putting their mechanisms on display, and, as I argued in my reading of "Express Yourself," subverting them by disclosing the artificiality, constructedness, and reversibility of relations of power and domination.

Yet in her "real" everyday relations with her cast, friends, and family in the documentary Truth or Dare, she also positions herself as the mother of her troop and is constantly affirming her power over them, often admitting in interviews that she is a "bitch" and "control freak." Before each performance, Madonna says a "prayer," much like a football coach propping his crew to go out and win the big one (in one sequence, she concludes by ordering her minions to go out and "kick ass"). In both work and leisure scenes in her concert film Truth and Dare, Madonna is clearly in charge and the opening song of the HBO documentary of the concert showed her with a whip in hand, proclaiming "I am the boss!"

One could, of course, argue that the film Truth or Dare is itself a put on that deconstructs the very genre of a film documentary by undermining the opposition between backstage and onstage. In Madonna's entourage, backstage is onstage with the omnipresent camera catching every nuance and Madonna and many of her circle are obviously playing to the film being shot. Yet one could argue that the many images, scenes, and comments of her family, tour ensemble, friends, and fans capture aspects of the "truth" of Madonna and present perspectives on the "real" Madonna.

For what is "Madonna" other than the effects she produces and generates, the public persona that she assiduously constructs? And the one thing that comes through repeatedly, reinforced by her many interviews and music performances, is that Madonna is in charge, that she totally dominates everyone around her. Madonna might be contrasted in this regard with avant-garde performance artist Laurie Anderson. While Madonna often presents herself as a sovereign subject who dominates her environment and controls those around her, Laurie Anderson presents more egalitarian images of social relations.

In Home of the Brave, a 1986 documentary of her concert performances, Anderson slides in and out of interactions with members of her cast, which often privilege the other performers, or present ensemble singing or dancing, in which Anderson sometimes slides off to the side and other times merges with her ensemble. Madonna, by contrast, always dominates her entourage and is always the center of attention with the musical performance numbers highlighting her talents, importance, and, especially, stardom.

Madonna is thus the sovereign and centered modern subject, always in charge, always in control, while Laurie Anderson is more fragmented, dispersed, and decentered à la postmodern subjectivity. In her 1990 music video collection, Anderson presents a male "clone" of herself to help her with production and publicity and then clones a female, and both clones are rather grotesque.

While Madonna grabs her crotch and prances in a male suit to symbolize her assumption of the prerogatives of male, phallic power, Anderson uses electronic devices to lower the octave of her voice, so that she sounds male - but an insecure, uncertain male voice signifying the frailty of personal and sexual identity. She dresses and sometimes looks androgenous, collapsing distinctions between "male" and "female" (themselves social constructs), while Madonna is invariably a "woman," even when she assumes male power (as when she bares her breasts after grabbing her crotch in the segment in

"Express Yourself in which she appears in a male suit, as if to say, "Look, I'm really a woman").

Madonna's texts are meaning-systems, which proliferate polysemic meanings and messages. Her performances on her music videos highlight the meanings of the words, or use images to undercut or subvert the meanings of the lyrics-as she chooses. Her music videos are often complex modernist systems of meaning, demanding interpretation and allowing multivalent readings.

Madonna is a meaning machine and her performances articulate her ideology, vision, and messages. Indeed, one level of meaning perpetually conveyed in her music videos and performances is that Madonna herself is a superstar, that Madonna is cool, that Madonna rules. This narcissistic self-reference and self-promotion in her performances is perhaps the underlying meaning of all of her images which relentlessly signify "Madonna! Madonna! Madonna!"

Laurie Anderson's performance in Home of the Brave, by contrast, provides fragments of meaning which do not add up to any clear system of meanings. Her texts thus disrupt, in postmodern fashion, the signifying chain, her images and sounds do not connect, or add up to anything in particular. Rather, they present a collage of disconnected signifiers, of sounds and images that do not signify, or that merely point to them.

Her performance is for the sake of performance, in the moment, and does not produce any particular statements, positions, messages or ideologies - unlike Madonna who is always in your face with her latest statement or message. Laurie Anderson thus enacts a postmodern-deconstruction of expression and identity, fragments and disperses her images and sounds, and resists developing systems of meaning. She follows David Byrne's injunction to "Stop Making Sense" and instead makes performances that are just that-performances.

Whereas Madonna is forever prancing around familiar everyday worlds (or exploring the utopian spaces of sexual fantasy), Anderson takes us to completely new and different worlds with different sights, sounds, and logic. One thus enters a new postmodern imagescape with Anderson where humans implode with technology, familiar instruments give out strange, electronically mediated sounds, and nothing is quite like it seems. Laurie Anderson herself often appears as an extraterrestrial and her Nietzschean Ubermensch (pointed to in her pop song "O Superman") is a curious synthesis of the human and technology, a new species of technohuman who produces new sounds, or as Sayre puts it, "a 'new noise'...in a new territory".

In fact, Anderson deterritorializes her performance spaces that are themselves strange and yet familiar. She also focuses attention on the musical instruments played and in a highly implosive set of gestures merges the human and organic with inanimate instruments. Ties become pianos which emit electronic sounds, guitars become organic, bending and flapping, while humans merge with technology or become mere shadows and photographic images.

Many of Anderson's performances are strongly compelling and emit intense and strange images and sounds that often take on a certain fascination and power. While Madonna's images signify and demand interpretation, Andersen's images resist interpretation. Her art is an erotics of surfaces and the play of light, sound, movement, word, and performance. Her texts are thus not polysemic, they resist reading, and revel in the their own play and deconstruction of meaning. While Madonna tends to exploit the familiar genres of popular music, Anderson mixes pop, rock, jazz, blues, gospel, classical, and other idioms with new electronic sounds and computer-generated images to produce a new multi-media performance art - a postmodern implosion of "high" and "low" art and familiar music genres.

At one point in Home of the Brave, she says "Welcome to difficult art," and then performs "Language is a Virus from Outer Space." The musical accompaniment mixes blues singers, with a jazz saxophone player, with rock percussion, guitar, and piano, mixed together in a hybrid pop sound. Words and images are flashed on the screen in the multi-media mode that Anderson uses, and she concludes by emitting electronic sounds by pounding on her head and gnashing her teeth.

In a sense, Anderson's work is not really difficult, it's just different: its fragments don't connect; it operates in a different space and time continuum, and its performances aim at otherness and strangeness rather than classical form, harmony and symmetry, or the proliferation of meaning à la modernism. By contrast, her gestures, sounds, images, and performance are simply strange and don't communicate anything at all - or what her signifiers communicate is simply themselves and no more.

Yet, in a manner typical of avant-garde art, Anderson raises questions concerning what art - and in particular music and performance - really is. Like John Cage, Anderson seems to imply that sound it is music and transgresses all musical boundaries mixing up familiar sounds with new electronically produced sounds. Likewise, performance in Home of the Brave combines musical numbers with storytelling, slices of everyday life, drama, comedy, and multi-media play.

Thus, in avant-garde fashion, Anderson uses some postmodernist techniques to interrogate what art is and expands its boundaries through her performances. Her performances do not add up to produce unifying meanings and her "text" is thus totally fragmented, with euphoric moments, but no deeper meaning. When she says "Language is a Virus From Outer Space," citing a phrase of author William Burroughs, who comes out on stage just before the performance to recite some typically Burroughsesque comments on eyes, images, and representations, followed by Anderson and company's performance of the song, there is no deep insight into language, and the performances and words that flash across the screen do not elucidate the phrase.

Rather, the performance simply raises questions concerning what language is that forces thought and reflection (and discussion if the song is performed in a group situation). Anderson is, of course, an avant-garde performance artist and

Madonna is the reigning queen of pop, so this comparison is between two rather different species of culture. Yet such a comparison reveals the limits of Madonna's novelty and creativity and the differences between opposing aesthetic strategies. Yet, curiously, the difference is not between a robust and creative modernism and a flat and dull postmodernism, as some might have it.

Instead, Madonna's aesthetic strategies are arguably modernist, while Laurie Anderson has been deploying arguably postmodernist strategies in some of her work, such as Home of the Brave. Madonna projects something of a individual style, vision, and voice, and attempts to produce innovative and complex texts within the form of music video. Some of her works do deconstruct familiar meanings, project a polysemic complexity of meaning that demands interpretation, and that provide texts in which sight, sound, and performance work together to generate a wealth of meanings.

Likewise, Madonna always has a political agenda and is frequently promoting her version of feminism, sexual liberation, and self-creation. Anderson, by contrast, deconstructs expression, fragments the signifying chain, implodes musical idioms, resists interpretation and produces a chain of signifiers that don't really signify, or that signify little beyond themselves-à la postmodernism. Yet such postmodern work doesn't "say anything," and evades the social commentary of Anderson's own earlier work in United States. Madonna by contrast is a commentary machine and constantly presents herself as a cultural revolutionary engaging in social critique, cultural innovation, and the promotion of social change. This brings us to some concluding reflections on Madonna's politics and effects.

Whatever the "truth" of Madonna (no doubt inaccessible in its multiplicity) it is clear that her music videos and concert performances constantly enact relations of power and domination and never portray egalitarian, reciprocal, or communitarian relations. As for Nietzsche, the will to power is at the center of Madonna's universe and Madonna represents herself as the subject of this will, as the center of power and all-powerful subject. Thus, whereas it is salutary that she presents images of powerful women overcoming male domination and while these images might help to empower women, they do not overcome the hierarchical structure of power and domination in our society.

Nor do they present an alternative to the relations of domination and oppression that currently structure everyday life in contemporary societies. Obviously, how one evaluates Madonna depends on one's specific politics and morality, and someone who cultivates an aesthetic of shock and excess, as does Madonna, is certain to offend and to become a target of criticism. Madonna, however, thrives on criticism, which, along with her deployment of fashion and sexuality, helps her produce an identity as a transgressor.

Her breaking of rules has progressive elements in that it goes against dominant gender, sex, fashion, and racial hierarchies and her message that identity is something that everyone can and must construct for themselves is also appealing. Yet by constructing identity largely in terms of fashion and image, Madonna plays into precisely the imperatives of the fashion and consumer industries which offer a "new you" and a solution to all of your problems through purchasing products, services, and buying into regimes of fashion and beauty.

By privileging image, she plays into the dynamics of the contemporary promotional culture that reduces art, politics, and the fabric of everyday life to the play of image, downplaying the role of communication, commitment, solidarity, and concern for others in the constitution of one's identity and personality. Madonna is thus emblematic of the narcissistic 1980s, a period still exerting a strong influence, in which the cultivation of the individual self and the obsessive pursuit of one's own interests was enshrined as cultural mythology. The imperative to "go for it!" echoes through the 1980s and Madonna went for it and got it.

Yet in becoming the most popular woman entertainer of her era (and perhaps of all time), Madonna produced works that have multiple and contradictory effects and that in many ways helped subvert dominant conservative ideologies. As I have argued, Madonna's deployment of fashion and sexuality pushed buttons of race, sex, gender, class, and religion that provoked contradictory responses, that highlighted the social constructedness of these phenomena, and that indicated these artificial categories of everyday life could be changed, or at least one's attitude toward such things as race and sexual preference could be changed.

In a sense, with the limitations that I have noted, Madonna helped bring marginal groups and concerns into the cultural mainstream and powerfully articulated the yearnings of young women for more independence and power. And yet there have been strong criticisms from the marginal and oppressed groups whose images and style Madonna has deployed that she exploits people of colour, gays and lesbians, and marginal sexual subcultures for her own purposes, bell hooks has argued that there is also a racist component in Madonna, who privileges herself and whiteness over people of colour. Madonna is always in center frame and is always the dominant figure, appearing to hooks more as "plantation mistress" than as "soul sister".

Hooks notes that Madonna ultimately privileges the "blonde look" over her natural dark hair and so when the chips are down, the image Madonna most exploits is that of the quintessential 'white girl.' To maintain that image she must always position herself as an outsider in relation to black culture. It is that position of outsider that enables her to colonize and appropriate black experience for her own opportunistic ends even as she attempts to mask her acts of racist aggression as affirmation.

Yet one could also argue that Madonna's constant changes of style, including hair colour, and her appropriation of black, Hispanic, gay and lesbian, and a vast array of other images circulate positive images of marginal subgroups through culture. In any case, Madonna is a site of genuine contradiction. On one hand, she promotes feminism, yet some of her images undercut feminist critiques of femininity, beauty, the objectification of women, and so on.

On the other, Madonna sanctions revolt and individual construction of image and identity, yet the form in which she carries out her revolt is that of the models of the fashion and consumer industries. Madonna calls herself an artistic revolutionary and celebrates modernist subversion, yet her work is circulated in the commodity form of popular music and music videos, which are, after all, at bottom, advertisements for the songs.

While there is sufficient material both to celebrate and to criticize her, one should grasp the many-sidedness of the Madonna phenomenon and her multiple and contradictory effects. Indeed, Madonna is a provocative challenge to cultural studies. Unpacking the wealth of her artistic strategies, meanings, and effects requires deployment of a full array of textual criticism, audience research, and analysis of the political economy and production of pop culture in our contemporary media society.

Her work has become increasingly complex and it is precisely this complexity, as well as her continued popularity, that has made Madonna a highly controversial object of academic analysis in recent years. Madonna allows many, even contradictory, readings which are grounded in her polysemic and modernist texts and her contradictory cultural effects. At dull gatherings, mention Madonna and you can be sure that there will be violent arguments, with some people passionately attacking and others defending her. Whether one loves or hates her, Madonna is a constant provocation who reveals the primacy of fashion and image in contemporary culture and the social constructedness of identity.

6

Construction of Femininity on Indian Television

Analysis of TV Programmes - An Eclectic Approach As noted in our discussion of theoretical considerations, the traditional approach of content analysis does not produce a complete picture of television programming. It was necessary, therefore, to supplement it with elements of structural analysis. This combination of approaches became particularly necessary since we decided to include all TV programmes, irrespective of their format, content, and duration, in the sample.

This led to our using semiologic analysis in order to understand how meaning was generated and conveyed through the various television programmes. As analytical tools, we used content analysis, semiology, structuralism, and the like, with all their potentials and shortcomings. We have attempted not only immanent criticism but, wherever possible, transcendent criticism of various media texts.While content analysis was sparingly used and that, too, mainly for the analysis of TV news, its aim was twofold. First, it was used to establish a quantitative base for more qualitative analysis of the message. Second, it helped us to categorize TV programmes according to content in a way not based on any prior assumptions or empirical categories previously applied to the depiction of women in mass media.

Three researchers watched TV programmes consistently for one month in order to ascertain the patterns of programme structure. Constant interaction and discussion enabled them to evolve a common perspective. This exercise also enabled them to categorize programmes and to evolve analysis sheets in order to study them. Seven different analysis sheets were designed to analyse seven different categories of TV programmes. These analysis sheets were piloted over a one-week period of TV viewing, then modified and finalized.

Thereafter, one master sheet for each programme was constructed on the basis of the sheets filled in by the three individual researchers. Each analysis sheet was discussed and debated until a consensus was reached.Sample Size The total sample consisted of every alternate day of Delhi Doordarshan programmes over a one-month period. The researchers watched TV programmes that

1. Start at 6 p.m. on weekdays and continue up to 11-11.15 p.m. every night;
2. Begin at 1.45 p.m. on Saturday and continue up to 4 p.m. and later continue from 6 p.m. to 11-11.15 p.m.; and
3. Begin at 9.30 a.m. on Sunday and continue all through the day, evening, and late evening.

Every single programme (inclusive of commercials) over a total of 15 days became part of the sample. However, the daytime educational broadcasts aimed at school and college students and the one- or two-minute 'fillers' and continuity programmes were not included in the sample.

There is a continuity of perspective that informs the total output of Doordarshan with regard to male and female roles. Two main trends were visible in the treatment of women and their concerns on this medium-that of affirmation and of denial. There was affirmation of a limited definition of womanhood as embodied by the physically and mentally housebound woman, engrossed in the minutiae of home-making, deriving meaning for her existence and achievements from her husband and children.

Together with the affirmation and entrenchment of passive, subordinate roles for women, Doordarshan programmes tended to deny viewers an insight into ongoing struggles of women to achieve personhood. Women in several parts of the country are engaged in isolated struggles for economic autonomy, political and legal rights, for a meaningful identity within marriage, and for relevant education. We got, if at all, token glimpses of such struggles, and even these were treated in a superficial manner.

The demarcation of public and private social spaces is a way of congealing the ongoing processes of affirmation and denial. The affirmed aspects of womanhood are situated and contained within the home, the most private of social spaces. The denied aspects of womanhood are largely located in public spaces which, as we shall see, are the domain of the male.

In effect, the construction of these two spaces results in the construction of femininity and masculinity, of gender. To retain the integrity of the public realm as male space, several exclusionary mechanisms are brought into force with the complicity of the inhabitants of the private realm. Our findings help to explicate the role of television in this hegemonic process, which is the maintenance of the integrity of the public and private realms.

THE PUBLIC REALM

In a commercial for soap, we see a young man working in his office. Later, through a crush of people in the elevator and on the road he goes to his club where he plays a hard game of tennis. When he returns home, he scrubs himself with the soap. Then, purified and sanitized after his interaction with the world outside, he goes to meet his wife. She is waiting in the garden, tea-table prettily set with lace and silver. She herself is young, soft, fresh, unhurried, quite untouched by the cares of the world, cushioned and contained within the home. She is enclosed, on one side by the walls of the house, on two sides by the garden, and in the front by the camera.

There appears to be only one way to gain access to the garden where she sits, that used by the man. He is her protector and he alone has access to her. The active energetic male goes to the passive, waiting, and accepting woman. In a commercial for a toothbrush, we are urged to enter a happy home contest. The house featured in the visual has large eyes, long eyelashes, and a large, painted mouth. The house is woman personified.

There can be no rigid, material distinction between the private and the public realms. In terms of activities we note that women often perform in public what are extensions of their private roles-that is, they work as childminders, nurses, maids, and housekeepers in hotels and hostels. In terms of the locus of decision-making, we note that both in our culture and in the media it is men who make the comparatively more important decisions within the home and wield greater economic autonomy. The distinction that we sense intuitively and emotionally will have to be crystallized in ideological terms.

O'Brien (1982) notes that the Marxists offer a partial explanation about why certain men had access to the public realm by defining that realm as the social space within which the ruling class is free to perpetuate the praxis of its own survival qua the ruling class. She goes on to add that for feminists, focusing on production processes as the basis for the establishment of ruling class hegemony is unsatisfactory and proposes that we concentrate instead on the reproduction process. Applying the dialectical model of the evolution of human consciousness to the analysis of human reproduction, she points out that for men, physiology is fate. They do not experience birth and therefore are alienated from integration with the actual continuity of species.

In Marxist terms, it is women who, through their labour, create a value that is the child. Men's reaction to their alienation from the product is to appropriate the child, that is bestow on it paternity, which is not a natural event, but an ideology. For men, therefore, potency and virility are essentially political and ideological attributes and stem from their need to cancel out the alienation built into the reproductive process. Together with the appropriation of the child comes the need to control the sexuality of the women. These twins needs result in the differentiation of the private realm from the public realm, with men effectively in control of both.

In describing the 'dualist' man, Arendt notes that the nature of man is said to be dual, composed of both animality and humanity, while a woman's nature is thought of as being single, composed of animality alone. This philosophy, cast in concrete terms results in the separation of public and private realms. The private realm is the realm of man's animality; it is where woman lives, and where she is governed by necessity. The public realm, on the other hand, is where man lives as a human being. This realm is created in freedom, and represents the space where man can overcome his animal nature.

The private or the domestic realm is seen by men as a work-free place, a refuge from the competing world of the market place and politics. In truth, however, it is women's unpaid labour within the home which enables men to work outside it. The distinction between these two social spaces and their respective inhabitants has also resulted in these inhabitants being marked in psychic and social ways, which differentiates them into two genders. The social construction of gender takes place through the working of ideology, which is a system of beliefs and assumptions-unconscious, unexamined, invisible - that represents 'the imaginary relationships of individuals to their real conditions of existence'.

Ideology is also a system of practices that informs every aspect of our daily lives, and though it originates in particular cultural conditions, it authorizes its beliefs and practices as 'universal' and 'natural'. In the context of gender it presents 'woman' as eternally and everywhere the same. Further, ideology as a universalizing mechanism offers partial truths in the interests of false coherence; it obscures the actual conditions of peoples' existence, and can often make them act contrary to their own existence. In the last section of this discussion, when we consider the support structures for male hegemony, we will enlarge on two major Indian epics, the Mahabharata, and the Ramayana, as universalizing ideological mechanisms that even today are implicated in the construction of femininity.

Cross-culturally, gender is found to be a learned quality, an assigned status, with quantities that vary independently of biology and an ideology that attributes these qualities to nature. Further, when woman as a social construct of contemporary industrial society is analysed, the gender stereotype so constructed is in fact found to be a sexual stereotype. Thus descriptors like docile, soft, passive, nurturant, vulnerable, weak, narcissistic, childlike, incompetent, masochistic, and domestic that are generally used for women, gain their validity only in apposition to 'male' activities.

Socially, femaleness means femininity which means attractiveness which, in turn, means sexual availability on male terms. Thus, through gender identification, women see themselves as sexual beings that exist for men. When women enter the public realm, they continue to be governed by gender stereotypes in diverse ways. Ferguson points out that the shift from patriarchal ideology based in the male-dominated family to a more diffuse masculinist ideology has resulted in a shift in power from fathers and husbands to male professionals and bosses.

Michel Foucault in tracing the history of sexuality notes that the rising bourgeois class gradually creates a new ideology for itself that shifts the emphasis from control of the social process through marriage alliance to the control of sexuality as a way of maintaining class hegemony. In public, this dynamic exhibits itself as a metaphorical father-daughter relationship, with the daughter as eternally ignorant and the father as consistently knowledgeable and discursive.

It is thus difficult to agree with Jane Gallop, who complains that both psychoanalysis and feminism flounder in the familial interpretation of power relations. While psychoanalysis considers revolutionary conflict along a parent-child model, thus reassimilating larger social issues into the familial domain, feminism, with its insistence on 'men-in-power', endows men with a sort of 'unified' phallic sovereignty that characterizes an absolute monarch and which bears little resemblance to the actual power in our social, economic structures. This model reproduces the daughters' view of the father.

We believe that Kakar and Ross come closer to enunciating the problem when they note that besides its roots in the unconscious wishes and desires of individual fantasy, the conception of the daughter as the sole creation and possession of the father also reflects the reality of the traditional Indian social structure. The creation myths which describe the birth of Saraswathi, the Goddess of learning, point out that she was the minddaughter or Manasaputri of Lord Brahma. Saraswathi is depicted without a consort, but stories abound of Brahma's subsequent sexual consumption of her.

If sexual consumption can be understood as intellectual control, this myth can help us understand the irreversible knowledge-giving-knowledge-taking interaction between men and women. We will examine three public service commercials and two fiction narratives to elucidate this point. The first, to explain the proper use of telephones, was made for the government department of telephones, and features a number of disruptive women. To begin with, there is a young pretty girl, whose extended love-talk over a public phone causes a log-jam of busy, irritated men.

The male authoritative voice admonishes, 'Keep love-talk to the minimum.' Never shown on screen is the male interlocutor, whose complicity made possible the long conversation. In the next scene, a man about to leave for work is obliged to call his female neighbour to his phone. As all women, she is loquacious and quite oblivious of the need to be brief. The busy man frets and fumes. In the third scene, two teenaged girls play a popular record over the phone; both dance for long minutes to the tune. Once again the male authoritative voice comes on to berate them.

A more serious problem is posed by another short film. Here a busy executive suffers a heart attack in his office. He tries in vain to reach his wife. She is busy gossiping about knitting patterns and parties. Finally, the man is taken to the hospital. This time, the woman secretary takes the wife to task, though the film ends with the mandatory male voice-over. It is not clear, however, why the man persisted in calling his wife.

Surely calling his doctor, or clinic or the nearest hospital emergency ward would have been more feasible?

The third short film is set in a hospital intensive care unit and purports to educate viewers about the correct deportment to adopt in such places. A young woman patient suffering from a heart attack is considerately cared for by everyone, but (unbelievably) her own mother. The mother, evidently the last to know of her daughter's condition, is loud, brash, overdressed, and stupid. She declares she is too busy with her social rounds to visit her daughter during the specified visiting hours, and argues so loudly with the nurse that the patient suffers a relapse. Once again, the male voice evaluates the woman's reprehensible behaviour. Two stereotypes clash in this film-the nurturing mother with the loud-voiced, strident woman-and the negative one wins.

In one serial, a retired judge, distressed by the plight of women in his immediate vicinity, resolves to help them through voluntary service. Several episodes of this serial show the judge and his friend, a retired police commissioner, tackle issues of dowry, widowhood, and so on. The judge's educated, wealthy, homebound daughter-in-law is shown involved in a women's club, attempting to raise money to build a swimming pool. She is educated about the need to use the money to build public toilets for slum dwellers. In another episode, the daughter-in-law is seen begging her husband for a page of his newspaper to read at breakfast.

Quite viciously, he informs her that the paper is not a deck of cards to be distributed, and anyway all she would be interested in is notices of garment sales and new face creams. Later the woman is shown with an egg mask on her face, and is again viciously baited by her husband. The metaphoric father's intelligence can be appreciated best if offset by the incredible stupidity of the metaphoric daughter. The elements of sarcasm and subterranean violence that inform this narrative and the three commercials discussed earlier are missing from the serial on the lives of Indian freedom fighters.

In the episode under review, the young freedom fighter notes his wife's restlessness. She expresses her loneliness and desire to be involved in his work. The husband takes her to meet his mentor. The mentor welcomes the idea and gives the woman a set of handspun clothes to wear. As befitting the followers of Gandhi, the symbolic father-daughter interaction is here imbued with gentle guidance. The woman's social and political initiation is in effect a rebirth, and to make this plain, the narrative shows her cutting off relations with her wealthy and unsympathetic father.

Thus in the public realm, whether through sarcastic coercion or sweet reasonableness, the preferred male-female interaction depicted is that of father-daughter. One mechanism which ensures the continued subordination of women within the public realm is the ideology of marriage as the ultimate goal for them. This results in women seeing themselves as temporary, part-time or emergency earners and seeking jobs that are extensions of their housekeeping roles and that capitalize on their socially acknowledged assets, their physical charm.

Television discourse confirms the 'woman as essentially homebound' ideal in many ways. In the commercials sampled, we did not come across a single case of young professional women endorsing any product. They were either young or unmarried, in which case they were seen in situations of leisure, or they were young and married, in which case they were seen engaged in domestic tasks. In programmes for women, interviews with women employed outside the home repeatedly stressed the effect of the woman's job on the family, and applauded her felicitous handling of both.

Women entrepreneurs, women judges, women police personnel were all routinely subjected to the same set of questions which focused on their husbands' responses to their jobs and the co-operation they obtained from them. The husbands were projected as exceptional, generous, and unusually co-operative. The real message being projected through these programmes was that of exceptional women engaged in juggling two jobs and a subtle warning to female viewers that if they were not fortunate enough to enjoy family support, they had better remain within the ambit of the home.

Training for women was usually discussed at the 'skills' level, that is, women were prepared for jobs that would enable them to function as supplementary or emergency earners. The options emphasized jobs that were mechanical and routine and which did not necessitate profound changes in household structure. Jobs like stenography, fashion design, beauty culture are flexible and do not have to be pursued as vertical-growth careers, with provisions for promotions, increased status and earnings, old-age and medical benefits, dependent on unbroken stretches of service. Teaching and nursing are also women orientated and, together with other jobs mentioned earlier, are seen as task rather than policy-orientated.

Thus teaching, which in its essence is a deeply intellectual and, at the same time, a subversive activity, is approached by our society as a mechanical chore, ill-paid and ill-prospected, and, as such jobs usually are, reified. Because of these reasons, all the jobs promoted as being ideal for women, are transplantable, that is, they can be relocated according to the needs of the husband's career. The women's real career thus lies within the private realm.

Another set of exceptional women seen on screen were the participants in the political arena and the revolutionaries. Considering the high visibility of women in our freedom movement and their much-lauded participation in it, it may appear strange to label them 'exceptional' especially as they were held to be complementary to men. But this dynamic of complementarity lasted only as long as the movement lasted. Once the situation became stable, women were once again excluded from the public realm. Two fictional narratives reiterated this 'emergency' role of women.

Mackinnon rightly notes that the concern of revolutionary leadership for ending women's confinement to traditional roles arises from the need to make their labour available to the regime. Women become as free as men to work outside the home, while men remain as free of it within. Women's labour and militancy are both co-opted. Just as our freedom movement remained a partial revolution (we only exchanged one set of rulers for another without disturbing the structure of Indian society), so women's participation remained partial. They operated within narrow, male-defined limits which did not alter the structure of male-female relationships.

Agriculture, no less than politics, was presented as a public realm in which women could negotiate roles only as wives or entertainers. In programmes for farmers, women invariably appeared as entertainers, singing folk songs or dancing. The actual work was presented as purely male activity, with hardworking men turning to dancing and singing as a respite. Commercials sponsoring farmers' programmes also reflected this theme, with males discussing fertilizer inputs, tractor hire, and crop prices, while the females adorned themselves. The man-as-earner and woman-as-consumer ideology was propagated even by public sector units.

Programmes about inputs to stimulate progress in agriculture also had male farmers as their target. Thus the visual of a mechanical paddy transplantor showed a man wielding the machine whereas in the field, this job is women-intensive. Women's involvement in agriculture was limited to kitchen gardens. In one programme, the camera travelled to the kitchen garden of the Vice-Chancellor of Haryana Agricultural University. His wife was interviewed on this programme. She was asked if she popularized kitchen gardens among her friends while her husband was asked 'technical' questions relating to fertilizers, pesticides, etc.

In the background could be seen labourers engaged in weeding and caring for the plants. The focus in this programme was on the women's role as home-maker, overseeing the homebased production of domestically consumed articles. The man, in command of technical expertise, was affirmed as one whose expertise was at the service of the public at large. Although in the programme on women artists the compère was female, two males were invited as experts. One of them noted that the works featured exhibited no tension, because in the Indian society women and men had equality of opportunity and expression.

This palpably absurd remark went unchallenged by the compère. One woman artist, who had changed her medium from oil to fabric collage, said that at first she felt like a housewife as she went about with her fabric and scissors. Her self-esteem and identity as artist was validated only when she went on to win awards for her work. We can now appreciate Barrett's remark that the meaning of gender in patriarchal discourse is not simply 'difference' but 'division, oppression, inequality and interiorized inferiority for women'. With the division of social space into public and private comes the labelling of public as superior and private as inferior.

When women enter into complicity with men in devaluing work within the home, they assist in the hegemonial process of valorizing men's work. The construction of the public realm as male space, as we have seen, confirms male authority. This is most evident in the news bulletins, which are records of male activity. News is information about recent events. To think about news is to make important assumptions about time, events, and ways of informing the people. These assumptions have their roots in socially defined reality; they reflect the way a society or culture views the world.

On Doordarshan the news bulletin is a highly structured programme. News relating to political, economic, and developmental activities is followed by news about sports and, finally, the weather. Mckinley notes that that news sequence is one which moves from events at the centre of culture that is problems of government, business, religion, and so on, to athletic competence, which is the cultural cultivation of natural abilities. Finally, concern is expressed over those aspects of nature not subject to human control that is the weather.

Our findings about the structure of news programmes support the findings of similar researches. We noted that political news formed about 45 per cent of the content of every bulletin. The first 10 items of every bulletin also dealt with political news; 66 per cent of the time in the case of Hindi bulletins and 66.3 per cent in the case of English bulletins. Smith reported that in his sample, the government was the dominant subject, the primary actor, and the primary acted-upon. Government investigations, hearings, and meetings provided the single largest category of news subjects, and governments at the city, state, and federal levels were the subjects of more than half the stories in the sample.

In our sample, more than 60 per cent of the newsmakers were celebrities, more often than not political leaders of the ruling party representing the government. Of the newsmakers in our sample, 72.4 per cent were male, and 40.3 per cent of them made news in the political context. Women made news in 6.5 per cent of the cases; here, too, they were largely politicians and government functionaries. Mckinley noted that the structure of society itself provides the context for interpreting newsworthy events. Since our society is deeply androcentric and class-divided, the criteria of significance and selection of newsworthy items are determined by this framework. Thus, not only women, but the poor and the disadvantaged are also excluded.

Our findings show that if women made news as individuals, they were celebrities like politicians or Wimbledon stars. In groups, they were shoppers during hours of curfew relaxation or victims of calamities. En masse they were featured as audiences at public rallies, passively listening to politicians. On the other hand, a report of an opposition-organized protest where women were described as participants was not supported with visuals. The collective strength of women as actors was thus rendered invisible.

Greene and Kahn help us to understand the invisibilisation of women in the news when they quote Lerner, who noted that as long as history (news) has as its primary focus 'the transmission and experience of power', and as long as 'war and politics are seen as more significant to the history of humankind than child rearing', women will remain marginalized or invisible. Women and the poor featured largely in the 'deaths and disasters' and 'development news' category. Even in the case of development news, as Ignatieff has noted, the government remains the actor.

The shift in focus to the disadvantaged sections of society is supposed to balance government hand-outs; instead, the inclusion of the so-called human interest stories, according to Ignatieff, has destroyed the coherence of the genre itself. While we do not completely agree with this, we hold that the inclusion of the human interest stories, embedded in the matrix of political stories, is more in the nature of providing relief from the grim business of life itself. It is a devaluation of the lived experience of the poor and the marginalized of society.

The Joshi Committee Report has strongly decried the tendency of television news to be orientated towards the activities of political and other celebrities. It notes: 'The viewers of Doordarshan live well above the poverty line and Doordarshan, through its VIP-oriented news programmes and triv ial entertainment, promotes complacency, and a drugged indifference to issues of social transformation, rather than any self-questioning of their lifestyle on the part of its middle and upper class viewers.' We agree, and feel with Ignatieff that 'television (news) is worshipping state power and insisting that we do so as well. It is power itself - the sacred offices of state - that is worshipped.'

Enrichment and sectoral programmes as well as commercials celebrate men's power to evaluate the world in general and women's activities in particular. The pattern of compèring followed by the enrichment and sectoral programmes illustrates this trend, as does the use of men as experts in all fields and on all occasions. Commenting on this disturbing trend, a media critic has pointed out that 'women lawyers, economists, women of real intellectual calibre and social conscience have been kept off the screen'. She points out that, by and large, only women sympathetic to the establishment participate in important interviews and discussion.

'One woman who was asked to participate in the Sach ki Parchaiyan programme on women was hastily dropped when she said she would mention Shah Bano'. The reference was to the controversial Muslim Women (Protection of Rights on Divorce) Act 1986, which most women see as a retrogressive measure. The medium thus persistently denies women's insights into what are seen as matters of public policy; their visibility is noted only at the level of tasks to be performed. Women are projected as reacting to situations, as if they never, at any point, have a dissenting voice to raise.

Alternatively, they are presented as expositors, not as original thinkers. Thus, on women's programmes and health programmes, women, as doctors and citizens can be heard talking of the need to delay marriage and childbirth in terms of rise in birth-rates, and the need to give the woman time to develop into a 'better' wife and mother. But we get to hear very little about the effect of early pregnancies on the physical and mental development of the woman herself.

Compères and experts on women's programmes repeatedly stressed the need for women to use clean water for drinking and cooking purposes. Women activists and development workers, and indeed citizens who have experienced the mirage of clean water at the most personal level and who can thus ask pointed questions relating to developmental priorities, are never heard on such programmes.

What are the effects of having significantly more prominent men than women on television? On the basis of her ongoing research into sex roles on Canadian television, Williams suggested that:

- There are fewer role models for females than males; this is especially important for children.
- It becomes difficult to provide variety in the portrayals of prominent females, which leads to stereotyping.
- The consistent portrayal of more men than women leads to the implicit message that females are less important than males.

She noted further that the consistency of such survey results and the apparent resistance to depicting women as important, knowledgeable, and authoritative appeared to be consistent with the 'keep men in power' viewpoint of Gerbner and Tuchman. With regard to Indian television, we hold that the drive is to shore up male ideology rather than males themselves. The activities of women ministers and politicians of the ruling party are also given fairly extensive coverage.

As we noted in our theoretical considerations, such apparently felicitous findings can result from the mechanical application of content analysis techniques. They need to be interpreted in the light of the Indian emphasis on the government as actor.Women are thus allowed a precarious foothold in the public realm under certain well-defined conditions. Such conditions serve as exclusionary mechanisms. Thus, the prescription states:

- Women are temporary or emergency earners/participants. They have to go back home once the emergency is over. The temporary, unmarried state is also emergency-related.
- Their choice of jobs should be limited to spheres which do not disrupt the household and do not challenge the importance of the male.
- When women aspire to careers rather than jobs, they can do so only because they are supported by exceptionally large-hearted men.
- Women are consumers, men are producers. Hard-working men can find respite either through their sheltered caring wives, or through programmes of music and dance.
- Women understand their presence in the public realm as an intrusion into male space and express this understanding through veiling their faces, modulating their voices, and hiding their intelligence.

We need to take note of the many dissenting voices that refuse to valorize the public realm. Rogers quoted in Greene and Kahn asks why research takes no note of women's involvement as matchmakers or as sharers in wealth or higher status. Further, if women are kept away from public life, are they necessarily inferior? Why should we give priority to public life, and why devalue women's importance in less formal, private roles?

We need to seriously address ourselves to this problem. While it is true that we should not use categories (such as private and public) to challenge the ideology from within which they arise, we have to note that however important women's work is within the private realm, it still places them effectively under male control. We need to challenge, as we noted earlier, the interiorisation of this control.

Further, in the Indian context, women are placed under male control precisely by apportioning to them such 'important' work. If autonomy was part of women's lived experience, would we, as a nation, experience ever-rising levels of female foeticide, female infanticide, and dowry-related deaths? All these phenomena require female complicity and such complicity arises only from women's interiorized inferiority.

IDENTITY IN FEMINIST TELEVISION CRITICISM

It is about fifteen years since the first feminist television criticism began to appear in Britain and the US, and it is now possible to begin to construct a history of this criticism, and particularly, a history of its personae, of the characters that are specific to feminist television criticism: the feminist television critic and the female viewer. This pair, and the drama of their identity and difference, seems one of the most interesting productions of feminist television criticism, and in the contours of their relationships I think we can see patterns of feminist intellectual work which are not specific to the criticism of television.

My argument is briefly, that the formative stage of feminist television criticism extends from about 1976 to the mid-1980s, and that the key feature of this formative stage is the move from outside to inside the academy. While in 1976 the feminist critic writes with a primary address to her movement sisters, in a tone quite hostile to the 'mass media', yet concerned to justify her attention to television, by the mid-1980s she inhabits a more academic position, tends to address other scholars, and is beginning to be anthologized in books used on both Communications and Women's Studies courses.

There are a series of journal special issues in the 1980s through which it is also possible to chart a rather more confident engagement with television specifically. Thus occasions such as the 'Console-ing Passions' conference held at the University of Iowa in 1992 and billed, correctly, as 'The first feminist conference on television and video', can properly be understood as one manifestation of the more academic second period of feminist television criticism, as can the recent rash of 'woman and television' books such as Mary Ellen Brown Television and Women's Culture, Christine Geraghty Women and Soap Opera, Andrea Press Women Watching Television, Lynn Spigel's Make Room for TV, Ann Gray Video Playtime, and Julie D'Acci Defining Women: Television and the Case of Cagney and Lacey.

If the formative period is marked, as I have suggested, at an institutional level, by a move from outside to inside the academy, it is also characterized, or perhaps I should say experienced, through the constitution of a new and as we shall see, contradictory, kind of individual, the feminist intellectual.

FEMINIST TELEVISION CRITICISM AND THE ACADEMY

One of the reasons for the shift from outside to inside the academy is that feminist concerns have had a particular impact in two critical areas in the study of television: first in relation to the study of a genre, soap opera, and second in relation to the study of the audience, a perennial concern for media studies and mass communications. This is not to suggest that there hasn't been substantial feminist work in other genres/ fields nor to underestimate the attention to audiences and serial drama in existing research on television, but to argue that it is in relation to soap opera and audience that feminist critical work on television has made a distinctive contribution which is recognized as such in the wider arena.

Thus Ien Ang, Dorothy Hobson, Mich'le Mattelart, Tania Modleski, Ellen Seiter, and the London Women and Film Group all conducted research on soap opera in the late 1970s and 1980s, work which either hypothesized about the female audience or, in Ien Ang's case, actually investigated it. All this work forms part of a much larger body of feminist research, begun in the late 1970s, which reevaluates traditional feminine genres and forms, like the women's picture, romantic fiction, the diary, and the magazine, and, either by implication or directly, investigates audience engagement.

Soap opera, as a genre, including US prime-time shows as well as much more localized national serials, has moved from being a ridiculed object of study to a mainstay of many syllabuses. Thus, in addition to the pioneering work mentioned above, there has been-and this is not an exhaustive list - the long Liebes and Katz Dallas project (1990), Robert Allen Speaking of Soap Operas (1985), Sandy Flitterman-Lewis's work on commercials and seriality (1983, 1988), David Buckingham's study of EastEnders (1987), Christine Geraghty's comprehensive analysis of the genre (1991), Sonia Livingstone's psychological study of audiences (1989), and the work of Kim Christian Schrøder (1988), Jostein Gripsrud (1990), Jane Feuer (1984), and Mark Finch (1986) on the prime-time soap Dynasty.

In the same period, there has been a general shift, across a whole range of social science and humanities disciplines, from a focus on the study of the text to an increased interest in the audience. In the study of television there has been a noticeable - if controversial - embrace of the virtues of qualitative methodology, a vogue for the work associated with the Centre for Contemporary Cultural Studies, and a series of detailed studies of particular audiences or audience sectors.

From its inception, this 'new' media ethnography has been marked by the problematic of gender in one of two ways. Either it has been mainly women who were the subject of the inquiry - as with the work of Hobson, Ang, Bobo, and Radway or, because the focus of the work is domestic, as with the work of Morley, Gray, Moores, and Spigel, gender (and generation) have been significant analytic and interpretative categories. Thus we could identify the feminist contribution to television research in the last fifteen years, in its most widely accepted form, to be the gendering of two key concepts, that of genre and that of audience.

We now have gendered genres, and we also have gendered audiences. This shift can be exemplified quite simply in the differences between early textbooks of television studies, such as Fiske and Hartley Reading Television and Len Masterman Teaching About Television, or textbook collections in communications such as Curran *et al.*, and later books such as John Fiske Television Culture, Robert Allen Channels of Discourse, and Curran and Gurevitch Mass Media and Society, which pay more specific attention to issues of gender both as an analytic category and object of study.

EXISTING ACCOUNTS OF FEMINIST TELEVISION CRITICISM

There are several surveys of feminist media criticism, only one of which, by Ann Kaplan, is specifically concerned with the study of television, although the introductions to the three collections on women and television- Baehr and Dyer (1987), Brown (1990), and Spigel and Mann (1992)-also offer some mapping of the field. What is striking about the more general surveys of feminism and the media such as those offered by Leslie Steeves (1987) and Liesbet van Zoonen (1991) is the similarity of the typologies used by both these authors and Kaplan (1987).

In each case, the typologies are a variant of the familiar political distinctions between liberal, radical, and socialist feminism. Thus Kaplan combines 'bourgeois, Marxist, radical and post-structuralist' feminism with the distinction between essentialist and non-essentialist approaches, while van Zoonen distinguishes between liberal, radical, and socialist feminism in her analysis of the range of feminist media research. Both authors, with slightly different emphases and inflections, argue for the methodological and analytic significance of the tradition of British cultural studies to the feminist analysis of television, seeing this as one way of avoiding essentialism.

The value of these typologies - the way in which they point to the differentiations within feminist thought, and the connection between media analyses and the analyses of wider social issues- should not obscure the fact that, as the authors themselves suggest, and Margaret Gallagher (1992) points out, very little criticism fits into only one category, and some work, such as Gallagher's own, is categorized differently in different schemas. Van Zoonen however, in a suggestive section entitled 'The Audience and "US" ' (1991: 43-4) raises issues about feminist research on popular culture which recur across all feminist work, and it is these ideas which I wish to explore in my own typology.

I want to construct a typology which is based on the conceptualisation of the relationship between feminism and women, or the feminist and other women as inscribed within the critical text. I offer this categorisation most immediately as a heuristic, rather than an historical typology. That is, I am not suggesting that feminist criticism has moved from stage one to stage three, although I would argue that there are discernible historical shifts in the type of paradigms that are dominant at any one moment. My three categories would be the following:

a. Transparent - no others;
b. Hegemonic-non-feminist women others;
c. Fragmented-everyone and other.

Each of these categories is defined through the relationship between the feminist and her other, the ordinary woman, the non-feminist woman, the housewife, the television viewer. It is this relationship, the way in which feminism constructs and has constructed itself in relation to the category 'woman', rather than the way in which women's subordination is theorized, which is essential to an understanding of feminist cultural criticism. That is, I am suggesting that feminist critical discourse itself constructs and produces, rather than simply analyses, a series of positions for 'women'.

TRANSPARENT

The positing of a transparent relationship between feminism and women is characteristic of the utopian, activist-

and could properly say formative-phase of post-1960s feminism. Although very rarely found without some articulation with the second 'hegemonic' relation, this utopian moment posits a shared sisterhood between all women, a consciousness of' women as a gender group who are subject to a global patriarchal subordination and who thus have gender specific experiences in common. The dream, and the frequently asserted reality, of this moment is that all women are sisters, there is no 'otherness' between feminism and women, and that the appropriate pronoun of criticism is 'we'.

It is this consciousness that dominates media reviews in, for example, early British movement magazines like Spare Rib in the 1970s, and it is this consciousness, this 'we', which has been most vulnerable to attack for its political exclusions (which women?) and its epistemological assumptions (do women know differently?). It is also, however, this notion of a shared gender experience which underpins part of the challenge that feminist work has offered to sociological and ethnographic research. Thus Dorothy Hobson's early research-which was scrupulous in its understanding of the complexity of the relationship between interviewer and interviewee, and which was consistently cautious about the class assumptions of the feminist 'we'-was not initially about the media, but about the experience of being a young working-class housewife/ mother, and she insists on the way in which reference to shared experience increased the richness of her interviews.

Similarly, the work of the distinguished sociologist Ann Oakley offers some of its most radical challenges to existing social science methodologies in her consistent refusal to occupy conventional positions of neutrality in response to the questions of her 'interviewee mothers'. She adopts this strategy as a specific response to what she calls 'the dilemma of a feminist interviewer interviewing women', when the topic of the interviews is the frightening, but eagerly anticipated experience of a first baby.

Ironically, given that it has partly been the political attacks on the unthinking exclusions of this feminist 'we' that have marginalized it as an enunciative position; it is currently in response to the writing of women of colour that we most often find the assumption of transparency. Thus we find Jacqueline Bobo's work often characterized as 'what black women think' and as the site for the investigation of ethnicity-as if all those white audiences were without ethnic identity-and as if the articulation of ethnicity and gender here is not also historical, contradictory, and sometimes provisional.

Indeed, in less academic feminism, it could be argued that the acceptance of the political critique of the transparency of the straight white Western feminist 'we' has led to a multiplication of special category, transparent, representative identities-older lesbians, working-class women, etc.- who are perhaps enabled to speak as a 'we', but also imprisoned by the inflexible demands of this identity fixing. This tendency is dearly represented by the British collection on women in the media, Out of Focus.

HEGEMONIC

What I am calling the hegemonic relationship between the feminist and the woman has been the most common position within feminist television criticism. It would also be possible to call this structure of relationship 'recruitist' to use Angela McRobbie's term, the impulse to transform the feminine identifications of women to feminist ones. The construction of feminist identity through this relation involves the differentiation of the feminist from her other, the ordinary woman, the housewife, the woman she might have become, but at the same time, a compulsive engagement with this figure.

The position is often profoundly contradictory, involving both the repudiation and defence of traditional femininity. In psychoanalytic terms, we could hypothesize that the encounter between the feminist and the housewife-a very dear arena for early and proto-feminist work from the 1960s on -involves not just the construction of an identity 'independent woman' against another possible one 'dependent woman', but, specifically, an engagement with the mother. In terms of feminist television criticism, this usually meant the television viewer, in relation to whom much of the early writing is profoundly ambivalent.

A key rhetorical device here, one with which we are familiar from other traditions of anthropological and sociological work, is the introduction of a guide or intermediary, who gives instruction to the researcher about the pleasures and procedures of television viewing. These figures are often to be found in acknowledgements-for example, Carol Lopate, in one of the first feminist discussions of soap opera: 'I should like to thank Irena Kleinbort, whose insights were invaluable in helping me develop some of the ideas in this paper, and who furnished me with examples from her more extensive soap opera watching'.

This disclaimer about soap expertise was anticipated by her earlier comment about learning how to watch, 'until I got to know the stories, the afternoon felt like one long, complicated saga...' It is almost as if the researcher must prove her not too competent within the sphere of popular culture to retain credibility within the sphere of analysis. Tania Modleski influential essay, The Search for Tomorrow in Today's Soap Operas, is marked by a similar ambivalence, particularly in its early version. For example:

Clearly, women find soap operas eminently entertaining, and an analysis of the pleasure that soaps afford can provide clues not only about how feminists can challenge this pleasure, but also how they can incorporate it. For, outrageous as this assertion may at first appear, I would suggest that soap operas are not altogether at odds with a possible feminist aesthetics. This passage displays a clear separation between the author and 'women', with the author explicitly addressing herself to 'feminists', a category in some ways opposed to 'women'.

The key words are 'clues' and 'outrageous'. 'Clues' reveals that this is an evangelical enterprise of detection; the analysis of soap opera will render information about other pleasures-pleasures that must be challenged. So the justification of the academic enterprise to other feminists is through its gathering of politically useful knowledge. However, within this address to an imagined sceptical feminist audience, Modleski is also making a polemical point: 'outrageous as this assertion may at first appear'. This 'outrageous' marks the other element in what I am calling the hegemonic relationship, the defence of 'women's culture'.

In 1979 this insistence is made against the grain of feminist attitudes to popular television, insisting that there is something here to be taken seriously. Both 'clues' and 'outrageous' disappear from the rewritten book version of the essay, where the two sentences are split. Clearly, women find soap operas eminently entertaining, and an analysis of the pleasure these programs afford can provide feminists with ways not only to challenge this pleasure but to incorporate it into their own artistic practices.

Indeed, I would like to argue that soap operas are not altogether at odds with an already developing, though still embryonic, feminist aesthetics. These rewritten versions, smoother, more confident, less embattled, also give much less sense of that author as caught between the positions of 'woman','feminist', and 'intellectual'. What we find, over and over again, in early feminist television criticism, is the complicated negotiation of the position from which the author writes.

There is a fleeting and fluctuating identification with a gender group (the residue of 'we women') which is at the same time a disavowal of many of the attributes of conventional femininity, crossed with the contradictory demands of intellectual credibility, which is of course conventionally ungendered. The identity of the feminist intellectual which strains to combine these identities is- necessarily - at this stage, profoundly unstable. What has called the hegemonic impulse within feminist criticism, apart from its straightforward desire for a political mobilisation around the inequities of gender, is also an attempt to make the femininity/feminism relationship less contradictory by recruiting the one to the other.

FRAGMENTED

The third way of thinking about the relationship between feminism and women I am calling 'fragmented' because it is founded on the possibility that there is no necessary relationship between these two categories. This moment is constituted by the force of the critiques directed at what I have called the 'transparent' moment both politically and theoretically as the implications of what is normally called the 'essentialism' debate percolate through the academy. 'Woman' becomes a profoundly problematic category - and arguably and ironically-'feminist' becomes rather more stable.

Franklin *et al.* have already offered one survey of the more general issues at stake here for cultural analysis in this journal. I want to sketch briefly two distinct directions in current research work which share a radical particularism. One is towards 'historical autobiography', the other towards a stress on the contingency of gender identifications, and the significance of the articulation of these identifications with the whole range of other formative identifications.

Valerie Walkerdine's work on the video-viewing of the Rocky films in the home of a working-class family can be understood in the context of a growing body of very sophisticated feminist autobiography, all of which can be understood as contributing to, or commenting on, the fragmentation of the 'transparent' relationship between feminism and women in their exploration of the constitutive dynamics of class, ethnicity, migration, and gender in the story of each self. All of these accounts suggest the impossibility of telling stories in which individuals are 'just' gendered.

The other thread, best exemplified by Ang and Hermes's radical review of the use of gender as an explanatory category in recent ethnographic projects, argues for the radical contingency of gender identifications, and against a research agenda which concentrates on 'women's culture' to the neglect of an articulation with ethnicity and class. The logic of Ang and Hermes's position is to jettison 'some fixed figure of "women"', and to argue that 'any feminist standpoint will necessarily have to present itself as partial, based upon the knowledge that while some women sometimes share some common interests and face some common enemies, such commonalities are by no means universal'.

Here, offered a typology of feminist television criticism in which the varying inscriptions of the relative identities 'feminist critic' and 'ordinary woman viewer' are seen as distinctive. The period of the institutional acceptance and development of feminist television criticism in the white anglophone academy (Britain, USA, and Australia) is a period in which we see the professionalisation of the enunciative identity 'feminist critic'.

The unconscious class and ethnic identity of the 'we' of this moment has been extensively documented elsewhere. The dominant mode of feminist critique in the period of academic institutionalisation is an hegemonic/recruitist one, hegemonic in the sense that this feminism has aspirations to dominate all accounts of the feminine. In this mode, the feminist critic is distinguished from her other, the ordinary woman, and the complicated defence and repudiation of conventional feminine culture which characterizes much feminist criticism of popular culture begins to be institutionalized. The pronouns here are 'we' and 'they', with the shifting referent of the 'we' being both 'feminists' and 'women', although the 'they' is always 'women'.

The third moment is that in which the epistemological grounding of the political category 'woman' is thrown into crisis-engulfed in a sea of what Dick Hebdige has called 'the Posts'. Here we have the confluence of the political critique of the 1970s with post-structuralist thought and the theorisation of the post-modern. Everyone here is an other - and there are no pronouns beyond the I - but there are, relatively, lots of women teaching and writing books about these ideas.

It is customary, in typologies of this type, for the approach or position being advocated to come at the end. However, I am not sure that this type of theoretical dean get-away is either possible or desirable. First, the logic of my own argument so far compels me to observe that my theoretically chic third category is itself dependent on its otherness from the first two categories. It too involves a repudiation of earlier femininities - in this case, feminisms. Second- and this is a point which can only make most tentatively - the apparent intellectual autonomy of the third category would reward sociological scrutiny. So if there are no theoretical dean get-aways, how can we reinterrogate this typology? Perhaps with the humility and sense of history that Christine Geraghty shows in the following passage which comes at the end of her book on soap opera:

> In marking a change in the experience of writing about Coronation Street in the mid-seventies and in writing about soap opera now, I am conscious of my own ambiguities about the project. What then was a desire to re-evaluate a cultural form which was denigrated, at least in part, because it was associated with women, now runs the risk of celebrating an illusion-the assertion of a common sensibility between women and a set of values sustaining us simply because we are women. In this context even to write 'we' rather than 'they' becomes problematic in its assumption and smacks of a community of interest which needs to be constructed rather than asserted.

Geraghty here gives an account of the historicity of identities and identifications, a micro-history of the identity 'woman' during the brief period of feminist work on television with which I have been concerned. She rejects the assumptions of shared interest - but she is still interested in sharing interests. The logic of her argument is recognition of the difficulties of any move outside the potential solipsism of a 'fragmented' feminist identity - but not an abandonment of the project.

7

Feminist Theory and Phenomenology

Philosophers rarely think about acting in the theatrical sense, but they do have a discourse of "acts" that maintains associative semantic meanings with theories of performance and acting. For example, John Searle's "speech acts," those verbal assurances and promises which seem not only to refer to a speaking relationship, but to constitute a moral bond between speakers, illustrate one of the illocutionary gestures that constitute the stage of the analytic philosophy of language.

Further, "action theory," a domain of moral philosophy, seeks to understand what it is "to do" prior to any claim of what one ought to do. Finally, the phenomenological theory of "acts," espoused by Edmund Husserl, Maurice Merleau-Ponty, and George Herbert Mead, among others, seeks to explain the mundane way in which social agents constitute social reality through language, gesture, and all manner of symbolic social sign. Though phenomenology sometimes appears to assume the existence of a choosing and constituting agent prior to language (who poses as the sole source of its constituting acts), there is also a more radical use of the doctrine of constitution that takes the social agent as an object rather than the subject of constitutive acts.

When Simone de Beauvoir claims, "one is not born, but, rather, becomes a woman," she is appropriating and reinterpreting this doctrine of constituting acts from the phenomenological tradition. In this sense, gender is in no way a stable identity of locus of agency from which various acts proceede; rather, it is an identity tenuously constituted in time-an identity instituted through a stylized repetition of acts. Further, gender is instituted through the stylisation of the body and, hence, must be understood as the mundane way in which bodily gestures, movements, and enactments of various kinds constitute the illusion of an abiding gendered self.

This formulation moves the conception of gender off the ground of a substantial model of identity to one that requires a conception of a constituted social temporality. Significantly, if gender is instituted through acts which are internally discontinuous, then the appearance of substance is precisely that, a constructed identity, a performative accomplishment which the mundane social audience, including the actors themselves, come to believe and to perform in the mode of belief.

If the ground of gender identity is the stylized repetition of acts through time, and not a seemingly seamless identity, then the possibilities of gender transformation are to be found in the arbitrary relation between such acts, in the possibility of a different sort of repeating, in the breaking or subversive repetition of that style. Through the conception of gender acts sketched above, I will try to show some ways in which reified and naturalized conceptions of gender might be understood as constituted and, hence, capable of being constituted differently.

In opposition to theatrical or phenomenological models which take the gendered self to be prior to its acts, I will understand constituting acts not only as constituting the identity of the actor, but as constituting that identity as a compelling illusion, an object of belief. In the course of making my argument, I will draw from theatrical, anthropological, and philosophical discourses, but mainly phenomenology, to show that what is called gender identity is a performative accomplishment compelled by social sanction and taboo. In its very character as performative resides the possibility of contesting its reified status.

FEMINIST AND PHENOMENOLOGICAL VIEWS

Feminist theory has often been critical of naturalistic explanations of sex and sexuality that assume that the meaning of women's social existence can be derived from some fact of their physiology. In distinguishing sex from gender, feminist theorists have disputed causal explanations that assume that sex dictates or necessitates certain social meanings for women's experience. Phenomenological theories of human embodiment have also been concerned to distinguish between the various physiological and biological causalities that structure bodily existence and the meanings that embodied existence assumes in the context of lived experience.

In Merleau-Ponty reflections in The Phenomenology of Perception on "the body in its sexual being," he takes issue with such accounts of bodily experience and claims that the body is "an historical idea" rather than "a natural species." Sigficantly, it is this claim that Simone de Beauvoir cites in The Second Sex when she sets the stage for her claim that "woman," and by extension, any gender, is an historical situation rather than a natural fact. In both contexts, the existence and facticity of the material or natural dimensions of the body are not denied, but reconceived as distinct from the process by which the body comes to bear cultural meanings.

For both Beauvoir and Merleau-Ponty, the body is understood to be an active process of embodying certain cultural and historical possibilities, a complicated process of appropriation which any phenomenological theory of constitution needs to describe. In order to describe the gendered body, a phenomenological theory of constitution requires an expansion of the conventional view of acts to mean both that which constitutes meaning and that through which meaning is performed or enacted. In other words, the acts by which gender is constituted bear similarities to performative acts within theatrical contexts. My task, then, is to examine in what ways gender is constructed through specific corporeal acts, and what possibilities exist for the cultural transformation of gender through such acts.

Merleau-Ponty maintains not only that the body is an historical idea but a set of possibilities to be continually realized. In claiming that the body is an historical idea, Merleau-Ponty means that it gains its meaning through a concrete and historically mediated expression in the world. That the body is a set of possibilities signifies

a. That its appearance in the world, for perception, is not predetermined by some manner of interior essence, and
b. That its concrete expression in the world must be understood as the taking up and rendering specific of a set of historical possibilities.

Hence, there is an agency which is understood as the process of rendering such possibilities determinate. These possibilities are necessarily constrained by available historical conventions. The body is not a self-identical or merely lactic materiality; it is a materiality that bears meaning, if nothing else, and the manner of this bearing is fundamentally dramatic. By dramatic I mean only that the body is not merely matter but a continual and incessant materializing of possibilities. One is not simply a body, but, in some very key sense, one does one's body and, indeed, one does one's body differently from one's contemporaries and from one's embodied predecessors and successors as well.

It is, however, clearly unfortunate grammar to claim that there is a "we" or an "I" that does its body, as if a disembodied agency preceded and directed an embodied exterior. More appropriate, I suggest, would be a vocabulary that resists the substance metaphysics of subject-verb formations and relies instead on ontology of present participles. The "I" that is its body is, of necessity, a mode of embodying, and the "what" that it embodies is possibilities. But here again the grammar of the formulation misleads, for the possibilities that are embodied are not fundamentally exterior or antecedent to the process of embodying itself.

As an intentionally organized materiality, the body is always an embodying of possibilities both conditioned and circumscribed by historical convention. In other words, the body is a historical situation, as Beauvoir has claimed, and is a manner of doing, dramatizing, and reproducing a historical situation. To do, to dramatize, to reproduce, these seem to be some of the elementary structures of embodiment. This doing of gender is not merely a way in which embodied agents are exterior, surfaced, open to the perception of others.

Embodiment clearly manifests a set of strategies or what Sartre would perhaps have called a style of being or Foucault, stylistics of existence." This style is never fully self-styled, for living styles have a history, and that history conditions and limits possibilities. Consider gender, for instance, as a corporeal style, an "act," as it were, which is both intentional and performative, where "performative" itself carries the double-meaning of "dramatic" and "non-referential." When Beauvoir claims that "woman" is a historical idea and not a natural fact, she clearly underscores the distinction between sex, as biological facticity, and gender, as the cultural interpretation or signification of that facticity.

To be female is, according to that distinction, a facticity which has no meaning, but to be a woman is to have become a woman, to compel the body to con form to an historical idea of "woman," to induce the body to become a cultural sign, to materialize oneself in obedience to an historically delimited possibility, and to do this as a sustained and repeated corporeal project. The notion of a "project," however, suggests the originating force of a radical will, and because gender is a project which has cultural survival as its end, the term "strategy" better suggests the situation of duress under which gender performance always and variously occurs.

Hence, as a strategy of survival, gender is a performance with clearly punitive consequences. Discrete genders are part of what "humanizes" individuals within contemporary culture; indeed, those who fail to do their gender right are regularly punished. Because there is neither an "essence" that gender expresses or externalizes nor an objective ideal to which gender aspires; because gender is not a fact, the various acts of gender creates the idea of gender, and without those acts, there would be no gender at all. Gender is, thus, a construction that regularly conceals its genesis.

The tacit collective agreement to perform, produces, and sustain discrete and polar genders as cultural fictions is obscured by the credibility of its own production. The authors of gender become entranced by their own fictions whereby the construction compels one's belief in its necessity and naturalness. The historical possibilities materialized through various corporeal styles are nothing other than those punitively regulated cultural fictions that are alternately embodied and disguised under duress.

How useful is a phenomenological point of departure for a feminist description of gender? On the surface it appears that phenomenology shares with feminist analysis a commitment to grounding theory in lived experience, and in revealing the way in which the world is produced through the constituting acts of subjective experience. Clearly, not all feminist theory would privilege the point of view of the subject, (Kristeva once objected to feminist theory as "too existentialist") and yet the feminist claim that the personal is political suggests, in part, that subjective experience is not only structured by existing political arrangements, but effects and structures those arrangements in turn.

Feminist theory has sought to understand the way in which systemic or pervasive political and cultural structures are enacted and reproduced through individual acts and practices, and how the analysis of ostensibly personal situations is clarified through situating the issues in a broader and shared cultural context. Indeed, the feminist impulse, there is more than one, has often emerged in the recognition that my pain or my silence or my anger or my perception is finally not mine alone, and that it delimits me in a shared cultural situation which in turn enables and empowers me in certain unanticipated ways.

The personal is thus implicitly political inasmuch as it is conditioned by shared social structures, but the personal has also been immunized against political challenge to the extent that public/private distinctions endure. For feminist theory, then, the personal becomes an expansive category, one which accommodates, if only implicitly, political structures usually viewed as public. Indeed, the very meaning of the political expands as well. At its best, feminist theory involves a dialectical expansion of both of these categories. My situation does not cease to be mine just because it is the situation of someone else, and my acts, individual as they are, nevertheless reproduce the situation of my gender, and do that in various ways.

In other words, there is, latent in the personal is political formulation of feminist theory, a supposition that the life-world of gender relations is constituted, at least partially, through the concrete and historically mediated acts of individuals. Considering that "the" body is invariably transformed into his body or her body, the body is only known through its gendered appearance. It would seem imperative to consider the way in which this gendering of the body occurs.

From a feminist point of view, one might try to reconceive the gendered body as the legacy of sedimented acts rather than a predetermined or foreclosed structure, essence or fact, whether natural, cultural, or linguistic. The feminist appropriation of the phenomenological theory of constitution might employ the notion of an act in a richly ambiguous sense. If the personal is a category which expands to include the wider political and social structures, then the acts of the gendered subject would be similarly expansive.

Clearly, there are political acts which are deliberate and instrumental actions of political organizing, resistance, and collective intervention with the broad aim of instating a more just set of social and political relations. There are thus acts which are done in the name of women, and then there are acts in and of them, apart from any instrumental consequence, that challenge the category of women itself. Indeed, one ought to consider the futility of a political program which seeks radically to transform the social situation of women without first determining whether the category of woman is socially constructed in such a way that to be a woman is, by definition, to be in an oppressed situation.

In an understandable desire to forge bonds of solidarity, feminist discourse has often relied upon the category of woman as a universal presupposition of cultural experience which, in its universal status, provides a false ontological promise of eventual political solidarity. In a culture in which the false universal of "man" has for the most part been presupposed as coextensive with humanness itself, feminist theory has sought with success to bring female specificity into visibility and to rewrite the history of culture in terms which acknowledge the presence, the influence, and the oppression of women.

Yet, in this effort to combat the invisibility of women as category feminists run the risk of rendering visible a category which may or may not be representative of the concrete lives of women. As feminists, we have been less eager, I think, to consider the status of the category itself and, indeed, to discern the conditions of oppression which issue from an unexamined reproduction of gender identities which sustain discrete and binary categories of man and woman.

When Beauvoir claims that woman is an "historical situation," she emphasizes that the body suffers a certain cultural construction, not only through conventions that sanction and proscribe how one acts one's body, the "act" or performance that one's body is, but also in the tacit conventions that structure the way the body is culturally perceived. Indeed, if gender is the cultural significance that the sexed body assumes, and if that significance is codetermined through various acts and their cultural perception, then it would appear that from within the terms of culture it is not possible to know sex as distinct from gender.

The reproduction of the category of gender is enacted on a large political scale, as when women first enter a profession or gain certain rights, or are reconceived in legal or political discourse in significantly new ways. But the more mundane reproduction of gendered identity takes place through the various ways in which bodies are acted in relationship to the deeply entrenched or sedimented expectations of gendered existence. Consider that there is a sedimentation of gender norms that produces the peculiar phenomenon of a natural sex, or a real woman, or any number of prevalent and compelling social fictions, and that this is a sedimentation that over time has produced a set of corporeal styles which, in reified form, appear as the natural configuration of bodies into sexes which exist in a binary relation to one another.

BINARY GENDERS AND THE HETEROSEXUAL CONTRACT

To guarantee the reproduction of a given culture, various requirements, well-established in the anthropological literature of kinship, have instated sexual reproduction within the confines of a heterosexually-based system of marriage which requires the reproduction of human beings in certain gendered modes which, in effect, guarantee the eventual reproduction of that kinship system.

As Foucault and others have pointed out, the association of a natural sex with a discrete gender and with an ostensibly natural "attraction" to the opposing sex/gender is an unnatural conjunction of cultural constructs in the service of reproductive interests. Feminist cultural anthropology and kinship studies have shown how cultures are governed by conventions that not only regulate and guarantee the production, exchange, and consumption of material goods, but also reproduce the bonds of kinship itself, which require taboos and a punitive regulation of reproduction to affect that end.

Leve-Strauss has shown how the incest taboo works to guarantee the channeling of sexuality into various modes of heterosexual marriage, Gayle Rubin has argued convincingly that the incest taboo produces certain kinds of discrete gendered identities and sexualities. My point is simply that one way in which this system of compulsory heterosexuality is reproduced and concealed is through the cultivation of bodies into discrete sexes with "natural" appearances and "natural" heterosexual dispositions. Although the enthnocentric conceit suggests a progression beyond the mandatory structures of kinship relations as described by Leve-Strauss, I would suggest, along with Rubin, that contemporary gender identities are so many marks or "traces" of residual kinship.

The contention that sex, gender, and heterosexuality are historical products which have become conjoined and reified as natural over time has received a good deal of critical attention not only from Michel Foucault, but Monique Wittig, gay historians, and various cultural anthropologists and social psychologists in recent years. These theories, however, still lack the critical resources for thinking radically about the historical sedimentation of sexuality and sex-related constructs if they do not delimit and describe the mundane manner in which these constructs are produced, reproduced, and maintained within the field of bodies.

Can phenomenology assist a feminist reconstruction of the sedimented character of sex, gender, and sexuality at the level of the body? In the first place, the phenomenological focus on the various acts by which cultural identity is constituted and assumed provides a felicitous starting point for the feminist effort to understand the mundane manner in which bodies get crafted into genders. The formulation of the body as a mode of dramatizing or enacting possibilities offers a way to understand how a cultural convention is embodied and enacted.

But it seems difficult, if not impossible, to imagine a way to conceptualize the scale and systemic character of women's oppression from a theoretical position which takes constituting acts to be its point of departure. Although individual acts do work to maintain and repro duce systems of oppression, and, indeed, any theory of personal political responsibility presupposes such a view, it doesn't follow that oppression is a sole consequence of such acts. One might argue that without human beings whose various acts, largely construed, produce and maintain oppressive conditions, those conditions would fall away, but note that the relation between acts and conditions is neither unilateral nor unmediated.

There are social contexts and conventions within which certain acts not only become possible but become conceivable as acts at all. The transformation of social relations becomes a matter, then, of transforming hegemonic social conditions rather than the individual acts that are spawned by those conditions. Indeed, one runs the risk of addressing the merely indirect, if not epiphenomenal, reflection of those conditions if one remains restricted to a politics of acts.

But the theatrical sense of an "act" forces a revision of the individualist assumptions underlying the more restricted view of constituting acts within phenomenological discourse. As a given temporal duration within the entire performance, "acts" are a shared experience and "collective action." Just as within feminist theory the very category of the personal is expanded to include political structures, so is there a theatrically-based and, indeed, less individually-oriented view of acts that goes some of the way in defusing the criticism of act theory as "too existentialist."

The act that gender is, the act that embodied agents are inasmuch as they dramatically and actively embody and, indeed, wear certain cultural significations, is clearly not one's act alone. Surely, there are nuanced and individual ways of doing one's gender, but that one does it, and that one does it in accord with certain sanctions and proscriptions, is clearly not a fully individual matter. Here again, to minimize the effect of certain gender norms which originate within the family and are enforced through certain familial modes of punishment and reward and which, as a consequence, might be construed as highly individual, for even there family relations recapitulate, individualize, and specify preexisting cultural relations; they are rarely, if ever, radically original.

The act that one does, the act that one performs, is, in a sense, an act that has been going on before one arrived on the scene. Hence, gender is an act which has been rehearsed, much as a script survives the particular actors who make use of it, but which requires individual actors in order to be actualized and reproduced as reality once again. The complex components that go into an act must be distinguished in order to understand the kind of acting in concert and acting in accord which acting one's gender invariably is.

In what senses, then, is gender an act? As anthropologist Victor Turner suggests in his studies of ritual social drama, social action requires a perfor mance which is repeated. This repetition is at once a reenactment and reexperiencing of a set of meanings already socially established; it is the mundane and ritualized form of their legitimation. When this conception of social performance is applied to gender, it is clear that although there are individual bodies that enact these significations by becoming stylized into gendered modes; this "action" is immediately public as well.

There are temporal and collective dimensions to these actions, and their public nature is not inconsequential; indeed, the performance is affected with the strategic aim of maintaining gender within its binary frame. Understood in pedagogical terms, the performance renders social laws explicit. As a public action and performative act, gender is not a radical choice or project that reflects a merely individual choice, but neither is it imposed or inscribed upon the individual, as some post-structuralist displacements of the subject would contend.

The body is not passively scripted with cultural codes, as if it were a lifeless recipient of wholly pregiven cultural relations. But neither do embodied selves pre-exist the cultural conventions which essentially signify bodies. Actors are always already on the stage, within the terms of the performance. Just as a script may be enacted in various ways, and just as the play requires both text and interpretation, so the gendered body acts its part in a culturally restricted corporeal space and enacts interpretations within the confines of already existing directives.

Although the links between a theatrical and a social role are complex and the distinctions not easily drawn (Bruce Wilshire points out the limits of the comparison in Role-Playing and Identity: The Limits of Theatre as Metaphor), it seems clear that, although theatrical performances can meet with political censorship and scathing criticism, gender performances in nontheatrical contexts are governed by more clearly punitive and regulatory social conventions. Indeed, the sight of a transvestite onstage can compel pleasure and applause while the sight of the same transvestite on the seat next to us on the bus can compel fear, rage, even violence.

The conventions which mediate proximity and identification in these two instances are clearly quite different. I want to make two different kinds of claims regarding this tentative distinction. In the theatre, one can say, "this is just an act," and de-realize the act, make acting into something quite distinct from what is real. Because of this distinction, one can maintain one's sense of reality in the face of this temporary challenge to our existing ontological assumptions about gender arrangements; the various conventions which announce that "this is only a play" allows strict lines to be drawn between the performance and life.

On the street or in the bus, the act becomes dangerous, if it does, precisely because there are no theatrical conventions to delimit the purely imaginary character of the act, indeed, on the street or in the bus, there is no presumption that the act is distinct from a reality; the disquieting effect of the act is that there are no conventions that facilitate making this separation. Clearly, there is theatre which attempts to contest or, indeed, break down those conventions that demarcate the imaginary from the real.

Yet in those cases one confronts the same phenomenon, namely, that the act is not contrasted with the real, but constitutes a reality that is in some sense new, a modality of gender that cannot readily be assimilated into the preexisting categories that regulate gender reality. From the point of view of those established categories, one may want to claim, but oh, this is really a girl or a woman, or this is really a boy or a man, and further that the appearance contradicts the reality of the gender, that the discrete and familiar reality must be there, nascent, temporarily unrealized, perhaps realized at other times or other places.

The transvestite, however, can do more than simply express the distinction between sex and gender, but challenges, at least implicitly, the distinction between appearance and reality that structures a good deal of popular thinking about gender identity. If the "reality" of gender is constituted by the performance itself, then there is no recourse to an essential and unrealized "sex" or "gender" which gender performances ostensibly express. Indeed, the transvestite's gender is as fully real as anyone whose performance complies with social expectations.

Gender reality is performative which means, quite simply, that it is real only to the extent that it is performed. It seems fair to say that certain kinds of acts are usually interpreted as expressive of a gender core or identity, and that these acts either conform to an expected gender identity or contest that expectation in some way. That expectation, in turn, is based upon the perception of sex, where sex is understood to be the discrete and factic datum of primary sexual characteristics.

This implicit and popular theory of acts and gestures as expressive of gender suggests that gender itself is something prior to the various acts, postures, and gestures by which it is dramatized and known; indeed, gender appears to the popular imagination as a substantial core which might well be understood as the spiritual or psychological correlate of biological sex. If gender attributes, however, are not expressive but performative, then these attributes effectively constitute the identity they are said to express or reveal.

The distinction between expression and performativeness is quite crucial, for if gender attributes and acts, the various ways in which a body shows or produces its cultural signification, are performative, then there is no preexisting identity by which an act or attribute might be measured; there would be no true or false, real or distorted acts of gender, and the postulation of a true gender identity would be revealed as a regulatory fiction. That gender reality is created through sustained social performances means that the very notions of an essential sex, a true or abiding masculinity or femininity, are also constituted as part of the strategy by which the performative aspect of gender is concealed.

As a consequence, gender cannot be understood as a role which either expresses or disguises an interior "self," whether that "self" is conceived as sexed or not. As performance which is performative, gender is an "act," broadly construed, which constructs the social fiction of its own psychological interiority. As opposed to a view such as Erving Goffman's which posits a self which assumes and exchanges various "roles" within the complex social expectations of the "game" of modern life, I am suggesting that this self is not only irretrievably "outside," constituted in social discourse, but that the ascription of interiority is itself a publicly regulated and sanctioned form of essence fabrication.

Genders, then, can be neither true nor false, neither real nor apparent. And yet, one is compelled to live in a world in which genders constitute univocal signifiers, in which gender is stabilized, polarized, rendered discrete and intractable. In effect, gender is made to comply with a model of truth and falsity which not only contradicts its own performative fluidity, but serves a social policy of gender regulation and control. Performing one's gender wrong initiates a set of punishments both obvious and indirect, and performing it well provides the reassurance that there is an essentialism of gender identity after all.

That this reassurance is so easily displaced by anxiety, that culture so readily punishes or marginalizes those who fail to perform the illusion of gender essentialism should be sign enough that on some level there is social knowledge that the truth or falsity of gender is only socially compelled and in no sense ontologically necessitated.

BEYOND AN EXPRESSIVE MODEL OF GENDER

This view of gender does not pose as a comprehensive theory about what gender is or the manner of its construction, and neither does it prescribe an explicit feminist political program. Indeed, this view of gender being used for a number of discrepant political strategies. Some of my friends may fault me for this and insist that any theory of gender constitution has political presuppositions and implications, and that it is impossible to separate a theory of gender from a political philosophy of feminism.

In fact, it is primarily political interests which create the social phenomena of gender itself, and that without a radical critique of gender constitution feminist theory fails to take stock of the way in which oppression structures the ontological categories through which gender is conceived. Gayatri Spivak has argued that feminists need to rely on an operational essentialism, a false ontology of women as a universal in order to advance a feminist political program.

She knows that the category of "women" is not fully expressive, that the multiplicity and discontinuity of the referent mocks and rebels against the univocity of the sign, but suggests it could be used for strategic purposes. Kristeva suggests something similar, I think, when she prescribes that feminists use the category of women as a political tool without attributing ontological integrity to the term, and adds that, strictly speaking, women cannot be said to exist. Feminists might well worry about the political implications of claiming that women do not exist, especially in light of the persuasive arguments advanced by Mary Anne Warren in her book, Gendercide.

She argues that social policies regarding population control and reproductive technology are designed to limit and, at times, eradicate the existence of women altogether. In light of such a claim, what good does it do to quarrel about the metaphysical status of the term, and perhaps, for clearly political reasons, feminists ought to silence the quarrel altogether. But it is one thing to use the term and know its ontological insufficiency and quite another to articulate a normative vision for feminist theory which celebrates or emancipates an essence, a nature, or a shared cultural reality which cannot be found.

The option I am defending is not to redescribe the world from the point of view of women. I don't know what that point of view is, but whatever it is, it is not singular, and not mine to espouse. It would only be half-right to claim that I am interested in how the phenomenon of a men's or women's point of view gets constituted, for while I do think that those points of views are, indeed, socially constituted, and that a reflexive genealogy of those points of view is important to do, it is not primarily the gender episteme that I am interested in exposing, deconstructing, or reconstructing.

Indeed, it is the presupposition of the category of "woman" itself that requires a critical genealogy of the complex institutional and discursive means by which it is constituted. Although some feminist literary critics suggest that the presupposition of sexual difference is necessary for all discourse, that position reifies sexual difference as the founding moment of culture and pre cludes an analysis not only of how sexual difference is constituted to begin with but how it is continuously constituted, both by the masculine tradition that preempts the universal point of view, and by those feminist positions that construct the univocal category of "women" in the name of expressing or, indeed, liberating a subjected class.

As Foucault claimed about those humanist efforts to liberate the criminalized subject, the subject that is freed is even more deeply shackled than originally thought. Clearly, though, I envision the critical genealogy of gender to rely on a phenomenological set of presuppositions, most important among them the expanded conception of an "act" which is both socially shared and historically constituted, and which is performative in the sense I previously described. But a critical genealogy needs to be supplemented by a politics of performative gender acts, one which both redescribes existing gender identities and offers a prescriptive view about the kind of gender reality there ought to be.

The redescription needs to expose the reifications that tacitly serve as substantial gender cores or identities, and to elucidate both the act and the strategy of disavowal which at once constitute and conceal gender as we live it. The prescription is invariably more difficult, if only because we need to think a world in which acts, gestures, the visual body, the clothed body, the various physical attributes usually associated with gender, express nothing.

In a sense, the prescription is not utopian, but consists in an imperative to acknowledge the existing complexity of gender which our vocabulary invariably disguises and to bring that complexity into a dramatic cultural interplay without punitive consequences. Certainly, it remains politically important to represent women, but to do that in a way that does not distort and reify the very collectivity the theory is supposed to emancipate. Feminist theory which presupposes sexual difference as the necessary and invariant theoretical point of departure clearly improves upon those humanist discourses which conflate the universal with the masculine and appropriate all of culture as masculine property.

Clearly, it is necessary to reread the texts of western philosophy from the various points of view that have been excluded, not only to reveal the particular perspective and set of interests informing those ostensibly transparent descriptions of the real, but to offer alternative descriptions and prescriptions; indeed, to establish philosophy as a cultural practice, and to criticize its tenets from marginalized cultural locations. I have no quarrel with this procedure, and have clearly benefited from those analyses. My only concern is that sexual difference not becomes a reification which unwittingly preserves a binary restriction on gender identity and an implicitly heterosexual framework for the description of gender, gen der identity, and sexuality.

There is, in my view, nothing about femaleness that is waiting to be expressed; there is, on the other hand, a good deal about the diverse experiences of women that is being expressed and still needs to be expressed, but caution is needed with respect to that theoretical language, for it does not simply report a pre-linguistic experience, but constructs that experience as well as the limits of its analysis. Regardless of the pervasive character of patriarchy and the prevalence of sexual difference as an operative cultural distinction, there is nothing about a binary gender system that is given.

As a corporeal field of cultural play, gender is a basically innovative affair, although it is quite clear that there are strict punishments for contesting the script by performing out of turn or through unwarranted improvisations. Gender is not passively scripted on the body, and neither is it determined by nature, language, the symbolic, or the overwhelming history of patriarchy. Gender is what is put on, invariably, under constraint, daily and incessantly, with anxiety and pleasure, but if this continuous act is mistaken for a natural or linguistic given, power is relinquished to expand the cultural field bodily through subversive performances of various kinds.

8

Psychoanalysis and Feminism

The hysteric most often named and discussed by Freud, although he never met her, and never encountered a case like hers, was "Fräulein Anna O.," the inventor of the "talking cure," introduced in the first case history of Studies on Hysteria, published by Freud and Breuer in 1895. Anna O., whose real name was Bertha Pappenheim, inspired what may be called the "legend" of the origin of psychoanalysis, and later in her life became an important figure in the history of the German Jewish women's movement and in the history of modern institutionalized social work.

She lived from 1859 to 1936, and in 1954, was honored by the Republic of West Germany as a "Helper of Humanity." Although feminists have recognized Pappenheim for the philanthropic and political activities of her public life, we have given less attention to her role as a contributor to psychoanalytic theory and technique. The Anna O. described in psychoanalytic writings, an attractive, highly intelligent young woman, suffered an hysterical collapse at the age of twentyone, during a period when she had been responsible for prolonged day and night nursing of her father, Siegmund, who was dying of tuberculosis.

For nearly two years, during and after her father's illness, "Anna" was a patient of the well-known and respected Viennese physician Josef Breuer, who described her case as "the germ-cell of the whole of psychoanalysis." Although Dr.

Breuer never fully recognized the meaning of his encounter with Pappenheim, he found the case remarkable enough to report to his young friend and colleague Freud, who was profoundly impressed when he heard about Pappenheim's unusual treatment by verbalisation and catharsis. That was in November of 1882.

Three years later, Freud was in Paris observing Jean-Martin Charcot's demonstrations of hypnosis and suggestion at the Salpêtrière hospital. At that time, Charcot's lessons on hysteria were as fashionable as the tirades of Sarah Bernhardt, and for much the same reason. In the late nineteenth century, hysteria was a chief subject in medical publications throughout Europe and in England. What Freud contributed to the work being done at this time in France was the idea of listening to what hysterics had to say. Bertha Pappenheim originated this technique, and another patient, "Elizabeth von R." (Ilona Weiss), refined it by suggesting to Freud the method of free association.

Although Breuer edited the story of Bertha Pappenheim's hysteria and suppressed her identity, we know her biography from later sources. She was born in Vienna, the third child in a family that already had two daughters. (Her two sisters died in childhood.) Her birth was followed by that of the family's only son, Wilhelm, whose privileges Pappenheim came to resent. She attended a Catholic school, although her home was traditionally Jewish.

Her grandfather, Wolf Pappenheim, a prominent personality of the Pressburg ghetto, devoted his fortune to the promotion of Jewish orthodoxy. Bertha's father, a wealthy grain merchant, cofounded the Jewish Schiffschul in Vienna. Bertha Pappenheim's mother, Recha, nee Goldschmidt, described as rather authoritarian, was originally from Frankfurt-on-the-Main, Germany, where she later returned with her daughter. This city was a center of charitable activities among Bertha's relatives on her mother's side. These relatives, connected to artistic circles, included Heinrich Heine.

Breuer remarks that some of Anna's more distant relatives had been psychotic, but she herself had been consistently healthy until her father's sickness in July 1880. She had received an education typical for girls of her class. She spoke perfect English, read French and Italian, and practiced embroidery and lacemaking, which remained a lifelong passion. There was a certain modernism about her training, however, since she rode horseback with her cousins.

A photograph of Bertha in riding costume, dated 1882, Konstanz, Germany, bears little resemblance to the patient Breuer describes, although he does mention that she had used a horsewhip in his presence once when her pet dog attacked a cat. Breuer describes Anna as a willful, energetic, intuitive, and compassionate person, someone who took pleasure in caring for the poor and the sick. According to Breuer, Anna could be obstinate, but "sympathetic kindness" was one of her essential character traits. Breuer reports that Anna had a "powerful instinct" toward charity work, but he does not mention that such work was one of the few forms of activity women were traditionally permitted outside the home.

During the time Bertha Pappenheim nursed her father, she stopped eating. Her weight loss was such that she was forbidden to continue her nursing duties. She had also developed a cough which resembled her father's. At this point, Dr. Breuer was called in for the first time. Over the next three months, a very complex hysteria developed. Pappenheim suffered rigid paralyses of her arms, legs, and neck muscles, headaches, and somnambulism. First her right arm, then her right side, then her entire body suffered contracture. She was intermittently deaf. She had a convergent squint and severe, inexplicable disturbances of vision. She had temper tantrums during which she would throw things about the room, tear the buttons off her bedclothes, and grow distressed when relatives appeared.

Pappenheim in her hysteria experienced a profound disorganisation of speech and, for a time, total aphasia. It is Pappenheim's aphasia and her use of her body as a signifier particularly concerned. Although many of what Freud refers to as Pappenheim's "museum of monuments" to "hyperaesthetic memories" have been richly and repeatedly analyzed, no one has sufficiently studied her unique use of languages. When she regained her ability to talk, Bertha Pappenheim was unable to understand or speak her native tongue although she proved surprisingly fluent in foreign languages, a circumstance Freud calls "strange" and other commentators call "bizarre."

She claimed to be divided into two selves: "a real one and an evil one which forced her to behave badly." Two states of consciousness would alternate, one of which would interrupt while the other was speaking. Breuer refers to the pauses in Pappenheim's speech by the French term absences. This suggests that for Breuer as well as for Pappenheim, the abnormal states of consciousness represented foreign parts of the self, parts alien to signification in her native tongue.

In the afternoons Pappenheim would fall into a somnolent state. After sunset she would wake up, repeating the words "tormenting, tormenting." She was unable to speak a whole sentence, and her whole body was paralyzed. Breuer first noticed that she was at a loss for words and then that she had lost her command of grammar and syntax as well. She no longer conjugated verbs, and eventually used only infinitives, which, says Breuer, were "for the most part incorrectly formed from weak past participles."

Neither infinitives nor participles specify a person; as Breuer notes, "tormenting" is an impersonal form. Pappenheim also omitted both the definite and the indefinite article. In the process of time she became almost completely at a loss for words. When words failed her, she would put them together laboriously out of four or five languages and became nearly unintelligible. Here is a reconstruction of Pappenheim's linguistic melange: "Jamais acht nobody bella mio please lieboehn nuit." She tried to write the same mumbo jumbo.

For two weeks Bertha Pappenheim was completely silent, and at this point, Dr. Breuer recognized for the first time the psychical mechanism of his patient's disorder: "She had felt very much offended over something and had determined not to speak about it." When Breuer guessed this and obliged her to talk about it during hypnosis, Pappenheim's linguistic inhibition disappeared, but she spoke only in English. In moments of extreme anxiety, her powers of speech either deserted her entirely or she used a mixture of languages.

At the times when she felt most free, Pappenheim spoke French and Italian. She had amnesia between these times and the times when she spoke English. During her illness, she baffled her family and servants with discourses in languages they did not understand and astonished her doctors by producing a rapid, fluent extemporaneous English translation of any text in French or Italian she was asked to read aloud. Pappenheim also made up words: gehäglich for behaglich, meaning comfortable and invented names in English for the process which she and Breuer had begun. She called it "chimney sweeping" when she was joking and "the talking cure" when she was being serious.

Freud and Breuer offer an inadequate explanation for Pappenheim's linguistic symptoms. We are told that one night while she was watching by her father's sickbed in a torment of anxiety, she fell into a twilight state, while her right arm, which was hanging over the back of the chair, went to sleep. Pappenheim was so terrified to find her arm paralyzed that she tried to pray, but could find no words.

At length she remembered a child's prayer in English. Therefore when her hysteria developed, she spoke and wrote English. This recollection of the child's prayer seems to bear no relation to Pappenheim's determination to keep silent. Nor does it explain her inventive nomenclatures, polylingual jargon, or amazing speeches in French and Italian. All it tells us is that Bertha was so upset she forgot her mother tongue. Although Breuer does not state what had offended Bertha, it is easy to infer that she resented and rejected her inferior position as a daughter in an orthodox Jewish family.

Although her intellectual and poetic gifts were remarkable, and she was a lively and charming person, Bertha Pappenheim at twenty-one was assigned routine and monotonous household tasks. Her brother, a year younger than she and not nearly as bright, had recently entered the University of Vienna, an institution closed to women at that time.

Breuer writes, "This girl, who was bubbling over with intellectual vitality, led an extremely monotonous existence in her puritanically-minded family. She embellished her life in a manner which probably influenced her decisively in the direction of her illness, by indulging in systematic day-dreaming, which she described as her 'private theatre.'" Speculating on the origin of "hypnoid" (dissociated, split) states, Breuer and Freud note that these conditions often seem to grow out of the daydreams which are common even in healthy people, "and to which needlework and similar occupations render women especially prone." That is, people left to embroidery are bound to embroider fantasies.

Pappenheim's daydreaming and her illness were heavily influenced by the necessity of spending hours tending her father's sickbed, a situation that cannot have failed to arouse wishes in such a lively and imaginative person, although Breuer does not mention this and seems not to have thought of it. Her squint developed while she was straining to see what time it was through her tears after she had waited up all night for a doctor who was late in arriving. In similar circumstances, Pappenheim hallucinated a black snake coming toward the sick man from the wall to bite him.

When she tried to drive away the snake, she found her arm paralyzed and saw her hands turn into little snakes with death's-heads at the fingertips. Her cough developed when she heard dance music coming from a neighboring house, felt a sudden wish to leave her father's bedside, and was overcome with self-reproaches. Thereafter, she coughed nervously whenever she heard rhythmical music. Pappenheim hallucinated her father's face as a death's-head and then saw her own reflection in a mirror as the same image.

Having lost her sisters to childhood deaths, and apparently wishing for the termination of her father's agonizing illness which she imitated with her cough, Pappenheim was preoccupied with skeletons. When Siegmund Pappenheim died, his daughter had to be removed to the country to protect her from suicidal impulses. Perhaps she wanted to join him in death, and perhaps she wanted to escape from guilt generated by what must have been liberation and a relief. She had lost a patient "of whom she was passionately fond."

Pappenheim's hysteria arose from sources in her life history typical of her time. It was not uncommon in the nineteenth century for the potential of daughters to be sacrificed while sons were educated and privileged; it was also in keeping with prevailing customs for young women to be called upon to nurse aging and ill parents. Neither Pappenheim nor Breuer could consciously express the ambivalent emotions such situations would arouse. Although Breuer recognized Bertha's grief for her father's death as a cause of her symptoms, he overlooked the hostility, anger, guilt, and frustrated sexuality apparent to psychoanalysts.

Even a nonpsychoanalytic reading of the case indicates that Pappenheim found her existence lonely and tedious. Late in her life Pappenheim thought of her lack of formal education as "defective spiritual nourishment," a reference that may illuminate the anorexic symptoms of her hysteria and her way of literalizing through her body her felt psychic condition. Breuer uses a similar metaphor of undernourishment to describe Anna O.: "She possessed a powerful intellect which would have been capable of digesting solid mental pabulum and which stood in need of it-though without receiving it after she had left school."

Once when Dr. Breuer interrupted his visits to her for several days because he had to leave Vienna, Bertha went entirely without food during his absence. At the time she fell ill, Bertha Pappenheim must have wanted someone to talk with, someone to listen to her elaborate stories. Breuer provided an audience for her mental creations. He increased by one the attendance at her "private theatre." Although Breuer had arrived as an old-fashioned physician with black bag in hand to treat Bertha Pappenheim's malady, she quickly changed the terms of the relationship by failing into autohypnosis and commencing to mutter in an apparently absent-minded state. She was clearly intrigued by the good looking and highly cultivated, successful doctor.

Although Breuer does not say so, his account of Bertha Pappenheim's behaviour suggests that she tried to seduce him, and that in a way she was successful. We are told about the various massages she received on her head and legs-standard procedures for treating paralysis. What was unusual, and the beginning of what developed into psychoanalysis, involved the long hours they spent in hypnosis together while Pappenheim told sad and fanciful stories and "talked herself out" until "she was clear in mind, calm, and cheerful." Breuer attributed her cheerfulness to the talking, not to his presence on the scene.

During the course of their treatment Breuer spent a medically unprecedented amount of time in his patient's company, visiting her nearly every day between the end of 1880 and the middle of 1882, often more than once a day, listening to the most minute details of her present and past life, repeating set phrases from her stories to get her narratives started each session. Although Breuer states that Bertha Pappenheim was "astonishingly underdeveloped" sexually, every commentator has remarked upon her physical attractions.

The case history suggests that Bertha fantasized a love affair with Breuer; and indeed, the infatuation seems to have been mutual, although unconscious on Breuer's part. Pappenheim failed to recognize her relatives and ignored all unwanted strangers, but she always had eyes for Breuer. According to Freud, her image of the treatment as "chimney sweeping" was a metaphor for sexual intercourse. After many months of hearing reports of this fascinating patient, Mrs. Breuer finally grew jealous and angry.

Surprised and probably feeling guilty as well, Breuer suddenly determined to end the treatment. He announced his intention to Pappenheim and prepared to depart on a trip to

Venice with his wife. According to Freud, Pappenheim responded with an "untoward event." She staged a hysterical childbirth to summon Breuer back for another session. He was shocked to find her in bed with abdominal cramps, which she explained with the words "Now Dr. Breuer's child is coming!" He calmed her with hypnosis and then fled the house, abandoning her to a colleague.

He never saw her again, and later when he heard that she was ill, he wished she would die and so cease to be miserable. Breuer chose not to report the fantasy childbirth in the published version of the case history of Anna O., and he never acknowledged the erotic element in their attachment. This suppression might be explained by Breuer's fear of a scandal; and if he perceived that Pappenheim had been playing a role to allure him, he might have feared that publishing the story would not only compromise him, but make him appear foolish as well.

However, his private obsession with the case after he had given it up, his reluctance to pre sent any account of it in public form, and his ultimate rejection of psychoanalysis indicate that there were other causes contributing to the absence of the final scene from his report in Studies on Hysteria, which gives the false impression that Anna's hysteria had disappeared. George Pollock traces Breuer's anxiety to the loss of his young and attractive mother in childbirth when he was three or four years old. She, as well as Breuer's oldest daughter, about eleven years old at the time of his relationship with the famous patient, was named Bertha.

When Freud began to uncover the role of transference love in hypnosis and psychoanalysis, and to stress the importance of sexuality in neuroses, Breuer dissociated himself from his controversial colleague. Although Pappenheim had led the way to the unconscious through her invention of the "talking cure" and her dramatisation of transference love in the doctor-patient relation, Breuer resisted the implications of their encounter.

Freud reports that Breuer repeatedly read to him pieces of the case history during 1882 and 1883, but objected vehemently to publishing the story of the treatment. Freud decided to report the case to Charcot, who listened but showed no interest. Ten years later Breuer agreed to a joint publication because Freud convinced him that Pierre Janet's work in French anticipated some of his results, such as the tracing back of hysterical symptoms to events in the patient's life, and their removal by means of hypnotic reproduction.

Although I think the oedipal configurations in Pappenheim's encounter with Breuer are significant, I want to focus for a moment on the oral dimensions of their relationship. Leo Stone's discussion of transference wishes links the unconscious meanings of the doctor-patient relation to the universal craving for the omnipotent mother of early infancy. Janet Malcolm summarizes:

> This craving... can be activated by doctors, politicians, clergymen, and teachers as well as by analysts. Stone draws a... distinction between the meaning of the primary transference generated by the physician and that generated by the analyst. While the physician's direct physical and emotional ministrations correspond to those of the "omniscient, omnipotent, and unintelligible" mother of the earliest period of infancy, the analyst's activities resemble (in unconscious reverberation) the not so agreeable ones of the mother in the months when the infant is learning to talk and to separate from her-"that period of life where all the modalities of bodily intimacy and direct dependence on the mother are being relinquished or attenuated, pari passu with the rapid development of the great vehicle of communication by speech." It is in this state of "intimate separation," or "deprivation in intimacy," that analysis is conducted, deriving its mutative power from the tension between verbal closeness and emotional distance.

In this stage of psychosexual development, linguistically constituted subjectivity ("I" versus "you," "he" versus "she," and syntactical relations) is superimposed upon our rhythmical, corporeal rapport with the mother. Prior to our accession to the grammatical order of language, we exist in a dyadic, semiotic world of pure sound and body rhythms, oceanically at one with our nurturer. Out of the infinite potential identities each newborn infant brings into the world, a single way of being is activated according to the way the mother behaves in oral symbiosis.

The mother's style of relating communicates the unconscious significance the infant has for her. Through her body language-holding, nursing, caressing, bathing, dressing-and then through mirroring, through the image the child forms of itself as it sees itself reflected in the mother's face, especially in her eyes, the mother communicates an identity to the child. As Heinz Lichtenstein describes it, the mother "seduces the child into life," in the same way that the sun activates tropism in a plant and so shapes its form and direction.

Our sense of ourselves as separate beings, as "subjects," is bound up with our entry into the order of language in which speech becomes a substitute for bodily connection. The world we as children enter is always already constituted and governed by language. When we accede to the world where communication in words allows both separation and intimacy, we are relinquishing the immediacy of semiotic and corporeal rapport with our nurturer, from whom we recognize our separation.

A child reared in a family such as Bertha Pappenheim's makes her transition to speech as part of a process according to which she recognizes the father's privileged relation to the mother. In the order of language, "I" and "you" conceptualize and mark separate persons, as "she" and "he," "mother" and "father," differentiate genders and roles. Although it is usually the mother who activates an infant's capacity for speech in the oral, semiotic stage, subjectivity in the sense of being a separate, syntactical agent, a grammatical "subject," comes later in childhood, when, in the patriarchal family, the father's role is being recognized.

Discovery of the father's role in the primal scene and recognition of male dominance in the social world conjoin with the integration of the patriarchal child into the systematic organisation of language. The interlocking of linguistic with cultural rules suggests an equation between the organisation of language and the systematic organisation of patriarchal culture and its sexually differentiated, oedipal subjectivity. In patriarchal socialisation, the power to formulate sentences coincides developmentally with recognition of the power of the father.

In this light, Bertha Pappenheim's linguistic discord and conversion symptoms, her use of gibberish and gestures as means of expression, can be seen as a regression from the cultural order represented by her father as an orthodox patriarch. Bertha Pappenheim failed to speak her native language, but could be fluent in alien forms of expression. She failed to speak coherent German, but she succeeded in getting Dr. Breuer to speak her language and enter a world repressed by patriarchal consciousness.

Breuer literally repeated Pappenheim's linguistic formulas; and in this way he came to an awareness of the unconscious. Bertha was twenty-one, on the brink of womanhood in a role offering little in the way of satisfaction or development of her intellectual gifts. When she looked into the mirror she saw a death'shead. Rejecting the cultural identity offered her; she tried to translate herself into another idiom. She regressed from the symbolic order of articulate German to the semiotic level of the body and the unintelligibility of foreign tongues.

Her communication in signs, mutterings, and made-up jargon indicates an attempt to re-create the special semiotic babble that exists between an infant and its mother. Pappenheim reached the point of having to be fed by Breuer. She turned Breuer into a surrogate oral mother; in the sense that she took over his role as doctor, she turned him into an identity-giver as well. Her birth fantasy, which put Breuer to flight, can be read as a wish to bring a new identity and perhaps a new reality into the world.

Dr. Breuer was evidently not prepared for the idea that Pappenheim was giving birth to psychoanalysis. But he seems to have understood her situation admirably. Here is his analysis of the predisposing causes of her hysteria: "First, her monotonous family life and the absence of adequate intellectual occupation left her with an unemployed surplus of mental liveliness and energy, and this found an outlet in the constant activity of her imagination. Second, this led to a habit of daydreaming (her 'private theatre'), which laid the foundations for a dissociation of her mental personality."

In other words, Bertha Pappenheim was schizoid because she was bored and needed to both watch and put on shows. She was alienated, split between what Breuer began to call "the unconscious" or "secondary" state and her "normal" state. Breuer adds that although her two states were sharply separated, not only did the "secondary" (or 'hypnoid') state intrude into the first one, but also "a clear-sighted and calm observer sat, as she put it, in a corner of her brain and looked on at all the mad business." Thus, Pappenheim confessed to Breuer the persistence of clear thinking in the midst of her madness.

After her conversion symptoms had ceased, and while she was passing through what Breuer called a temporary depression, Pappenheim told him that "the whole business had been simulated." He concludes:

> I have already described the astonishing fact that from the beginning to the end of the illness all the stimuli arising from the secondary state, together with their consequences, were permanently removed by being given verbal utterance in hypnosis, and I have only to add an assurance that this was not an invention of mine which I imposed on the patient by suggestion. It took me completely by surprise, and not until symptoms had been got rid of in this way in a whole series of instances did I develop a therapeutic technique out of it.

Pappenheim actually treated herself, with Breuer as her student. One may ask how it was that Bertha Pappenheim managed to achieve such a breakthrough. It seems that she was influenced by the widespread interest in catharsis that followed the publication of a book by the uncle of a friend of hers. This friend was Freud's future wife, Martha Bernays, whose uncle, Jacob Bernays, published a study of the Aristotelian concept of catharsis in 1880.

Bernays's book was widely discussed by scholars and became an important topic of conversation in Viennese salons. Perhaps Pappenheim had been introduced to the concept of catharsis as a method of dramatizing and expelling emotions, and she then put it to use as a means of capturing and holding the attention of her scientifically minded physician. Since women of Pappenheim's day remained outside the official cultural institutions transmitting knowledge, she was limited in her forms of discourse. She made a spectacle of herself in order to resolve the tension between her guilt and her desire to escape familial exploitation. Her knowledge of the unconscious (her "clouds") was expressed in a distressed and distressing way.

This knowledge had then to be theorized by men. She presented a startling and engaging demonstration of the psychological, affective causes of hysteria, but Dr. Breuer away still believed in the somatic foundation of hysterical phenomena. It was left to Freud to complete the shift from physiological to psychological study and to articulate in a scientific way the central role of eros in therapeutic relationships, a major transition in the history of psychiatry.

Bertha Pappenheim invented the "talking cure" during an epoch that needed to tell itself its troubles. An important figure in the history of consciousness, she expressed in the language of the body what psychoanalysis says in words. I think we can regard her in the terms Erik H. Erikson has used to describe ideological leaders: "Individuals with an uncommon depth of conflict, they also have uncanny gifts, and uncanny luck with which they offer to the crisis of a generation the solution of their own crisis."

In the process of talking herself out to Breuer, Pappenheim converted a nonverbal message, expressed in body language or pantomime and called an hysterical symptom, into a verbal language. That is, her narratives converted or translated a message from one language into another. She was a psychodramatist, complete with appropriate scenic arrangements for the reproduction of crucial events; and she devised the method of narrating back piece by piece the story of each symptom to reach its source.

In a technique comparable to Shakespeare's in the play-within-the-play in Hamlet, Pappenheim put on a dumb show in distraction, muttered, and then spoke out the story behind the show. She restaged the origins of her symptoms in order to undo them. This is ritual as catharsis. Breuer said that the patient's symptoms disappeared as soon as the event which had given rise to them was reproduced in a trance, making it "possible to arrive at a therapeutic technical procedure which left nothing to be desired in its logical consistency and systematic application."

Each individual symptom in her museum of "hyperaesthetic" memories was taken up separately, and the occasions on which it had appeared were described in reverse order, starting before the time when she became bedridden and going back to the event which had led to its first appearance. According to Breuer, "when this had been described the symptom was permanently removed." In dramatizing her past, Pappenheim was also dramatizing the unconscious, and she was engaging her audience in an oedipal repetition in the form of Breuer's countertransference.

The Pappenheim turned Breuer into a substitute oral mother, audience, and identity-giver in order to escape the crisis of cultural identity occasioned by her father's terminal illness, as a psychodramatist who enacted the birth to consciousness of a new psychic reality. Through her clever manipulations of languages, she managed to avoid the role of dutiful orthodox daughter and find an intelligent, stimulating, and sympathetic listener. Pappenheim's entry into public life remains to be discussed.

She became a feminist in an epoch when women felt compelled to speak up against the abuses that paralyzed their development. In the same year that Freud and Breuer published their Studies on Hysteria, Pappenheim at the age of thirty-six became headmistress of an orphanage in Isenburg, Germany, near her mother's birthplace. This became the central headquarters for her forty-year career in philanthropic social work later commemorated by the West German government. She spent her life rescuing and sheltering abandoned and abused women and children.

In linking the two phases of her career, Lucien Israel classifies Pappenheim as one of a number of celebrated hysterics who later led altruistic public lives, substituting themselves for a male mentor who failed them. Israel analyzes such women as "successful hysterics," whom he sees as founding their vocations on a fantasy of universal love and a sense of rivalry with men.

The Pappenheim case, claims Israel, demonstrates very clearly that the universal love embodied in her career as rescuer of women and children was originally directed at a specific person chosen as mentor. But the mentor, or more precisely, "master" (maître), Breuer, failing to reciprocate her love, became an object of identification that was replaced by Pappenheim herself. Having discovered that the doctor is not all the patient had hoped, "successful hysterics" decide to incarnate his role as therapist, savior, "helper of humanity."

Israel's analysis overlooks the charity work tradition among Pappenheim's maternal relatives. Pappenheim chose to make Breuer the gift of her symptoms and their treatment because of what he stood for as a doctor. She chose him for a significant encounter involving issues that were bigger than both of them. Her identification with the role of savior is consistent with her status as an Eriksonian leader who forged her charisma out of her post-adolescent identity crisis, for Eriksonian ideological leaders feel that their lives must be made to count in the great historical movements of their day.

The two great historical movements of Pappenheim's day were the discovery of the unconscious and the liberation of women, and she made herself heard in both of them. The range of her career as a reformer indicates that Bertha Pappenheim was "in love with activity on a large scale," a phrase Erikson adopts from Woodrow Wilson to describe the qualities of which charismatic leaders are made.

The nature of Pappenheim's symptoms and their treatment connect her with several other remarkable women. Although it may be true that Pappenheim's performances for Breuer were inspired by a book she had read or heard about on catharsis, one must speculate about what currents might have been at work among her hysterical counterparts in Germany and France throughout the nineteenth century, and slightly later in Switzerland when psychoanalysis was introduced into the Burgholzli clinic in Zurich; and one must wonder what inspired Ilona Weiss to suggest the free associational method to Freud. As Henri Ellenberger observes, aspects of Pappenheim's hysteria have never been satisfactorily explained. First of all, between December 1881 and June 1882, Pappenheim's two personalities were sharply distinct, and Breuer was able to affect a shift from one to the other by holding up an orange, the food she had chiefly lived on during the previous year.

While one part of Bertha existed in the present, another part relived the previous year precisely, day by day. Thanks to a diary Mrs. Pappenheim had kept, Breuer was able to verify that the events Bertha hallucinated had occurred, day by day, exactly one year earlier. Second, certain of Bertha's symptoms supposedly occurred without an incubation period and could be made to disappear simply by recalling the circumstances under which they had appeared the first time. Bertha had to recall each instance when the symptom had appeared, whatever the number, in exact chronological order, a unique feature of her treatment.

These remarkable exercises in memory, and the idea of the patient dictating appropriate therapeutic procedures to the physician, although extraordinary in the 1880s in Vienna, were not unheard of in the history of medicine. Ellenberger links Pappenheim's case with the great exemplars of "magnetic illness" who achieved fame during the early part of the nineteenth century. Katharina Emmerich, a poor peasant and former nun from Dülmen, Westphalia, had dreams every night that followed one another in a regular sequence according to the cycle of the liturgical year, a mnemonic feat comparable to Pappenheim's hallucinations recalling each day of the previous year in exact sequence.

Another subject, Friedericke Hauffe, "the Seeress of Prevorst," spoke frequently in an unknown language, and although uneducated and the daughter of a gamekeeper, she delivered recitatives in the purest High German instead of the Swabian dialect commonly spoken by the people around her. In her magnetic trances, the "Seeress" often prescribed treatments which unfailingly cured her exactly when predicted, just as Pappenheim predicted the date of her recovery to Breuer. Estelle L'Hardy, who fell ill upon her father's death, was cured of a dual personality through the dictations of a comforting angel appearing to her during "magnetic" sleep. Her doctor managed a gradual fusion of her normal and "magnetic" states by establishing an emotional rapport that challenged Estelle's dependency on her mother.

Like Bertha, Estelle relied on a special relationship with her physician for her cure. Ellenberger sees Pappenheim as a kind of revenant of the "magnetic" patients who performed miraculous feats of memory, spoke in tongues, controlled the forms of their treatments, and predicted the dates of their "cures." Another analogue to Bertha Pappenheim is her Parisian contemporary Blanche Wittmann, known as "queen of the hysterics" because of the impressive sculptural forms of her poses and the longevity of her tenure at the Salpêtrière hospital. The experiments with traumatic paralysis and their reproduction under hypnosis which Freud witnessed at the Salpêtrière are today regarded with skepticism, and Ellenberger concludes that Pappenheim's treatment was a clever trick. Yet her story and Charcot's seances at the Salpêtrière were major inspirations to Freud.

During her hysteria, Anna O. had taken up writing in a curious fashion. Her right hand being paralyzed, she wrote with her left hand and used Roman printed letters copied from her edition of Shakespeare. Such incorporation of foreign signifiers might have been linked to her desire for psychic integration and prefigures Pappenheim's later role as a translator. She resurrected and translated the memoirs of her ancestor Glückel of Hameln, who was "a born writer and storyteller." Wishing to transmit Jewish culture to a world ignorant of Yiddish, Pappenheim translated into German sagas and legends from the Talmud and Midrash, together with folk tales and The Women's Bible.

Special significance adheres to the sundry languages Pappenheim spoke in her hysteria and in later life because her use of translation as a verbal strategy reverberates in psychoanalytic preoccupation with the term and the process. Jacques Lacan, for example, calls psychotherapy the "repatriation of alienated signifiers." Freud refers to the Anna O. case more than forty times in his collected works and frequently in his letters. The intensity of interest these references indicate suggests that she emblematized something essential for him.

At the time he was working out his theory of hysteria, Freud was translating Hippolyte Bernheim and Charcot from French into German; his and Breuer's "Preliminary Communication" on the subject was immediately translated into Spanish, French, and English. Later on Freud conducted several analyses in translation, and psychoanalysis has been a multilingual movement.

Freud compared the symptomatology of hysteria to a "pictographic script which has become intelligible after the discovery of a few bilingual inscriptions." Freud uses the word "translation" to discuss the work of psychoanalysis and the work of the unconscious. In the "dream-work," the latent wish is "translated" into the imagery of the manifest content of the dream. Freud writes: "The dream-thoughts and the dream-content are presented to us like two versions of the same subject-matter in two different languages.

Or, more properly, the dream-content seems like a transcript of the dream-thoughts into another mode of expression, whose characters and syntactic laws it is our business to discover by comparing the original and the translation." In hysteria, says Freud, psychic messages are "translated" into somatic expression. Analytic interventions he considered "translations" of the unconscious into the conscious. The "talking cure" is the "translation of affects into words." Repression for Freud was a "failure of translation." Thus the forms in which Anna O. communicated her distress and her shifts between languages to express levels of consciousness metaphorize what developed into what one may call a psychoanalytic concept of translation.

Aragon and Breton's celebration of nineteenth-century hysterics as fellow artists indicates that the surrealists recognized hysteria as an expressive discourse; and we may add, it was a discourse of femininity addressed to patriarchal thought. Lucien Israel notes that the question of whether or not hysteria is an illness has received no answer. His own analysis of Bertha Pappenheim ventures close to the idea that feminism is transformed hysteria or more precisely, that hysteria is feminism lacking a social network in the outer world. In popular culture the word "hysterical" has often been used in attempts to discredit feminist expression, for both hysterics and feminists are "out of control": neither hysterics nor feminists cooperate dutifully with patriarchal conventions.

Attempts to discredit feminists as "hysterical" derive from a repressive impulse similar to the defense that creates hysterical symptoms in the first place: repudiation-of socially untoward feelings such as anger and resentment. Thus one may call hysteria a self-repudiating form of feminine discourse in which the body signifies what social conditions make it impossible to state linguistically.

Although hysteria had mainly been associated with women, Charcot and Freud demonstrated the existence of male hysteria and opened to analysis the repressed femininity of men. If we valorize hysteria as a form of making the unconscious conscious, we can call Bertha Pappenheim a forebear of psychoanalytic feminism. We note that psychoanalysis entered the history of consciousness in dialogue with feminine subjectivity, for Freud's discovery of the unconscious was a response to the body language of nineteenth-century hysterics. Thus, psychoanalysis can be read as a translation into theory of the language of hysteria.

Both psychoanalysis and hysteria subvert the reigning cultural order by exploding its linguistic conventions and decomposing its façade of orderly conduct. Both the psychoanalytic and the feminist movements have been international and interlingual. Thus the psychoanalysis of hysteria in Europe in the nineteenth century may be seen to contribute to the multilingualism, internationalism, and communication in translation of contemporary linguistic feminisms.

This theme finds its perfect metaphor in The Dream of a Common Language, where Adrienne Rich writes, "we are translations into different dialects/ of a text still being written/ in the original." As a speaker in tongues and as a psychodramatist of the relationship between the body language of hysteria and psychoanalytic entrance into the history of consciousness, Anna O. represents a significant event in this unfolding multilingual text.

9

Some Problems for Feminism

The representation - and visual representation in particular - poses certain problems for both feminist thinking and feminist politics. I want to take a look at one or two of these problems as they presented themselves to me in the context of a recent cinema - going experience. Early in 1986 I attended a commercial screening in London of a film called Pumping Iron II - The Women. The screening was organized for an all-women audience and was followed by a discussion between the audience and a panel, consisting of two film critics and a bodybuilder.

It is possible there were more critics and bodybuilders in the audience, but most of the women present apparently fell into neither category. Though, being mostly feminists, they were not the "ordinary women" of the populist Imaginary, either. Few "ordinary women" - if such beings exist - would in any case have the opportunity to see Pumping Iron II. Although the film received an enthusiastic critical reception on its U.S. and British releases, it has had no general release, nor as far as it been shown on television in Britain. And the video version circulating in Britain for a while has now been withdrawn.

None of this matters very much in the present context since the film figures here largely as a peg or point of departure for a set of general observations on visual representation and feminism. My argument, in other words, is applicable to more than this one film: and an argument based on Pumping Iron II might even shed some light on cinema in general.

Nevertheless, a summary of the storyline of Pumping Iron II is probably in order here. The film is about a women's bodybuilding championship held in Las Vegas in 1984. It may be called "semi-documentary," in that while all the characters play "themselves," they are placed in situations set up expressly for the camera. Indeed, the contest was proposed in the first place by the film's director, George Butler: its initial raison d'être, therefore, was that a film would be made of it. Suffice it to say - without entering into debates about "truth" and "fiction" in cinema - that certain fictionality underlies the film's cinema verite appearance. This double status makes it entirely appropriate to look at the film as a narrative in the classic mold.

The main protagonists are real-life bodybuilding champions Rachel McLish, Carla Dunlap (the only black contestant), and Australian weightlifter-turned-bodybuilder Bev Francis. The first part of the film shows these and other women in the run-up to the contest - their training, their relationships with their (male) coaches and with each other. The film's climax is the competition itself, held in the plush surroundings of Caesar's Palace.

The narrative hook is simple: Who will win? But there is more to the story than that: the competition and its outcome turn upon the question of what sort of body a female bodybuilder ought to have. Before the 1984 championship, women bodybuilders had produced lithe and sinewy, as opposed to overtly muscular, physiques. But in the film, Bev Francis's entry into competition challenges this order of things. For hers is a body so extremely muscular that it can only be seen as "masculine' by judges and contestants accustomed to previous competition "form." Francis clearly has more muscles than any of the other women in the contest: the question is, can she win on these grounds?

This question, which becomes crucial to the progress of the narrative, is addressed quite explicitly in the film. When all the contestants are assembled in Las Vegas for their final few days of training before the championship, several discussions on this very issue take place. First of all, a group of competitors-all minor characters - relax together in the pool at Caesar's Palace, surrounded by classical statuary.

They are all more or less in agreement that the judges should stick with the "feminine look." This is followed by a scene in which these very judges - all but one male - confer on "the official [International Federation of Bodybuilding] analysis" of the word "femininity." Then, following a short scene in which Carla Dunlap, under the gaze of a facsimile Winged Victory, does some synchroswimming practice alone in the pool, she and Bev chat about the judging of the contest, muscles, and, again, "femininity." Finally, Rachel McLish is seen expressing doubt to an interviewer that the world is yet ready for Bev Francis. But although the question "Who will win?" is duly answered at the end of the film, the conundrum of the appropriate body for a female bodybuilder is never really resolved - a point to which I shall return.

On its British release, Pumping Iron II was hailed by some as the feminist film of the year, on the grounds that it holds up conventional notions about the relationship between femaleness, femininity, and the body not only to scrutiny, but also to a certain amount of ridicule: this feminist reading sanctioned the women-only screening which I attended. Aside from the allfemale audience, this was an extraordinary event in a number of respects. Most unusual, perhaps, was the packed auditorium.

And the audience behaved not in the customary (in Britain, at least) manner as a gathering of individuals, couples or small groups of friends on their separate night out at the pictures, but as a single social group: talking back to characters on the screen, cheering on the "goodies," booing the "baddies," and so on. All the viewers, it seemed, were having a wonderful time, enjoying both the film and the circumstances in which they were watching it. Although the potential of female or feminist audiences as communities is an issue of obvious relevance to questions of feminism and representation, I want to concentrate more specifically here on the question of what is involved for audiences of this sort in the reception of a film like Pumping Iron II.

This question was raised quite forcefully after the screening was over, during discussion of the film. Many of those who spoke were critical of the film. Criticism tended to be expressed in terms of the nature and value of women's bodybuilding as a sport. In particular, the view was put forward that aside from being competitive (A Bad Thing), the sport was narcissistic (An Even Worse Thing). If criticism from this feminist audience was not directed at the sorts of things that preoccupy film theorists (the film text, the specifically cinematic, the spectator-text relationship, and so on), it did in a way highlight some key problems - not just for feminist thinking around cinema and visual representation in general, but for other feminist practices as well.

The apparently inconsistent responses of this audience-enjoyment during, negative criticism after, the screening-might well betoken a certain discomfort with the pleasures evoked by the film. In this context, viewers' references to narcissism could be regarded as symptomatic. In relation to activities represented on the screen, this invocation of narcissism assumes a certain transparency on behalf of the cinematic image: a "naive" reading from which critics and theorists of cinema would undoubtedly hasten to dissociate themselves.

Yet narcissism also describes a potential mode of relation to the film text, and its invocation in this displaced manner may well be an expression of the difficulty of such a relation, highly foregrounded, perhaps, in this particular text, but by no means confined to it. One of the central and most productive insights of feminist film theory concerns the ways in which sexual difference is constructed, and spectators addressed as male/masculine and female/feminine, within the cinematic apparatus.

To summarize and grossly oversimplify a substantial body of work, it might be argued that the options on offer to spectators in cinema are basically either to take up a masculine subject position as, so the argument goes, is proposed by the huge number of films in which the enunciating instance is male/ masculine; or to submit to a masochism of overidentification, as is evoked, for example, by the Hollywood "women's picture"; or to adopt the narcissistic position of taking the screen as mirror and becoming one's own object of desire.

In their inscription within a complex and unstable libidinal economy, these spectator-text relations are not mutually exclusive; each is, in theory, available to all spectators, regardless of gender. However, in the social, historical, and ideological space inhabited and produced by cinema, certain constraints are imposed upon such polymorphy. For example, the Hollywood women's melodrama of the 1940s and 1950s, proposing a mode of identification culturally marked as characteristically feminine, was deliberately marketed to female audiences: in this instance, social relations and psychic relations intersect in the actual reception of films.

Nevertheless, while the pleasures of cinema are obviously available to women as well as to men, I would contend that for women there is an additional degree of instability in the relations of subjectivity upon which these pleasures depend. In Pumping Iron II, for instance, an important source of pleasure for female spectators must lie in its construction of the female body not only as strong but also as capable of being shaped and defined by women themselves.

And yet while this film might evoke such new and technological narcissistic identifications, the pleasure of this position may at the same time be undercut in at least two ways: first of all, by a construction of the female body as potentially monstrous; and secondly, as a consequence, by the fact that, for a woman, assenting to the pleasures afforded by cinema is tantamount to becoming caught up (to use Foucauldian terminology, on which I shall elaborate later) in certain relations of power, held in place by these relations and by the constructs of sexuality they inscribe.

These power relations and their associated instabilities characterize a good deal of classical cinema. Pumping Iron II is exceptional only in that it brings such contradictions to the fore at the levels of both narrative and spectacle. For example, on both these levels the film is quite clearly "about" the female body in ways that most films are not. That is to say, while - as feminist film theorists have argued - the female body may figure crucially in the production of both meaning and pleasure in classical cinema, Pumping Iron II transcends this inscription of the female body to interrogate that body and its limits.

The film's narrative is governed by the question of who will win the contest. But since in this context "who?" must mean "which body?," the trajectory of the narrative is harnessed to a further set of questions: What is a woman's body? Is there a point at which a woman's body becomes something else? What is the relationship between a certain type of body and "femininity"? These are challenging questions in a cultural context in which the body figures as an irreducible sign of the natural, the given, the unquestionable. Foremost among these cultural effectivities of the body is its function as a signifier of sexual difference.

But the concept of sexual difference is itself an ideological battleground: it holds together - or tries to - a range of discourses and meanings centering on biological sex, social gender, gender identity, and sexual object choice. The encapsulation of all these within constructs of sexual difference is a historically grounded ideological project which works to set up a heterogeneous and variably determinate set of biological, physical, social, psychological, and psychic constructs as a unitary, fixed, and unproblematic attribute of human subjectivity.

One of the effects of this is that, at a social level at least, every human being gets defined as either male or female. From this fundamental difference flows a succession of discourses and powers centering upon identification and sexuality. Pumping Iron II can be read if not as actually unraveling this discursive formation, certainly as unpicking it a little around the edges. The film does this most distinctively by constructing the body in a particular manner as performance. Performance is an activity that connotes pretense, dissimulation, "putting on an act," assuming a role.

In other words, in the notion of performance a distance of some sort is implied between the "act" and the "real self" concealed behind it. Performance proposes a subject which is at once both fixed in, and called into question by, this very distinction between assumed persona and authentic self. Performance, in other words, poses the possibility of a mutable self, of a fluid subjectivity. If performance proposes fluidity and the body connotes fixity, the combination of the two in the instance of bodybuilding confers a distinctly contradictory quality on the activity.

For bodybuilding involves more than placing the body on display, more than simply passive exhibition. The fact that bodybuilding is an active production of the body, a process of acting upon and determining its contours, is impossible to ignore. In Pumping Iron II, for example, innumerable scenes emphasize the sheer hard work involved in the production of the women's bodies. In bodybuilding - the willed construction of a certain physique-nature becomes culture.

Performance and the body are instrumental in the operations of classical cinema as well; but rarely in ways which in the final instance challenge the natural order of the body and its inscription of sexual difference. For in cinema, performance is usually appropriated to the self-evidently cultural and mutable instances of clothing and gesture. In bodybuilding, muscles function in much the same way as clothing does in other types of performance. But muscles, unlike clothes, are supposed to be natural. What happens, then, when muscles enter the cultural domain? In a sense, of course, they already do inhabit it, for muscles carry a heavy burden of cultural meanings.

Not least among these are meanings centered upon sexual difference and its naturalness. Within such a discourse, muscles are constituted as "essentially" masculine. Thus when women enter the arena of bodybuilding, a twofold challenge to the natural order is posed. Not only is the naturalness of the body called into question by its inscription within a certain kind of performance: but when women have the muscles, the natural order of gender is under threat as well.

Muscles are rather like drag, for female bodybuilders especially: while muscles can be assumed, like clothing, women's assumption of muscles implies a transgression of the proper boundaries of sexual difference. In Pumping Iron II the limits of the female body are the object of obsessive concern, to the extent that the opposite poles of the issue are represented in the "feminine" body of Rachel McLish against the "masculine" body of Bev Francis.

The woman's body as muscular may also be regarded as tantamount to a fetish, a point which brings me back to the question of cinema. For it is an axiom of feminist film theory that one of the masculine subject positions available to the spectator in cinema is constructed through a fetishistic look, a look which effects a disavowal of the threat of castration posed by woman. The phallic woman imaged in this process of disavowal is either overvalued as a glamorous figure, or punished as a monstrosity. Such an operation, it is argued, is characteristic of the spectator-text relations proposed by classical cinema. Again, this operation is foregrounded in Pumping Iron II.

In particular, Bev Francis's body can only, within the terms of the body/gender/culture problematic, be seen as "masculine," or at least as "not-feminine." How is such a disturbing body to be looked at when translated on to the cinema screen? Indeed, can it be looked at? At the level of spectacle, then, the threatening quality of Bev's body can be neutralized by its construction - in a fetishistic look - as monstrous. And yet at the level of narrative, Bev figures as a key character - indeed as a sympathetic character - in the film. Whether she will receive her just narrative deserts as a "good person" or her just, "specular" deserts as a phallic woman is a question entirely central to the suspenseful trajectory of Pumping Iron II.

In the end, Bev loses the championship, coming in at a humiliating eighth place. But ultrafeminine Rachel McLish does not win, either: and of these two it is Bev who, by her magnanimity in defeat, scores the moral victory.

First prize, in fact, goes to Carla Dunlap, whose body is represented in the film as a midpoint between Bev's and Rachel's. But there is more to this resolution than mere compromise. Carla is set up as an outsider, as different from the other contestants - and not just by virtue of race: she is the most articulate of the group, a self-sufficient loner, the only one with no man to coach her and provide moral support. Carla's dea ex machina win does not so much answer the film's central question, then, as sidestep it.

The issue of the appropriate body for a female bodybuilder is not actually resolved: rather it is displaced on to a set of discourses centering on-but also skirting-race, femininity, and the body, a complex of discourses which the film cannot acknowledge, let alone handle in Pumping Iron II's terms. Carla's body can be "read" only as a compromise: other major issues are left dangling. These contradictions overdetermine the ways in which Pumping Iron 11 foregrounds a number of dilemmas facing female spectators at the cinema. Most especially, the film makes it clear that to adopt a narcissistic position in relation to the cinematic image is to run the risks of identifying with womanas - fetish: of identifying with her overidealisation, certainly - and, more commonly, perhaps, in the cinema of the 1980s-with her victimisation and punishment.

The difficulties of such a mode of identification effectively become a topic of Pumping Iron II, so that the instability of femininity as a subject position, and the discomfort involved in identification with it, is liable to become evident in looking at this film in ways they are not when such relations are more embedded, more submerged in the text.

This brings me back to the question of the powers at work in cinema's relation of spectatorship: powers through which, it is argued, sexual difference - and indeed perhaps other kinds of difference, too - are constructed. To take pleasure in cinema is to be seduced by these operations; to be subject to, to submit to, the powers they inscribe. The spectator becomes caught up in, and constituted by, a set of powers which produce (among other things) discursive constructs of femininity and masculinity. She/he is positioned, defined, set in place, within these powers and constructs. The gendered subjectivities so produced are not interchangeable, however.

This is one reason - and a very important one - why visual representation presents special problems for feminist politics. In this context two questions present themselves: Is it possible for women/feminists to take pleasure in visual representation, particularly in cinema? And, more generally, what is to be done about the problems all this poses for feminism?

Representation sets in play certain relations of power through which, among other things, discourses around sexual difference and subjects in and for those discourses are ongoingly produced. In this sense, representation may be regarded, once more to adopt Foucauldian terminology, as a strategy of normalisation. Representation participates in the various relations of power with which we are surrounded and in which we are always in one way or another implicated. Representation can be understood, then, as a form of regulation.

This theoretical position suggests that no one, no social group, no structure, can stand outside the powers and the normalizing instrumentality of representation. Therefore if "women" are positioned and produced through these powers in specific ways as social subjects, it follows that they are not excluded from these powers. Nor, in the classic sense of the term, can women be regarded as "oppressed" by them. For power, in this model, is not a thing, is not imposed from outside its subjects, but is rather a process, the outcome of a series of interacting and potentially contradictory relations in which these subjects are necessarily involved.

If power operates in this way as a network of countervailing "force relations," then resistance becomes an integral part of processes of power. Given this, what kinds of resistance to the normalizing effectivities of representation are available to feminism? In current circumstances, three sets of feminist strategies of resistance present themselves: censorship, feminist practices of representation, and feminist critical practice. My main concern here is with feminist critical practice, but a few words on the other two are perhaps in order first.

If censorship deserves attention, this is not because (at least in its legal or quasilegal manifestations) it constitutes an important feminist strategy of resistance to the normalizing powers of representation: on the contrary, generally speaking it does not. However, since feminist protests against visual representations of women are often appropriated (in Britain and the U.S., at least) in support of prefeminist and even antifeminist arguments in favour of censorship, it might be worthwhile making a few distinctions here.

While censorship - to the extent that it seeks to repress certain representations - can be regarded as a prohibitive operation, it can also be seen as productive. At the most basic level, for example, it produces the "unrepresentable" precisely as a set of images that should not be seen. What censorship both pro hibits and produces is most especially that category of representations named the "obscene."

However, constructs of femininity produced by representation cannot simply be mapped directly on to constructs of the obscene produced by censorship. On the contrary, in fact: in both psychic and economic terms, "femininity" may be regarded as exactly a condition of representation. If feminists and censors seem to be at one in objecting to certain images of women, the objects of their objections are in fact completely different. It might be added, moreover, that censorship, in inciting desire for the unrepresentable, in the final instance acknowledges and reinforces the power of the image. To this extent, censorship is complicit in those very normalizing processes which feminism seeks to resist.

Feminist practices of representation, on the other hand, embody - in the quest for a "new voice," a transformation of vision - a wholly understandable desire to stand outside these powers. This is not necessarily an essentialist project, though given the appeals often made to an authentic feminine voice, "writing the body" and suchlike, it certainly looks like it at times. A good deal of exciting and valuable work in film, as in other areas of cultural production, has appeared in recent years, some of it indeed claiming to speak a "feminine voice." Nevertheless, the search for new forms of expression is more productively seen in terms of resistance to the powers of representation than as taking place outside their "field of force."

This argument is more than just a corollary of the notion that power is allpervasive: it also registers a discomfort with a distinction between feminist cultural production on the one hand and feminist theory and criticism on the other. Such a polarisation perpetuates the assumption that while theory and criticism are of necessity implicated in "discourses which negate or objectify [women] through their representations," feminist cultural production is somehow capable of transcending these limitations. At stake here, of course, is a separation of theory and practices: precisely one of the dualisms of patriarchal thought which feminist thinking seeks to challenge.

This brings me to the third and final strategy of resistance, strategically termed in this context feminist critical practice. Feminist critics and theorists among my readers may be relieved to hear that, in arguing that criticism can be a political practice in its own right, I have masculine authority on my side. I refer here to the quotation from Foucault which heads this chapter.

If feminist critics can place themselves among those who, in Foucault's words, "resist and refuse what is," we might well then ask: Where lies the specificity of feminist as against other forms of oppositional cultural practice? Perhaps it resides in the possibility that feminist critical practice may constitute not only a resistance to the powers of visual representation, but also an attempt to bridge the gap between woman as spectacle, as object of the look, and women as historical subjects.

Alongside feminist cultural production, then, feminist critical practice can be a fundamentally deconstructive strategy which questions the possibility of universals or absolute meanings and exposes the constitution of power at stake in their assertion. However, I shall not end with any fanfares, for one further question remains unanswered: can feminists (and indeed women in general) take pleasure in visual representations, and if so, how? I have suggested that the feminist audience at the screening of Pumping Iron II was uncomfortable with its own pleasure in the film.

If this is so, then their discomfort was simultaneously expressed and dealt with in a process of disavowal. This is evident in the negative criticisms directed at-but actually missing - the film: and it may be seen in itself as a form of resistance to the film's powers of seduction and subjection. The question remains, though: Can there be a feminist critical position which neither refuses nor disavows the pleasures of cinema?

RACE AND GENDER IN POPULAR FILM

Issues of race, gender, and ethnicity come together in an especially bizarre manner in one of the earliest sound films, The Jazz Singer, at the end of which the Jewish son, played by Al Jolson, donning black face for a theatrical performance, hears "the call of the ages - the cry of my race," sings "Mammy" to his mother, and rushes home to his dying father, promising to take up momentarily the father's role as cantor. Subsequently - and the coda is added to the film version of the stage play - the son returns to his show - business career, thus being permitted the best of both worlds, old and new.

Here, of course, are the familiar oedipal themes of Hollywood cinema: the son's accession to the role of the father entails a modification of the stern and unyielding patriarchal attitude, thereby, in the case of The Jazz Singer, accommodating the assimilationist ideologies of the period. The mother is a key figure in the process of the hero's growth and acculturation, since in her unconditional love for her child she can serve as the mediating force between father and son, old world and new, the desire for cultural difference and the desire for cultural integration.

But the mother in the film is not the only mediator, not the only person whose sole significance lies in the meaning she holds for the white man and his drama; the other such figure is, of course, the black man, metonymically summoned to represent the unalterable fact of "race," and thus to form one pole of the assimilationist continuum, at the other end of which stands the Jolson character's shiksa girlfriend.

It is ironic, if utterly characteristic that the essentialist notion of race the film draws upon is asserted through masquerade and in a space of illusionism, i.e., the theatre. That is to say, the jazz singer recognizes his supposed racial authenticity as a Semite in the process of miming another race - assuming black skin and black voice - so that the film is situated squarely in the realm of the fetish, whereby the notion of ineradicable racial difference (one which defies history and calls out across "the ages") is simultaneously affirmed and negated.

Recent work by Homi Bhabha has shown how colonialist discourse as a whole involves a process of mimicry that is related psychoanalytically to the mechanism of fetishisation, the play of presence and absence. By mimicry, I take Bhabha to be referring to an imposition by one nation of its structures, values, and language upon the colonized nation, an imposition that rather than completely obliterating difference speaks of "a desire for a subject of a difference that is almost the same, but not quite" and hence is, Bhabha continually emphasizes, ambivalent.

Although Bhabha's terms of reference concern the British Empire, they apply equally to the American situation, for, as Thomas Cripps points out in his somewhat dated but still useful study of blacks in American film, the position of blacks in relation to the dominant culture and its representations has been an "ambivalent" one: blacks had "absorbed American culture but could not expect to be absorbed by it." Moreover, Cripps himself points out that the British colonial system "resembled American racial arrangements" in the way "it encouraged cultural assimilation while denying social integration".

One fairly ludicrous result of such "arrangements" was that, for example, in cinema what used to be called "race movies" often had to do without white people. "Without whites, the requirements of dramatic construction created a world in which black characters acceded to the white ideal of segregation, and unreal black cops, crooks, judges, and juries interacted in such a way as to blame black victims for their social plight." But the lack of verisimilitude, which Cripps sees as a problem, can cut two ways: for it is easy to see how how such copies of white cinema could easily reflect back on the model itself, mocking it, defamiliarizing it, casting doubt upon its accuracy as, in the words of one film concerned with the perennial theme of "passing," an "imitation of life".

Eddie Murphy Coming to America furnishes a contemporary example of a movie in which black mimicry of whites is both a source of humor and a fundamental structuring principle of the text. In this movie, Prince Akeem leaves Africa to come to America-to Queens - in order to find a queen of his own choosing, one with a "mind of her own" rather than the woman destined and trained from birth to be his wife. Although on his arrival Prince Akeem discovers a world where black poverty seems to be the rule, the film rapidly moves beyond this world to enter middle-class black society, represented by the owner of a hamburger stand called McDowell's.

The owner, whose daughter becomes Akeem's choice for a wife, explains the differences between his business and the McDonald's franchise: "they have golden arches, we have golden arcs.... Their rolls have sesame seeds, ours don't, etc."-distinctions, in other words, without a difference. The joke here, in which mimicry itself is foregrounded, may be said to cut a variety of ways, potentially mocking the white model for black middle-class ambitions but also, at least in the eyes of prejudiced white audiences, affirming white capitalism as the "real thing" and appearing to expose black aspirations as ridiculous and pathetic.

There is also another sense in which mimicry operates throughout the text. Insofar as the film may be said to belong to a recognizable genre, the screwball comedy, the film participates in, mimes, a fantasy unreal enough when it concerns whites and doubly so in relation to blacks. In a gesture reminiscent of the classic screwball hero Godfrey of My Man Godfrey, Akeem disguises himself as a penniless floor-washer in order to win over the father of the (motherless) woman he loves.

As the barber advises, "If you want to get in good with the daughter, you got to get in good with the father." The film is clearly situated squarely within the bounds of the oedipal drama, the only twist being that the arrival of Akeem's real father is the decisive event in winning over the future father-in-law, who is bowled over on discovering the richness and royalty of his daughter's suitor. The film's major conflict thus turns out to be not an interracial or class conflict but one between the wealthy black Americans and the even wealthier Africans.

That the film resolves its conflict according to the traditional dictates of the genre by ending with a wedding (between Burger Queen and future African king) that promises the harmonious union of two worlds - a black imitation of white corporate America, represented by McDowell's, and a black African nation represented by its royal family-takes on a particularly sinister irony in light of the role played by American corporations in the destruction of the environment of Third World peoples.

The ending of Coming to America may be seen as an attempt to resolve at the level of fantasy the ambivalence or doubleness Bhabha sees operating in representations of race: the black man as alien, African other (an otherness always already denied because it is the familiar, Americanized Eddie Murphy who plays the lead role) and the black man as assimilated dreamer of the American dream. Such ambivalence, according to Bhabha, is explosive; there is an incipient menace in mimicry, and from "a difference that is almost nothing but not quite" it is but a step to a "difference that is almost total but not quite." Switching genres, from comedy to horror, we may note that the film Alien Nation provides a vivid illustration of the thesis.

In this film a group of aliens from another planet have been residing in Los Angeles as an oppressed minority, clearly meant to serve as allegorical figures for blacks. (Here we see vividly illustrated the dominant culture's tendency to collapse all racial groups into one undifferentiated mass which serves as the "Other" of white society. For, clearly, the notion of an alien nation draws on the existence of the Latino population of illegal "aliens.")

The aliens are almost like white but "not quite" (they get drunk on sour milk; the males have larger penises than the Americans; their heads are strangely shaped, hairless, and mottled), and in the liberal surface text, the bigoted white cop must learn to accept his new alien partner, Sam Francisco, as someone whose differences are in fact insignificant in the face of the men's overriding common humanity.

The two are involved in tracing down a deadly drug that has nearly destroyed the people on the alien planet, and at one point Sam forces his partner to witness the hideous physical transformation of a victim who has overdosed so that he may see "just how monstrous" his people "are capable of becoming." Yet, plot details aside, is it not the case that the threat of monstrosity - that is, of black monstrosity - has been present all along in the film as a consequence of the decision to make it an allegory rather than to treat the situation of blacks directly?

And has not the tendency of films from the very early days of cinema to cast white people in blackface served a similar function - i.e., to suggest that blackness may be so monstrous it can only be signified but not directly represented? When in Birth of a Nation we watch the lecherous man in blackface pursuing the young white girl to her death, do we need to know about, in order to feel the force of, Griffith's reason for casting mostly white actors in the film: i.e., to protect the purity of white womanhood on the set?

We need, then, not just to analyze the function of mimicry on the part of the colonized people, but to understand its role in the life and art of the colonizer - to understand, that is, the function of minstrelsy. Bhabha writes of the way the "not quite/not white" element of difference displayed by colonized races is related to the psychoanalytic notion of the fetish: "black skin splits under the racist gaze, displaced into signs of bestiality, genitalia, grotesquerie, which reveal the phobic myth of the undifferentiated whole white skin."

Minstrelsy would be a method by which the white man may disavow-acknowledge and at the same time deny-difference at the level of the body; as a process of fetishism, it seeks, like all fetishes, to restore the wholeness and unity threatened by the sight of difference, yet because it enters into the game of mimicry it is condemned to keep alive the possibility that there may be "no presence or identity behind the mask."

The concept of fetishism enables us to understand why minstrelsy has never really died out - why it lives in a different form in the "trading places" and "black like me" plots with which Hollywood is enamored, the most recent example being Paul Mazursky Moon Over Parador (actually an instance of "brownface"), in which the Richard Dreyfus character, an unemployed Hollywood actor, is pressed into masquerading as the leader of a Central American country and in effect winds up playing the "Tootsie" of Latin American dictators.

Some of Bhabha's discussion covers familiar territory for a feminist reader, since he draws on material elaborated in feminist theory. The problematics of difference and sameness have, for example, been brilliantly analyzed by Luce Irigaray in her readings of Freud essay "On Femininity" and Plato Republic. Irigaray shows that for all Western culture's emphasis on the difference between the sexes, there is an underlying negation of the difference - and the threat-posed by the female sex, a negation evidenced for example in Freud's theorizing of the woman as an inferior man, as bearer of the "lack." In Freudian theory, of course, the fetish is precisely the means whereby "lack" and difference are disavowed - accepted and negated simultaneously.

It is the means, in other words, whereby "a multiple belief" may be maintained and hence serves to support the wildly divergent stereotypical associations that accrue around the fetishized body. For it is not just the black who is marked in the dominant discourse as, in Homi Bhabha's words, "both savage... and yet the most obedient and dignified of servants;... the embodiment of rampant sexuality and yet innocent as a child;... mystical, primitive, simple-minded and yet the most worldly and accomplished liar, and manipulator of social forces."

Much of this description also applies to the representation of woman, who in the male Imaginary undergoes a primal splitting into virgin and whore. The importance of Bhabha's work, like Fanon's before him, lies partly, for me, in the way it insists on understanding the psychosocial dynamics of colonialism and racism, bringing psychoanalysis to bear on questions that have unfortunately all too often been viewed as not susceptible to a psychoanalytic understanding.

Yet, unaccountably, although Bhabha utilizes the very concepts originally developed in the theorisation of sexual difference, he almost entirely neglects the issue of gender and slights feminist work. In virtually ignoring the "woman question," while retaining the terms in which it has been posed, Bhabha commits the same kind of error for which Freud can be and has been criticized. The latter was undoubtedly being both racist and sexist in designating "woman" as the dark continent. But the answer is surely not to reverse the proposition and implicitly posit the "dark continent" as woman - not, at the very least, without carefully theorizing the relation.

Although he does not examine how race and gender intersect, Bhabha nevertheless notes at one point, "Darkness signifies at once both birth and death; it is in all cases a desire to return to the fullness of the mother, a desire for an unbroken and undifferentiated line of vision and origin." For the heart of the matter, the heart of darkness, is, after all, "Mammy"- she who, absent in her own right, is spoken by man as guarantor of his origin and identity.

In the face of the male desire to collapse sexual and racial difference into oceanic plenitude, feminism needs to insist on the complex, "multiple and cross-cutting nature of identity and to ask: how do we rid ourselves of the desire for a "line of origin," how avoid positing either sexuality or race as theoretically primary, while we at the same time undertake to understand the vicious circularity of patriarchal thought whereby darkness signifies femininity and femininity darkness? I would like in this chapter to address this question by examining first the way our culture through its representations explores the highly charged taboo relationships between black men and white women (specifically focusing on Gorillas in the Mist and a scene from an early film, Blonde Venus) and then to focus on the representations of black women in popular film, looking especially at the ways in which the black woman functions as the site of the displacement of white culture's (including white women's) fears and anxieties.

In Gorillas in the Mist, the question of origins is posed at the outset by, of course, a white man - in this case the anthropologist Dr. Louis Leakey, who is seen in a large hall lecturing about gorillas: "I want to know who I am, and what it was that made me that way." As if conjured up by his words, Dian Fossey appears, the woman who will journey alone to the heart of darkest Africa and whose story may be viewed as a phantasmatic answer to the white man's question.

It is an old story; an updated, middlebrow version of the King Kong tale, which itself is part of a tradition of animal movies that have functioned as thinly disguised "allegories for black brutes." Of the perennial popularity of the film King Kong, for example, X. J. Kennedy wrote:

A Negro friend from Atlanta tells me that in movies houses in coloured neighborhoods throughout the South, Kong does a constant business. They show the thing in Atlanta at least every year, presumably to the same audiences. Perhaps this popularity may simply be due to the fact that Kong is one of the most watchable movies ever constructed, but I wonder whether Negro audiences may not find some archetypical appeal in this seriocomic tale of a huge black powerful free spirit whom all the hardworking white policemen are out to kill.

Putting aside the way this passage provides a textbook example of how white racism gets projected into the psyches of the black audience, we may note that Kennedy's remarks are paradoxically couched in a liberal frame which tacitly acknowledges the legitimacy of black political grievances while employing an ahistorical notion of "archetype," which would deny the humanity of blacks (imaged as beasts) and so function to prevent them from achieving social and political equality.

This is not to say that Kennedy's response is idiosyncratic: on the contrary, films like King Kong, made by whites in a racist society, lend themselves to this kind of interpretation, which is situated in the space of disavowal characteristic of colonialist discourse (the fetish indeed being a means by which two apparently opposed beliefs, "one archaic and one progressive," may simultaneously be held). This is a space, as we shall see, increasingly occupied in a postfeminist, post-civil rights era by a mass culture that must on one level acknowledge the political struggles of the last few decades and on another, deeper level would ward off the threat these struggles pose to the white male power structure.

Thus, for example, Gorillas in the Mist seems to respect the notion of a woman sacrificing the opportunity for a husband and family in order to pur sue a career, a career that, indeed, involves her living the sort of adventurous and dangerous life usually reserved for men in popular films and that also accords her the kind of single-minded dedication to a cause typically attributed to the male scientific investigator. But the film takes it all back, as it were, by "deprofessionalizing" Fossey, neglecting to mention her growth as a scientist who in the course of her research in the mountains of Rwanda earned a Ph.D. from Harvard. The film further subverts its apparently liberal attitude to woman's independence by suggesting that Dian is merely channeling and sublimating (or should it be desublimating, since she goes "back" to the apes?) her sexual desires and maternal instincts into her cause. In the last scene, for example, after her death, the image track shows the son of the slaughtered gorilla swinging in the trees-clearly Fossey's son, since her tryst with its father, the gorilla Digit (in which the romantic music swells as Dian lies on her back, smiling blissfully when the gorilla slowly takes her hand, leaving a precious little deposit of dirt in her palm) is followed by her coupling with the National Geographic photographer.

The soundtrack records a conversation between her and Roz Carr, the plantation owner, in which Fossey remarks, "I expected to get married and have children," and her friend replies, "Instead there's a mountain full of gorillas who wouldn't be alive if it weren't for you." The titles at the end tell us that Fossey's work "contributed significantly to the survival of the species"-woman's function, after all, even if it isn't quite the right species.

The transfer of Fossey's affection from her fiance to Digit and his "group" is visually marked by the film through its replacement of the photo of the fiance, which we see early in the film placed on a little typing table outside Dian's hut, with photos of the gorillas ("gorilla porn," as one of my friends remarked) that she passionately kisses right before her murder, while a song of Peggy Lee's ("I'd take a million trips to your lips") plays on the phonograph.

But perverse as all this may sound - and in my view is - the most remarkable aspect of the film is the way in which it manages to make its psychosexual dynamics seem innocent. Indeed, the very title of the film points to a kind of disavowal, suggesting a tamed, romanticized, "misty" view of beasts and bestiality: a film whose own sublimating efforts work on every level to deny the perversity of the gorilla/woman sexual coupling it continually evokes.

Black skin "splits" in this film, to recall Homi Bhabha's words, into images of monstrosity and bestiality on the one hand and of nobility and wisdom on the other. Fossey's tracker, Sembagare, represents the latter option; he is presented as a man whose family has been wiped out along with their tribe and thus, having no story or plot of his own, he is free to live a life of self-sacrificing devotion to the white woman.

It is impossible to overestimate the importance of this character - a common type in Hollywood cinema - in serving as a guide to the audience's interpretation and judgment of events, and it is interesting to reflect on the fact that such a character's possession of the gaze may be concomitant with a radical dispossession in relation to the narrative. Throughout the film, the camera continually cuts to shots of Sembagare, usually gazing approvingly on some action performed by the heroine, but also, occasionally, registering disapproval and dismay.

Mostly what Sembagare cares about is that the heroine's sexual and romantic needs be fulfilled, and this is made clear from the very outset when he first sees and comments on the picture of the fiance. By attributing a kind of maternal concern to the black male as well as granting him a degree of moral authority, the film can appear to be, in liberal fashion, empowering the character while at the same time relieving the audiences' anxieties about the proximity of white womanhood and black manhood.

That fears about the threat posed by the black male to white woman are not far beneath the surface can be seen in the film's treatment of all the other black men, who are usually shown in menacing groups, surrounding our heroine, gesturing and muttering in their "savage" languages, and touching her hair in awe. Early in the film, some black soldiers come to Fossey's hut, destroy her possessions, and evict her from their country. The film treats African civil wars as nothing more than a nuisance impeding Fossey's crusade-a crusade aligned with the film's project of substituting a timeless, pastoral "gorilla nation" for the eminently less important struggles of emerging black nations.

Significantly, as the men attempt to force her to leave, Fossey furiously tells them not to touch her, to get their hands off her. Now, given that the big love scene with the gorilla involves Fossey holding hands with him, and indeed that the love interest is given the name "Digit" by Fossey because of the webbing of his fingers, and finally that the film is most horrified by the castration of the gorillas' heads and hands, the latter made into curio ashtrays for rich Americans, we might be justified in seeing in this motif of the hand a condensation of the film's basic conflict: a pitting of animals against black men, with the former ultimately viewed as less physically and morally repellent than the latter.

Here we might note that we come full circle to Griffith film Birth of a Nation, which had intercut shots of Flora being stalked by Gus with ones of squirrels framed in an iris. The black man thus becomes, as Cripps observes, "a predator about to pounce upon a harmless animal". Thus it is that in Gorillas in the Mist, the machete-wielding black men who earn their living destroying gorillas are depicted as less truly and movingly human than the tragic and noble gorillas - as was the case in King Kong, as well.

Of course, at the level of its script, the film suggests a more complicated view, and at one point the photographer Bob cautions an angry Fossey that the black men are simply pawns in an economic power game that chiefly benefits rich Americans. In this respect too, then, the film operates in the realm of disavowal, verbally disputing its own visual scapegoating of the black men and, moreover, projecting the scapegoating onto the character of Fossey, who at one point terrorizes a little black boy by pretending to be a witch and at another point conducts a mock lynching of a black male poacher.

It is the white man, then, who in the end seems to be the most fully human character, while the black men are either self-sacrificing servants or threatening monsters, and the white woman is at the same time both a noble savior of innocent creatures and a witch whose unholy alliance with the beasts of the forests turns her into a raving monomaniac.

In other words, into the space hollowed out by the film's fetishistic splittings steps the white man, equipped with the photographic apparatus which apparently enables him to establish the proper voyeuristic distance from the perversity that surrounds him. Interestingly, since this is Dian Fossey's story, and most of the film is from her point of view, the film gives the point of view over to Bob on several occasions. I have already referred to one instance - when Bob stares in fascination at Dian's "mating" with Digit, the camera cutting to tight close-ups of him as he crouches near his photographic equipment and stares intently at the coming together of woman and ape.

Another such moment occurs when he first arrives on the scene, and we see Dian squatting on the floor, imitating the gorillas' movements and noises. So vertiginous does the film's play with mimicry become that the woman is constantly shown copying the gorillas, aping the anthropomorphized apes; like the blacks, she seems to occupy a position one step below the animals, to be not quite capable of achieving the same degree of humanity attained by the beasts.

But while an analysis of the point-of-view structure of Gorillas in the Mist suggests that, like most Hollywood films, and despite its biographical claims, this one is largely concerned with white male fears and fantasies and seems designed to assure the white man of his full humanity in relation to the animals, the female sex, and other races, it is important to understand that the voyeuristic distance between the white male and his "others" ultimately collapses.

Bob, it turns out, is drawn to gorillas too, and he gets to act out his bestial lusts vicariously when he and Dian become lovers after he sees her with Digit and during an elaborate verbal play in which references to the beauty of the animals serve as double entendres applying to Fossey herself. Here we encounter the perennial thematics of homosocial desire, according to which the woman functions in a triangular relationship between two males, the woman becoming attractive to the second male as a result of being sought after or possessed by the first: a matter of, in Rene Girard's words, mimetic desire-of, in the film's case, man imitating beast. Thus, we might say, by the end of the twentieth century, homosocial desire, long the cornerstone of patriarchal society, has expanded to include the entire order of Primates.

In Gorillas in the Mist, then, woman serves to initiate man into the secrets of his origin, whereupon he goes off to a new job in the wider world, escaping the carnage and destruction visited on the other players. Such violence is made to seem an appropriate ending to a film that touches on so many taboo areas, situating itself at the shifting borders between man and woman, whites and blacks, humans and animals, nature and society. One might expect that because of its unsettling obsession with these taboos, its nearly uncontrollable play of iteration, audiences would be troubled by the film's perversity.

Seldom, however, did reviewers even mention the film's bizarre psychosocial dynamics; instead, the main "controversy" surrounding Gorillas in the Mist had to do with its accuracy as representation of Fossey's life - a question, once again, of mimicry, or mimesis. It is tempting to speculate that this question arises as a response to the disturbances created by the film at a phantasmatic level, instilling in us a longing for an authentic human life to serve as ground and source of the film's meaning, just as the film itself attempts to foreclose the historical process and establish a natural, pastoral space which would preexist the struggles of feminists and black nationalists. Such a question would take on a special urgency precisely because the lines toed by the film are so thin that it comes perilously close to mocking its own quest, making monkeys of us all.

In his book The Signifying Monkey: A Theory of Afro-American Literary Criticism, Henry Louis Gates praises Jean Renoir's silent film Sur un air de Charleston for its parody of the literature of discovery popular in Renaissance and Enlightenment Europe. In the film, a black man in blackface discovers a postholocaust Europe and its only survivors, "a scantily clad white Wild Woman... and her lascivious companion, an ape." Gates sees in this scenario a "master trope of irony," which operates a "fairly straightforward... reversal... of common European allegations of the propensity of African women to prefer the company of male apes."

That Gates can see nothing dubious in Renoir's "surrealistic critique of... fundamental conventions of Western discourse on the black" and can entirely neglect to consider the potency of myths like King Kong (which long precede the 1933 film) suggests a very large blind spot indeed-blind, that is, to the way the female Other, regardless of race, has been frequently consigned to categories that put her outside the pale of the fully human. (Why, we might inquire, did it not occur to the "master" ironist to depict a scantily clad white man lewdly gyrating with his pet ape?)

Most pertinently we need to ask if, given the fetishistic nature of discourses on race and gender, a politically effective representational strategy can ever operate via "reversal." Gates's own lucid discussion of the complexity of black American "signifying," which he argues both participates in and subtly undermines white discourse, implicitly repudiates the viability of "straightforward reversal" as political critique. If, as Gates argues, blacks have developed a double-edged discourse capable of responding to what W. E. B. DuBois called the "twoness" of their existence in American culture, how much more pertinent is the theorisation of such a discourse for anyone concerned with understanding the complex articulations of race and gender in American life and with avoiding the "reversals" that keep us continually veering between the Scylla of racism and the Charybdis of sexism.

To illustrate this point, I want to return to a scene in a film by a director whose presence is strongly felt at the "originary" moment of feminist psychoanalytic film theory: namely, Josef von Sternberg, the auteur who was the focus of Laura Mulvey's comments on the way popular narrative cinema tends to fetishize the female body. The film - Blonde Venus - has been as riveting to contemporary theorists of cinema as the sight of Dian Fossey lying among the apes was to the character Bob in Gorillas in the Mist. A still from the scene graces the cover of an issue of Cinema Journal which includes an article about the subversiveness of the film's treatment of female sexuality.

In the plot leading up to this scene, the heroine Helen, played by Marlene Dietrich, has recently left her humble home and her husband and son to return to a career on the stage; in the still, she has just emerged from an ape costume, although hairy bits of the costume remain around her genital area, her shoulders, and her derrière, and she is about to sing "Hot Voodoo." On her head is a blonde Afro wig and behind her stand a group of women in blackface holding spears and giant masks painted with large mouths and teeth.

Nowhere does Sternberg more forcefully reveal himself to be the master fetishist of the female body than in this scene, which for an adequate reading requires us to apply the insights of both a Homi Bhabha and a Laura Mulvey. Too often feminist film critics have alluded only parenthetically to the film's racism while devoting themselves chiefly to considering whether the film is "progressive" in its emphasis on performance and spectacle, its subtle visual undermining of the domestic ideal that the narrative purports to uphold.

Yet the racism is not an incidental, "odd" moment to be bracketed off in order to pursue more pressing concerns, but is, in fact, central to the evocation and manipulation of desire that begins with the Hot Voodoo number and continues up to and beyond Helen's flight south to increasingly exotic locales, the last of which is a Louisiana boarding house run by a black woman. In the Hot Voodoo sequence, the fetishistic working of presence and absence, difference and sameness, depends, as it does in Gorillas in the Mist, on the interplay of the elements of white woman, ape, and blacks.

If it can be said that the film draws on the stereotypical association, referred to by Gates, of apes and black women, it can also be that said the white woman is the ape. But then again, of course, she is not the ape. Part of the sexual charge of the spectacle derives from the disavowal, the doubleness, the contradictory belief structure whereby she is posited as simultaneously animal and human, as well as simultaneously white and not white (suggested by the blonde Afro wig).

Similarly, the white women in blackface and black Afro wigs who stand behind Dietrich are also affirmed and denied as African "savages" (and are fetishized further in that the war paint on their faces resembles the painting on the masks they carry in front of the lower halves of their bodies - the teeth on these masks clearly symbolizing the vagina dentata). I think we can take this fully theatricalized image as emblematic of some of the complex interrelations of gender and race in popular representation.

In doing so, however, we are forced to recognize that while everyone in this scenario (except for the white male, played by Cary Grant, who is looking on) is relegated to "the ideologically appointed place of the stereotype"), the black women in the film are in the most marginalized position. If it is true, to cite Claire Johnston's famous formulation, woman as woman has largely been absent from patriarchal cinema, this has obviously been much more literally the case for black women than for whites.

And if the white woman has usually served as the signifier of male desire (which is what Johnston meant when she spoke of the absence of woman as woman), the black woman, when present at all, has served as a signifier of (white) female sexuality or of the maternal ("Mammy"). In the last part of this chapter I would like to explore the way in which black women in contemporary popular film are reduced to being the signifiers of signifiers.

The use of the black woman to signify sexuality is vividly illustrated in one of the most recent films in the tradition of The Jazz Singer. In this case, however, the protagonist is a woman who finds herself going back to her Jewish roots. In Crossing Delancey, directed by Joan Micklin Silver, Amy Irving plays Izzy, a thirty-three year-old white woman who lives alone in Manhattan, works in a prestigious bookstore organizing readings by the literati, and, vehement disclaimers to the contrary notwithstanding, is clearly desperate to find a man. Indeed, she is so desperate that after ridding herself of an infatuation with a self-absorbed and pretentious writer, she overcomes a strong distaste for a Jewish pickle salesman, who has been chosen for her by a marriage broker in collusion with Izzy's grandmother.

In a brief scene occurring rather early in the film, Izzy is trying to decide whether or not to call the writer to ask him out, and she asks the advice of a friend as the two relax in the sauna after a workout in the gym. While the women recline in their towels, the camera pans down to reveal two black women, one of whom, a very large woman whose ample flesh spills out of a tight bathing suit, loudly recounts to her friend an anecdote about love-making in which while performing fellatio ("I'm licking it, I'm kissing it, he's moaning") she discovers a long-"I mean long"-blonde hair, which the man rather lamely tries to explain away. The camera tilts back up, as Izzy, having listened intently to the conversation, thoughtfully remarks, "Maybe I will call him."

Clearly the black woman, small as her role is, represents sexuality and "embodiment" in a film that never mentions sex at any other time (to be sure, the fact of sex is hinted at when Izzy spends an occasional night with a married male friend, but it is never shown or discussed). Even the framing of the scene we have been discussing suggests in amazingly exemplary fashion the hierarchical division between black and white women, with the uptown Manhattanite princess-"on-her-high-horse" (to quote the grandmother), who will be forced to accept as a lover a Jewish man from lower Manhattan, placed in the upper part of the frame and the sexualized black females situated, as always, on the bottom (a spatial metaphor with both social and psychic dimensions).

The black woman's story not only hints at the threat of miscegenation - for, just as this woman's lover has strayed, so too is Izzy straying from her roots - but represents directly all those desires that this postfeminist film is disavowing: both a voracious sexuality and a voracious hunger in general, resulting from the deprivations suffered by single middleclass white women in the modern world.

Thus the fact that the one sexual act mentioned in the film (which is about a woman's love for a pickle salesman, no less) is the act of fellatio is not surprising given the ubiquitous presence of food in the film (scenes of Izzy and her friend eating hotdogs on Izzy's birthday after she lies to her boss about going to a fancy restaurant [obviously women cannot nurture themselves or each other]; of lonely women picking at food in salad bars and eating Chinese takeout while watching television; of a baby nursing at his mother's breast while the heroine looks on in envy-envy not, it is quite clear, of the mother but of the suckling child; and finally, of the [as the film portrays her] obnoxiously loud female marriage broker continually gobbling down other people's food, eating with greasy fingers and talking with her mouth crammed full).

The horror of the body expressed in contemporary culture, the anorexic mentality to which this horror gives rise, and the tendency on the part of men to deal with these fears by displacing them onto the body of the female; what we need to note here is the special role played by the woman of colour as receptacle of these fears. The function of the fat, sexually voracious black woman in Crossing Delancey is to enable the white Jewish subculture, through its heterosexual love story, to represent itself in a highly sentimentalized, romanticized, and sublimated light, while disavowing the desires and discontents underlying the civilisation it is promoting. (Once again, then, we see the need for feminist analysis to consider the ways in which ethnic and racial groups are played off against - and play themselves off against - one another.)

If in Crossing Delancey - a film written and directed by women - the black female body is the sexualized body, in other films the black woman functions not only as the sexual other, but as the maternal body, as psychic surrogate for the white mother-in short, as "Mammy." Recent feminist theory has shown that the nursery maid in Freud's own time played an important, although largely unacknowledged, role in initiating the child into sexual knowledge.

In America, as black feminists have pointed out, the black woman has more often than not served a similar function in the acculturation of white children. Clara's Heart, starring Whoopi Goldberg, provides an unusually stark illustration of the process whereby the young white male achieves maturity through penetrating the mystery of the black woman - "her wisdom, her warmth, her secret," as the poster proclaims. That (returning to the metaphor of the Dark Continent) we are dealing here almost literally with the "heart of darkness" is suggested by Clara's last name, which is "Heart" - an organ that turns out to be a euphemism for a more libidinally cathected body part.

For Clara's secret, which her young charge David, suffering from neglect at the hands of his narcissistic parents, attempts to discover, is that she has been raped by her own son. The horror, the horror, indeed. The black male thus literalizes the psychic reality of the bourgeois male, for the rape is in fact the logical result of the white boy's - and the narrative's-probing.

At one point, for example, David sits at Clara's knee and begins slowly and sensually to feel her leg, moving inexorably upward until Clara screams at him - an "overreaction" explained when we learn of the son's rape. Moreover, David not only continually badgers Clara to reveal her story but reads in secret the letters he finds in a suitcase under her bed. Again, Clara reacts furiously, saying he has ruined their friendship, although at other times she says he can never do anything to destroy her affection.

The intense aggression aroused by the promise and withholding of unconditional love ultimately finds expression in the revelation of incest and rape - a rape that is enacted by the sexually monstrous black male, who is presumably incapable of sublimating such feelings and thus destined to remain forever a casualty of Oedipus, while the recognition of his own desires in the mirror provided by the black male enables the white boy to rechannel his hostilities and become a man: previously unathletic, we now see him win a swimming championship under the approving eye of his father!

Thus the black man comes to serve as as the white male's oedipal scapegoat, and the black woman is positioned, as in so many popular representations (like Spielberg The Colour Purple), as sexual victim - not of the white man, of course, the historical record notwithstanding - but of black men, including even their own sons. And black people in general are once again consigned to the level of bestiality.

A more recent, enormously popular film in which Whoopi

Goldberg again has a major role shows yet another way the black woman serves the function of embodiment. In Ghost, Whoopi Goldberg plays a spiritual medium, Oda Mae Brown, who stands in for the body of the white male, Sam, played by Patrick Swayze. Sam has died as a result of a mugging, which turns out to have been engineered by a coworker embezzling funds. When he learns of the plot and of his wife's danger at the hands of the mugger, he seeks out Oda Mae to help him communicate to his wife.

After a great deal of mutual mistrust between the wife and Oda Mae, climaxed by a scene in which Oda Mae stands outside the door trying to convince the wife of her "authenticity," as it were, she is allowed inside the house, and the wife expresses a great longing to be able to touch her husband one last time. Oda Mae offers up her body up for the purpose, and Sam enters into it. The camera shows a close-up of the black woman's hands as they reach out to take those of the white woman, and then it cuts to a shot not of Oda Mae but of Sam, who in taking over her body has obliterated her presence entirely.

This sequence, in which Goldberg turns into a man, may be seen as a kind of logical extension of all her comedic roles for she is always coded in the comedies as more masculine than feminine. For example, there is a scene in Jumping Jack Flash in which she dresses up in a sexy evening dress that nearly gets chewed up by a shredding machine, and, as she climbs the stairs to her apartment at the end of the evening, she is heard muttering in anger because the taxi cab driver mistook her for a male transvestite.

In Fatal Beauty, too, Goldberg's donning of women's clothes is seen to be a form of drag - of black female mimicry of (white) femininity, and when she dresses in such clothes she walks in an exaggeratedly awkward fashion like a man unaccustomed to female accoutrements. Two important points need to be made here. First, the kind of "gender trouble" advocated by Judith Butler and others in which gender, anatomy, and performance are at odds with one another does not necessarily result in the subversive effects often claimed for it; on the contrary, in certain cases, such as those involving the woman of colour who has often been considered, in Bhabha's words, "not quite" a woman, this kind of "play" may have extremely conservative implications.

Second, when both extremes of the Whoopi Goldberg persona are considered together - those in which she represents the maternal/female body (as in Clara's Heart) and those in which she is coded as more or less male - we see that we are not all that far from the situation addressed by Sojourner Truth: The black woman is seen either as too literally a woman (reduced to her biology and her biological functions) or in crucial ways not really a woman at all.

I must acknowledge, however, although it places me in an uncomfortable position, that I personally find the Goldberg character in the comedies both attractive and empowering (and I know some young white girls who have made Goldberg a kind of cult heroine), and that part of this attraction for me lies in the way she represents a liberating departure from the stifling conventions of femininity. Yet I have to recognize as a white woman the extent to which these images are at least in part the creation of a racist mentality and to acknowledge how such images and my own reaction to them may serve to keep me and black women at odds (although I would also argue strongly that Goldberg's powerful acting allows her frequently to transcend some of the limitations of her material or else to bring out the subversive potential buried within the text).

It is urgent that white women come to understand the ways in which they themselves participate in racist structures not only of patriarchal cinema - as in Crossing Delancey - but also of contemporary criticism and theory. In an important article surveying the work of white women newly addressing issues of race, Valerie Smith points out that some white feminist theorists may be participating in an old tradition of forcing the black woman to serve the function of embodiment:

It is striking that at precisely the moment when Anglo-American feminists and male Afro-Americanists begin to reconsider the material ground of their enterprise, they demonstrate their return to earth, as it were, by invoking the specific experiences of black women and the writings of black women. This association of black women with reembodiment resembles rather closely the association, in classic Western philosophy and in nineteenth-century cultural constructions of womanhood, of women of colour with the body and therefore with animal passions and slave labour.

What Smith's remarks clearly suggest is the black woman's need to refuse to function as either the man's or the white woman's bodily scapegoat, just as some white women are refusing any longer to function this way in male discourse. I would like to end, however, with a fantasy, which involves reading the scene I have discussed in Ghost against the grain. This may be a fantasy that for many reasons black woman will not fully share, since it points in a utopian direction and wishes away some of the contradictions I have been analyzing.

Without for a moment forgetting these contradictions, without denying the force of Hazel Carby's observation that feminist criticism (to say nothing of a "woman's film" like Crossing Delancey) has too often ignored "the hierarchical structuring of the relations between black and white women and often takes the concerns of middle-class, articulate white women as the norm," I nevertheless want to point to an alternative to the dominant fantasy expressed in Ghost.

If in the film the black woman exists solely to facilitate the white heterosexual romance, there is a sense in which we can shift our focus to read the white male as, precisely, the obstacle to the union of the two women, a union tentatively suggested in the image of the black and white hands as they reach toward one another. I like to think that despite the disturbing contradictions I have pointed out in this chapter, a time will come when we eliminate the locked door (to recall an image from Ghost) that separates women (a door, as we see in the film, easily penetrated by the white man), a time when we may join together to overthrow the ideology that, after all, primarily serves the interests of white heterosexual masculinity and is ultimately responsible for the persecutions suffered by people on account of their race, class, and gender. But since it is white women who in many cases have locked the door, it is their responsibility to open it up.

Bibliography

Abel, Marco (2009) *Violent Affect: Literature, Cinema and Critique After Representation.* Lincoln: University of Nebraska Press.

Ahmed, Sara (2004) *The Cultural Politics of Emotion.* New York: Routledge.

Best, Susan (2007) "Rethinking Visual Pleasure, Aesthetics and Affect," *Theory & Psychology* Vol. 17(4): 505–514.

Blackman, Lisa. (2008) "Affect, Relationality and the `Problem of Personality'," *Theory, Culture & Society.* Vol. 25 (1): 23–47.

Cheek, J., Doskatsch, I., Hill, P. & Walsh, L. (1995) *Finding Out : Information Literacy For the 21st century,* MacMillan Education Australia, South Melbourne.

Dowling, Emma (2007) "Producing the Dining Experience: Measure, Subjectivity and the Affective Worker," *Ephemera: theory & politics in organization* Volume 7 Number 1.

Duncombe, Stephen (2007) *Dream: Re-Imagining Progressive Politics in an Age of Fantasy.* New York: New Press.

Federici, Silvia (2004) Caliban and the Witch: Women, the Body, and Primitive Accumulation. Brooklyn, NY: Autonomedia.

Federici, Silvia (2008) "Precarious Labor: A Feminist Viewpoint," In The Middle of a Whirlwind: 2008 Convention Protests, Movement, and Movement. *Los Angeles: Journal of Aesthetics & Protest Press.*

Gibbs, Anna (2002) "Disaffected," *Continuum: Journal of Media and Cultural Studies.* 16: 3.

Gorton, Kristyn (2007) "Theorizing emotion and affect: Feminist engagements," *Feminist Theory Vol.* 8(3): 333–348.

Gregg, Melissa (2006) *Cultural Studies' Affective Voices.* New York: Palgrave.

Hochschild, Arlie (1983) *The Managed Heart: Commercialization of Human Feeling. Berkeley*: University of California Press.

Katsiaficas, George (2001) *The Subversion of Politics: European Autonomous Movements and the Decolonization of Everyday Life.* New Jersey: Humanities Press.

Moir, A. & Jessel, D. (1991) *Brain Sex: The Real Difference Between Men and Women*, Mandarin, London.

Negri, Antonio (1999) *Insurgencies: Constituent Power and the Modern State.* Trans. Maurizio Boscagli. Minneapolis, MN: University of Minnesota Press.

Pruchnic, Jeff (2008) "The Invisible Gland: Affect and Political Economy," *Criticism* Volume 50, Number 1: 160-175.

Redding, Paul (1999) *The Logic of Affect.* Melbourne: Melbourne University Press.

Simons, R. C. (1996) *Boo!: Culture, Experience and the Startle Reflex, Series in Affective Science,* Oxford University Press, New York.

Sjostrand, S. (ed.) (1993) *Institutional Change: Theory and Empirical Findings,* M.E. Sharpe, Armonk, N.Y.

Terranova, Tiziana (2004) "Communication Biopower," *Network Culture: Politics for the Information Age.* London: Pluto Press.

Thoburn, Nicholas (2007) "Patterns of Production: Cultural Studies after Hegemony," *Theory, Culture & Society.* Vol. 24(3): 79–94.

Thrift, Nigel (2007) *Non-Representational Theory: Space, Politics, Affect.* London: Routledge

Titchener, E.B. (1895) "Affective Memory," *Philosophical Review.* Volume 4 Number 1: 65-76.

Vaneigem, Raoul (1994 [1967]) *Revolution of Everyday Life*. Trans. Donald Nicholson-Smith. London: Rebel Press.

Vaneigem, Raoul (1994) *The Movement of the Free Spirit*. Trans. Randall Cherry and Ian Patterson. New York: Zone Books.

Index

G

H

I

L

M

O

P